Ayrshire Cattle in the county of Deux Montagnes, Quebec. *Nickel mine and smelter at Thompson in Northern Manitoba.*
A cruise ship passes under the Thousand Islands Bridge at Ivy Lea, Ontario.
Fishermen of Northwest Cove, on Nova Scotia's South Shore. *The Trans-Canada Highway in the Selkirk Mountains, British Columbia.*

Patterns of Canada

Edited by

WILLIAM J. MEGILL

Compiled for

THE ROYAL CANADIAN GEOGRAPHICAL SOCIETY

1867 1967

THE RYERSON PRESS, TORONTO

Tulips in full bloom along the Rideau Canal in Ottawa, the Nation's capital.

FOREWORD

Any attempt to tell the whole story of the hundred years since confederation in Canada would obviously require a much thicker book than this one. We have, therefore, not attempted to do so, but instead to present a series of accounts of events and activities which may serve to re-create the atmosphere of the periods in our history from which they were drawn.

"We", in this case, means the editorial committee of the *Canadian Geographical Journal,* the official organ of the Royal Canadian Geographical Society. With a few exceptions, all the articles which go to make up this book have appeared in the *Journal* at some time during the past thirty-six years. Each was chosen because of the particular contribution it could make to portrayal of the changing pattern of Canada's growth, a process which consumed a good many hours of the committee's time.

My own task as editor has been to prepare the selected articles for publication. Many have necessarily been reduced in length, but when this has been done I have tried to use the author's words so far as possible and have avoided re-writing. The resulting text has been approved by all the authors with whom I have been able to correspond. I hope that those I have been unable to find, and who may be still living, will approve what has been done with their words.

Several facets of our life and industry are depicted at one period of time only. Just four cities — Halifax, Montreal, Ottawa, and Vancouver — are covered specifically and the emphasis is on their early history. They have been chosen to show the rich variety of the foundations on which we have built the Canada of the present day. Similarly, the only article on aviation is one which describes the first trans-Canada flight, which was made in 1920. Our modern cities and the world-wide operations of Air Canada are described in other books.

The development of our agriculture, forestry, fisheries, mining, manufacturing, and power resources has had to be treated in general terms, showing where we have arrived at the present time. Only a few of the individual projects are described separately. They must serve as examples of the number and great variety of major engineering achievements which have transformed parts of our sub-continent and are continuing to do so.

We have not tried to see far into the future. Where Canada may arrive in ten, twenty or fifty years' time will depend entirely on how we respond to the challenges of the coming years. As we have attempted in this book, by careful selection from a wide range of material, to create an impression of the changing mosaic of Canadian life throughout the last hundred years, so we can forecast only the broad lines of future development as we now see them.

My thanks are due to the editorial committee of the *Canadian Geographical Journal* who have discussed, approved and rejected material for this book as the work of compilation has progressed. For them it has been an extension of the time and thought they give regularly to the *Journal*, willingly and without reward. If I mentioned them by name my list would be too long, so they must remain anonymous.

Whatever artistic merit you may find in the layout of the text and pictures must be credited to Harry Metras of the Gazette Printing Company in Montreal. We have now worked together on layout of the *Canadian Geographical Journal* for almost seven years — my task being to ensure that text and pictures complement each other, his to choose the size and arrangement of the illustrations to make an attractive page.

Finally, I would thank all who may read this introduction. My words in this volume are few but I am nevertheless pleased to think that they may be read. However, the merit of an editor does not lie in his own literary expression but in how he presents the work of other hands and minds.

W. J. M.

Ottawa, 1966.

Printed in Canada at THE GAZETTE PRINTING COMPANY (LIMITED), *Montreal.*

Bound at THE RYERSON PRESS, *Toronto.*

TABLE OF CONTENTS

Lying southeast of Banff, Alberta, Mount Rundle towers over the town like a giant rampart. The Reverend Terrill Rundle was a Methodist missionary to the Indians of the Northwest more than a century ago, from 1840 to 1848, and the mountain was named in his honour. Also, in 1843, the Hudson's Bay Company granted him a "commissioned gentleman's allowance", in recognition of his work.

TABLE OF CONTENTS *(Continued)*

The Rock Garden of Royal Botanical Gardens May. Created in 1929-19 from sand and gravel p along the entrance to the c of Hamilton, this well-lo garden displays Spring bu in May, Summer flowers fr July to September, and chr anthemums in October.

The location of this beauty spot is not known, but the picture could have been taken in any one of many different parts of Canada in October. The fall colours and the mud-flats leading out to the shallow bay with its browning reed beds will recall many a pleasant day to sportsmen and to all who like to ramble in the unspoiled countryside.

*Harvesting apples near Brockville, Ontario. This scene is repeated in
many parts of Canada from coast to coast every fall, as the different
varieties of apples ripen. The feel of the sun warm on the back and the
rich smell of the ripe fruit is a part of our heritage which more and more
Canadians will miss as we become increasingly city-dwellers.*

Grain elevators have well been called "Castles of the New World", not only because of their characteristic shape but also because they provide secure storage for grain on the western prairie. Here, grain is received from the farmer, classified for grade, and stored until it is moved forward to elevators at lake or ocean ports. These are at Vulcan in Southern Alberta.

The Rocher Déboulé Range, overlooking the confluence of the Skeena and Bulkley Rivers, near Hazelton, British Columbia, seems to blend into the clouds as the sun lights up the steep slopes through the haze.

A typical reconnaissance engineer's camp, located on the shore of Fred Wright Lake, sixty-five miles northwest of Hazelton. Waterways, in this case the Kispiox and Skeena Rivers, are still the highways in Canada's wilderness.

14

A rocky passage in the Big Eddy Rapids on the Black River near Washago, Ontario. This scene is characteristic of the rivers of the Canadian Shield, which here is near its southern limit. The tall white pines which were once predominant have long since been logged off and other species have replaced them for the most part, but the natural beauty which has made the Muskoka and Kawartha Lakes area a favourite vacation-land is still unspoiled.

La Vérendrye was probably the first European to see Painted Rock, on Lac la Croix. Stained many subtle-toned colours with minerals and seepages of vegetation, this is one of the many scenes in Canada which have changed little since the days of the early explorers.

16

THE PATTERN OF THE LAND

Canada is a land of rocks, lakes and rivers. She has her fertile lowlands and the broad prairie of the mid-west but these are the smaller part of the land, the strip near the southern boundary which has been settled and developed so far. North of this settled belt is a wide strip of sub-arctic forest land; then the true tundra, north of the tree line; and beyond the mainland are the Arctic islands, whose topmost point is less than five hundred miles from the North Pole.

The first settlers found Canada an inhospitable land, a land of long, bleak winters and short, hot summers, a land that would yield to the plough only after back-breaking toil in clearing the primeval forest. Why did they stay ? Some had no choice, some felt the challenge and the promise and knew that one day it would provide a good life for their descendents. They have been followed by others of their kind, men and women of various races and creeds. Between them, they pushed back the frontiers and disclosed the pattern of the land as we know it today.

The principal topographical feature is the Canadian Shield, which surrounds Hudson Bay and extends south to the line of Lake Superior and which is made up of some of the oldest and hardest rock in the world.

East of Lake Huron, between the Shield and the international boundary, lies the narrow strip of the Great Lakes-St. Lawrence Lowlands which ends on the east at the Appalachian Region, an area of tumbled rocks interspersed with small, fertile plains. West of the Shield lie the Prairies and the Mackenzie Lowlands, which end at the Cordillera, a series of mountain ranges sharp and new in geological age compared to the rest of the land.

The first Europeans to arrive found few local inhabitants. Life in this land and climate was difficult for primitive people. The Indian tribes were semi-nomadic, changing location with the seasons to ensure their food supply. The woods were full of animals and birds and the rivers teemed with fish but this wild-life also yielded to the necessities of the seasons and moved its habitat to ensure survival and growth. The creation of ordered, settled communities required courage and endurance of a high order.

This is the land as it was. The southern fringe is changed beyond all recognition now, but this is only a small part of the whole. Much of it remains as the first explorers found it, because the Shield is but sparsely populated. Apart from the mining communities, the farms of the clay belt in Northern Ontario and the hydro-electric power plants which are putting the rivers to work and curbing their turbulence, the principal change is that large areas of second-growth timber replace the accessible forest which has been cut over. Also, the canoe and the dog team have yielded pride of place to the aeroplane and the helicopter as the chief means of transportation.

17

The late Dr. Charles Camsell, C.M.G., LL.D., at his desk in 1944 when he was Deputy Minister of Mines and Resources.

WHAT GEOGRAPHY MEANS TO CANADA

by CHARLES CAMSELL

GEOGRAPHY is our oldest and most comprehensive science. It encloses within its compass the whole of the earth and all the things of the earth, particularly as related to the sustenance and well-being of man. Our common ancestor was our first practical geographer. By necessity he was an explorer, and by necessity he had to provide himself with food, shelter, and protection.

Canada is a new land. The geography of primary interest to Canadians is therefore not the geography that mainly concerns the nationals of old, densely-populated and progressive countries of which Great Britain is the outstanding example. The physical layout of Great Britain is exactly known — every foot of its limited area having been mapped in detail many years ago. The character and extent of its natural resources have been subjected to thorough examination. It is compact, with simple

This address by Dr. Charles Camsell, first president of the Royal Canadian Geographical Society, was delivered at the University of Toronto on 7th November, 1935, on the occasion of the installation of Dr. Griffith Taylor as Head of the first separate department of geography to be established at a Canadian University. His words are still valid and will remain so.

internal transport problems. It has a teeming energetic population much beyond the capacity of its natural resources to support. The British people have therefore long since looked beyond their own boundaries for the wherewithal to provide a large part of the necessities and comforts of their highly developed civilization. They have been world explorers and world exploiters, and in the course of time have built up the British Empire upon which the sun never sets. They are thus mainly

concerned with world geography.

Canada, on the other hand, has an immense area, little of which has been thoroughly explored. It is made up of a number of extensive natural regions with distinctly different physical characteristics. Its climate ranges from temperate to frigid. Its comparatively small population is distributed over a width of 3,000 miles and mostly within a depth of 200 miles. Its transport problems are peculiarly difficult. Its natural resources, while widely diversified, are as yet only sketchily known. The Canadian people are therefore primarily concerned with Canadian geography, since their main problems — both economic and political — have their origin therein.

It is generally recognized that the character and extent of a nation's development are largely dependent upon two main facts — its geography and its people. As the character of a people depends in large degree upon environment it is apparent that the geography of a country must not only furnish the foundation upon which the superstructure of its national life is to be built, but also the materials for its construction. However, while it is true that the stability and general character of a national structure thus depends upon its geography, it must be kept in mind that the magnitude of the structure, its architectural balance, and its durability depend upon the completeness with which the builder has searched out and collected the available geographical building material, his mastery of the art of design, and the skill in workmanship — or in other words upon the intelligent co-ordination of full geographical knowledge.

To no country in the world does this apply with greater force than to Canada. As already mentioned, practically all its major economic and political problems have their origin in its geography. Such being the case, the solutions of those problems cannot be final until that geography is fully known and thoroughly understood.

As an outstanding example of radical revaluation of a part of Canada's national estate brought about by advancement in geographical knowledge, I might refer to the huge shield-shaped wilderness of Precambrian rock centering on Hudson Bay and covering the whole of eastern Central Canada except a narrow strip of agricultural land along the Lower Lakes and the St. Lawrence. This great natural region, usually known as the Laurentian Upland or Canadian Shield, has long been the stumbling block to Canadian development — entered in our inventories as a dead liability, except for its comparatively small production of fur, and, latterly, timber.

Having no counterpart in the United States it is the one geographic feature which above all others has placed the two countries in distinctly separate categories as national properties. Largely because of the Canadian Shield, Canada today has a population only one-twelfth of the United States. For the most part useless for agriculture, it separates by a thousand miles of rugged rock and swamp the relatively small farming lands of Southern Ontario from the vast expanse of fertile plain — ready for the settler's plow — lying to the west.

It thus brought early Canadian settlement to an abrupt halt with the filling of the narrow agricultural areas of Southern Ontario and Quebec — not to be resumed for a period of roughly fifty years when its bridging by the railway had been completed. It is the cause of Canada's major transport difficulties. An effective barrier to western movement for half a century, it is primarily responsible for that concentration of industry in southern Ontario which has created pronounced sectional differences of opinion across the Dominion and makes for difficulties in government. Its only saving grace was its fur, and its white pine along the Ottawa.

But with the progress of geographical exploration, and the advancement of geographical knowledge, it has been found that the grim forbidding aspect of the Canadian Shield covers a heart — literally and figuratively — of gold. A sharp revision of this one-time worthless item in Canada's inventory is in progress. That it is a veritable treasure vault of mineral wealth — gold, silver, copper, nickel, zinc, platinum, and the like, even radium — has already been established by Porcupine, Kirkland Lake, Cobalt, Sudbury, Rouyn, Flin-Flon, Eldorado and a host of other mining camps. And intensive exploration and prospecting has really only begun.

Second in importance in this revaluation are the forest resources producing each year, in addition to lumber, scores of millions of dollars worth of wood pulp and paper. It has a rapidly-expanding value in its recreational attractions — hunting, fishing, canoeing, and camping — sold for increasing millions of dollars in cash each year. And it still produces many bales of fur — for years Canada's only money crop.

The story of the Canadian Shield is a fascinating romance. It is the story of Cinderella with geographical knowledge as the Fairy's wand. I refer to it only as an apt illustration of the truth that a thorough knowledge and appreciation of a country's geography is vitally essential to its fullest economic development.

However, it is not enough that Canadians should know Canadian geography. In these days of world interdependence they must also have a working knowledge of world geography. Canada requires goods which cannot be produced at home. She must therefore sell Canadian produce in competitive world markets. She occupies an advantageous world site practically midway between the markets of Europe and Asia. Knowledge of the geography of world trade, world transportation, and world competitors is essential if Canada's natural advantages are to be fully realized for the benefit of Canadians.

How is this needed geographical knowledge and understanding to be acquired? The answer is in our educational institutions, in our public service, in private business, in scientific and educational societies, and in individual research.

I think you will agree that sound instruction in geography in our educational institutions is the keystone of sound geographical knowledge and appreciation. Practical recognition of that fact has been delayed overlong in Canada. On behalf of the Canadian Geographical Society, I congratulate this great university upon taking the lead in closing up this serious gap in our higher educational instruction.

CANADA'S DEBT TO THE INDIANS

by DIAMOND JENNESS

Vast would be Cartier's amazement if, revisiting the basin of the St. Lawrence to-day, after the lapse of 400 years, he could observe the thousands of his countrymen vigorously puffing smoke from short-stemmed wooden bowls, and gathering from mile after mile of rich farm

Dr. Jenness, recipient of the Society's Massey Medal for 1962, was Chief Anthropologist at the National Museum for many years and gained his reputation as an expert on Canada's Indians and Eskimos as a result of his numerous scientific expeditions across Canada and in the Arctic. This assessment was written in 1939.

land the green stalks and leaves of the tobacco. Not because he himself never smelt the fragrance of the burning leaves. The poor uncultured Indians, he remarked,

"people whose bodies are fairly well formed, though they are wild and savage folk . . . have a plant of which a large supply is collected in summer for the winter's consumption. They hold it in high esteem, though the men alone make use of it in the following manner. After drying it in the sun, they carry it about their necks in a small skin pouch in lieu of a bag, together with a hollow bit of stone or wood. Then at frequent intervals they crumble this plant into powder, which they place in one of the openings of the hollow instrument, and laying a live coal on top, suck at the other end to such an extent, that they fill their bodies so full of smoke, that it streams out of their mouths and nostrils as from a chimney. They say it keeps them warm and in good health, and never go about without these things. We made a trial of this smoke. When it is in one's mouth, one would think one had taken powdered pepper, it is so hot."

Tobacco was but one of many plants, native to America alone, that the Indians brought under cultivation and then handed on to Europeans. Cartier's successors evidently found its smoking much more agreeable than he did, for a century later the custom spread with astonishing rapidity over large parts of Europe and Asia, and the cultivation of tobacco became so firmly rooted in West Africa, and in Malaysia, that its origin from America alone remained in doubt until quite recently. The cities of Quebec and Montreal now cover the fields where Cartier saw it growing, but it now ranks as one of Canada's major crops, yielding in 1938 a revenue of approximately 20 million dollars.[1] Two of the Dominion's crops that exceeded it in value, corn and potatoes, the white man also derived from the Indians

---

[1]1960 figure: $114,699,000.

and did not enjoy before the discovery of America. It is, indeed, a remarkable tribute to the intelligence of the aborigines that of the numberless new species of plants Europeans found in the New World, all that possessed any great economic value were already being cultivated or utilized by its inhabitants.

The precise origin of corn is obscure. We can still recognize, in the Old World, the wild grasses from which our ancestors developed wheat, oats, barley and rye, but we cannot discover any wild species of corn, except what has escaped from cultivation. Some botanists believe that it is a hybrid, derived from the crossing of a grass called teosinte, that grows wild in the highlands of Mexico, with some other plant not yet identified. The Indians, though lacking in scientific knowledge, must have bred the plant with great skill, for they developed varieties both for the humid tropics and for more temperate climes. Champlain and other early travellers in south eastern Ontario speak of the miles and miles of corn fields around the Huron villages, cultivated with the crudest

of tools, but yielding bountiful harvests. Interspersed with the corn, too, were rows of squash and beans, of species previously unknown to Europeans, though grown by them to-day throughout the length and breadth of Canada.

Quite as remarkable, perhaps, was the cultivation of cassava by the "savages" of the New World, this time in South America. There are two species of cassava, a sweet and a bitter. The latter is the more importantly economically, but in its raw state contains a deadly poison, hydrocyanic acid. The Indians, who had long discovered this, taught Europeans how to decompose the acid by heat, so that now cassava is a staple food throughout the Old World tropics no less than in the New. Although the plant cannot thrive in Canada, the Dominion imports every year an immense quantity of tapioca, which is merely the starch of the cassava root agglomerated into pellets on hot plates.

Our early colonists in Eastern Canada were a hardy temperate folk who seldom pined for the mellow

Crowfoot and his family. Elected head chief of the Blackfoot confederacy in 1877, he died in 1890.

wines and ciders they had left behind them in sunny France. Yet they were not slow to imitate the Indians in extracting a delicious liquor from one of the native trees. "When the Sap begins to rise", wrote Charlevoix, "they make a Jag or Notch in the trunk of the Maple, and by Means of the Bit of Wood which they fix in it, the Water runs as by a Spout". The Indians reduced this 'Maple-water' to syrup, but in pre-European times they could not evaporate it to sugar because they possessed no iron pots or pans. However, they used the syrup to sweeten their corn flour, so that when our children demand corn-bread and maple syrup for breakfast, should we not impress on them that they owe both these luxuries to the Indians?

Must we not bless the Indians, also, for our Christmas turkey? Our forefathers in Europe had to content themselves with roast beef at Christmas, because the bird was not known in the Old World. Wild turkeys were fairly numerous in Southern Ontario until the 19th century, when they succumbed to the guns of both Indians and whites; the last recorded survivor, shot in 1879, rests now in the National Museum. To-day, in

Hector Crawler, a former chief of the Stoney Indians.

place of the wild birds, we have the birds from our farms, which raise a breed of turkey first domesticated by the Indians of Mexico.

What untold suffering we have escaped through the use of cocaine, quinine, and other medicines first taught us by the natives of this hemisphere. Though we now use cocaine mainly as an analgesic, the Indians of Peru prized it also for its stimulating qualities, and invariably chewed coco leaves whenever they

were called upon for exceptional exertions. Likewise, for malaria, they chewed the bark of the cinchona tree, which derived its name from a certain Countess of Chinchon, the wife of a Peruvian governor, who herselfwas cured of malaria by this means When the medicinal value of its bark became known in Europe, largely through the Jesuits, the tree was introduced into Java, so that to-day nearly all our quinine comes not from Peru, but from the East Indies.

Tomatoes, cocoa, and the potatoes that have given prosperity to at least two of our provinces, Prince Edward Island and New Brunswick, all come to us from the Indians of South America. (One wonders how Irishmen managed to exist prior to the 16th century, when the potato first made its appearance in Western Europe). Even the sweet potato that we are now beginning to grow in Southern Ontario had its origin in Peru. True, the Maoris of New Zealand, the Hawaiian islanders and other Polynesians were cultivating this vegetable when European navigators first explored the Pacific. This does not mean, however, that the sweet potato, which was certainly

Ojibwa Indian women with their birch-bark canoe.

indigenous to South America, was indigenous also to Polynesia; still less that it was native to any part of the Old World, or even known there before the 16th century. What it does mean is that the Polynesian islanders crossed the Pacific and discovered the west coast of America long before Columbus discovered its Atlantic coast. Unlike the Spaniards, however, they did not return to conquer and colonize the New World, but carried the sweet potato to their island homes and remained there.

Columbus, when he discovered the West Indies, admired the garments the inhabitants were wearing (whenever they wore any clothes at all). Actually the Indians have given us our finest cotton plants, the Sea Island varieties that yield the longest staple. The same navigator, during his second voyage to America, marvelled at the resilience of a heavy black ball, made from a vegetable gum that the Indians tossed about in some game. Other Spaniards also reported the same peculiar substance, rubber, but Europe paid no attention to it until the 18th century, when she imported small quantities from Brazil to erase the marks of lead pencils. To-day Canada alone imports on the average 7 million dollars worth of crude rubber each year, and exports manufactured rubber goods to the value of about 13 million.[2]

We have not exhausted, even yet, the many contributions that the Indians have made to modern civilized life. If, as some believe, it was not they, but their ancestors or relatives in northern Asia who invented the snowshoe, the toboggan, the dog-sled, and the bark canoe, they at least improved these means of transport and handed them on to us. Birch-bark canoes modelled after theirs carried all the goods of the

1961 figures:
Imports, $16,587,000;
Exports of rubber products $7,575,000, a lower figure than for 1938 due to wide use of plastics and synthetic rubber, not shaped, whose exports totalled $103,832,000.

early fur-traders, and conveyed explorers like Mackenzie, Fraser and Thompson from the Gulf of St. Lawrence to the Arctic, from Hudson Bay to the Pacific Ocean. It is only in modern times that we have transformed them into the canoes of cedar, basswood and canvas that

Iroquois Indians husking corn.

now skim over our lakes and rivers, and are beginning to invade the inland water-ways of our mother continent, Europe. Nor is it only the bark canoe that we have assimilated. The Eskimo *kayak*, the cleverest one-man vessel afloat, has been used in Scandinavian waters, and a craft that copies its construction is slowly winning ground among the pleasure-seekers of both hemispheres.

Less than 100 years have gone by since the great English explorer, Sir John Franklin, sailed with 129 men for the Canadian Arctic. Like nearly all his contemporaries, he pitied the "benighted Eskimos of the frozen North", and counted their experience through the centuries of little or no value to the intelligent white man.

Yet where the Eskimos wandered at will with their dog-teams, his seamen fell exhausted beneath the weight of their heavy hand-sledges; and they died of starvation where the Eskimos found abundant fish and seals. To-day no traveller in the Arctic fails to equip himself with a dog-sled, and many an expedition beside Peary's has owed most of its success to the skill of its Eskimo dog-drivers.

The lighter side of our lives, too, owes something to the Indians. We learned the game of lacrosse from them, and we pit college against college just as they pitted village against village. The only difference is that the Indian game was far more exciting, because, being less obsessed by rules, they reckoned victory not by the number of goals, but by the number of broken heads.

So far I have listed only the material things that the Indians have contributed. Canada's debt to them goes far deeper. Hundreds of square miles that to-day yield furs or minerals would still be virgin territory if the Dominion had not been inhabited at the time of its discovery. It was the Indians who guided Champlain up the Ottawa River to Georgian Bay, and led him from one village to another along trails that

The last wild turkey, preserved in the National Museum.

23

have since become a part of Ontario's highway system. Fifty-five years later other Indians conducted Henry Kelsey from Hudson Bay to the edge of the prairies, and showed him the numberless herds of bison that grazed over its wide expanses. As protégé of an Indian chief, Samuel Hearne explored the barren lands and located, near the mouth of the Coppermine River, the deposits of copper that are now one of our great reserves of that mineral. A few years later another Indian chief piloted Alexander Mackenzie down the mighty river that bears his name until they reached the Arctic Ocean; and when the same explorer made the first overland crossing of Canada the year afterward, he followed Indian routes up the Peace and Parsnip Rivers over the continental divide, and actually accompanied an Indian trading party from the upper waters of the Fraser River to the Pacific Coast at Bella Coola. Mackenzie's fur-trading successors, David Thompson and others, crossed and recrossed the Rockies over passes discovered by Indian hunters, who, unknown to their contemporaries, were really blazing the trails for our transcontinental railways. Finally, coming down to more recent times, it is to the keen observation of lonely Indian trappers that we owe the discovery of several gold mines, among them the well-known Metachewin.

Even in Canada's political history individual Indians have played a notable part. Every school-child knows of Joseph Brant, the Mohawk chief who espoused the English side in the American Revolution, became a colonel in the British army, and received a tract of land six miles wide on each side of Ontario's Grand River on which to establish his followers. One of the treasures in the National Gallery at Ottawa is a portrait of Brant, painted by the celebrated English artist George Romney. Less well-known, though his services to Canada were no less

great, was Crowfoot, the warrior-statesman of the Blackfoot Indians, who restrained his excited tribesmen from joining Louis Riel's rebellion and driving every European off the Canadian prairies. The Canadian Pacific Railway recognized Crowfoot's services by giving him a life pass; and his prosperous tribesmen to-day laud his foresight in selecting for them an excellent tract of farm-land, and in diverting their energies from buffalo-hunting to the raising of cattle and growing of wheat.

An Indian cowboy in the Chilcotin district of British Columbia. The life of a cowboy often demands the strength, skill and endurance that the life of a mounted warrior once did.

No one can estimate the number of Indians who have merged with Canadians of European extraction and passed unnoticed into the general population. The figure certainly runs into the thousands and even ten thousands; certainly also many of their descendants have held prominent places in the political, social and economic life of the Dominion. When we speak of Indians to-day,

however, we forget this Indian blood that flows in the veins of an appreciable percentage of our population, and think only of the Indians, largely of mixed blood also, who remain on their reserves or roam over Northern Canada trapping the fur-bearing animals. Yet they too are taking an increasingly important part in our economic life. It is true that the value of the furs they contribute is steadily diminishing, partly through a diminution in the numbers of the wild fur-bearing animals and the successes of fur-farms, partly also through the absorption of the Indians into other occupations; even so, it still reaches the respectable total of about $1,500,000 yearly. Against the decrease in the fur catch we must place the increasing yields of Indian farms and gardens, and the growing number of Indians who are finding employment as mechanics and dockhands, or who work for fishery companies, in lumber camps and mills, and on ranches. The Mohawk Indians of Caughnawaga, near Montreal, enjoy so high a reputation as steel-workers that they were employed on San Francisco's mammoth bridge; and last summer no less than 24,000 bushels of wheat were raised by the little Blackfoot tribe that Crowfoot settled in Alberta.

There is no reliable estimate of the population of the New World, or even of North America, in the years preceding European colonization; but Canada, from the Atlantic to the Pacific and from the Arctic Ocean to the United States boundary, seems to have carried only about 200,000 inhabitants. It is remarkable, to say the least, that this mere handful of "savages" should have influenced so greatly the development of our Canadian civilization. Does it not argue also that their 115,000 descendants, those who remain on reserves and are still classed as Indians, will some day become admirable citizens, provided we give them a reasonable opportunity?

Indians playing lacrosse. At the time of the coming of Europeans, the game was popular among nearly all tribes between Ontario and the Gulf of Mexico.

Guarding Ontario's corn fields.

"Hoeing in the Seed." This was the early practice on newly cleared land. Stumps were left to rot, sometimes for several years, before removal.

BIRTH OF AGRICULTURE IN CANADA

by RAYMOND P. GORHAM, B.S.A.

Raymond P. Gorham, a professional agriculturist, who was a member of the first graduating class of Macdonald College and whose hobby was agricultural history, wrote this account for the January, 1932, issue of the Canadian Geographical Journal.

WHEN JACQUES CARTIER first came in contact with the Canadian Indians on the coast of Bay Chaleur in 1534, he found them well supplied with bread although at the time on a fishing expedition far from their usual village. In the following year, when he visited Hochelaga (later to become the city of Montreal), he saw extensive fields planted with corn and noted, also, that they had beans, peas and cucumbers; and that they grew and used tobacco. The success achieved by the Indians did not fail to impress Cartier with the agricultural possibilities of the country, and on his

"Bread Oven, Cap à L'Aigle." Most of these ovens have now disappeared, but many of them continued in regular use for a century or more after they were built.

third voyage he started out prepared to establish a colony on the St. Lawrence which should support itself, at least in part, through agricultural efforts. He had on his ship, cattle, goats and swine, and the narrative of the voyage mentions that they were intended for breeding in the country.

Due to adverse weather conditions, his voyage was protracted, and it was near the end of July before he reached Newfoundland and August 23 before he arrived at the Indian village of Stadacona. Cartier did not fail, however, to have land broken up, and to plant in September, 1541, the seeds of cabbage, lettuce and turnips. The

seeds of some grain, either winter wheat or fall rye, were sown also; but as Cartier, after some trouble with the Indians, abandoned the place early in the following spring, he did not see the result of his planting or harvest the crop. The journal of Jean Alphonse, a pilot of Roberval's expedition, mentions harvesting grain which had been sown by Jacques Cartier. This appears to have been the first grain sown and harvested by white men in Canada, and the place where it grew was Charlesbourg Royal, near the present Cap Rouge.

The expedition of Roberval was also fitted out with the object of colonization, but, like that of Cartier,

was delayed during the Atlantic passage and did not reach Stadacona until the end of July, 1542. When supplies had been landed and buildings prepared, the members of this expedition found themselves in August already short of food. When the ice broke up in the spring, the survivors of this somewhat unlucky expedition abandoned the colonization project and sailed for Europe.

With their departure appears to have ended the attempt at the development of European agriculture in Canada for more than half a century. There is no doubt that fishermen and traders continued to frequent the coast during this period, but they left no written record of their activities. It was not until the arrival of de Monts and Champlain in 1604 that further known efforts were made. The Sieur de Monts had received a grant of territory with power to govern and trade, and his object was to establish a permanent settlement to hold possession of and develop this land. Amongst those who accompanied him were Samuel de Champlain, who had made a voyage up the St. Lawrence the previous year, Pontgravé, who had tried to settle at Tadoussac, and the Sieur de Poutrincourt, a French gentleman interested in colonization. Proceeding around the coast of the present Bay of Fundy, and after exploring and naming Port Royal this expedition attempted to settle upon an island in what is now the St. Croix River — as it appeared later, a most unfavourable place.

At the falls of the St. Croix, according to Champlain, wheat was sown which grew and ripened well. As the seed was sown in late summer, this must have been winter wheat

which ripened in 1605. It is probable, also, that fall rye was sown, for mention is found in the "Nova Francia" of Marc Lescarbot, who visited the St. Croix in 1606, that in that year there was gathered self-sown rye which the soil had brought forth without tillage following the sowing in 1604. Lescarbot adds the note that he saw there no wheat. Both statements are in accord with our present knowledge of Maritime conditions, wheat seldom perpetuating itself in the field while rye commonly does so.

In 1605, the colony was moved from St. Croix Island to Port Royal, where new habitations were erected during the early summer. The Sieur de Monts, after seeing his colony housed, departed for France to obtain more supplies. Champlain remained at Port Royal and noted in his journal:

"As soon as the Sieur de Monts had departed (for France), some of the 40 or 45 who stayed began to make gardens. I, also, not to remain idle, made one which I surrounded

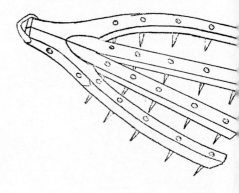

A wooden harrow.

with ditches full of water wherein I placed some very fine trout. I sowed there some seeds which throve well."

The Sieur de Poutrincourt was so impressed with the possibilities of the new land about Port Royal that he sought and obtained from de Monts a grant of that region for the purpose of settlement. Accordingly, he became the first individual to have a direct interest through land ownership in the development of the country. Going back to France in the

"*View from Retreat, Windsor, N.S.*" *One of the notable features of pictures of agriculture in Canada until even comparatively recent times is the number of men at work, as in this harvest scene.*

"Clearing Land Around the First Cabin." Oxen were the preferred draught animals for this work, which was often done on a
"shared labour" basis, part of each man's land being cleared in turn.

autumn of 1605 to obtain supplies, he returned in 1606 with equipment, assistance, and the seeds and plants necessary for the practice of agriculture. With him came Marc Lescarbot, the Parisian advocate, who was to aid in the first successful gardens and write the first history of New France, and the apothecary, Louis Hébert, in after years to be known as the first farmer of Quebec.

In this work Lescarbot took great pleasure and in his history has left us this first written description of the joy to be found in tilling the Canadian soil:

"For I can truly say that never before did I derive so much pleasure in physical work as I did in dressing and tilling my gardens; to enclose and hedge them against the gluttony of the hogs, to make plots, to straighten the paths, to build arbours, to sow wheat, rye, barley, oats, beans, peas, garden-herbs, and to water them. So much did I desire to know the goodness of the ground by my own experience that summer's days were but too short, and very often did I work by the light of the moon."

In another place in his history Lescarbot mentioned tillage as "the first mine that must be sought, for it is more than the treasures of Atahualpa."

In March and April, 1607, the

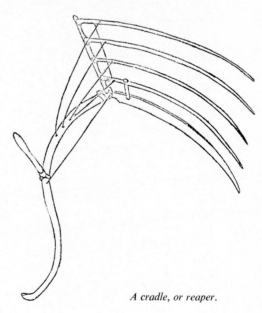

A cradle, or reaper.

29

preparation of the gardens was resumed and all rejoiced at the prospects for success. Champlain kept note on the conditions for planting and made record that early May appeared to be the most favourable period, although some seeding could be done in April.

When all were thus looking forward to a successful year there came the news from France that de Monts had encountered financial difficulties and that the colony would have to be abandoned. Lescarbot, the happy, cheery writer lamented:

"It was a great grief to us to abandon a land that had produced to us fair corn and so many fair adorned gardens. It is a land of promise. We have made trial of it and have taken pleasure therein which never did them that have gone before us, whether it be in Brazil, whether it be in Florida or in Canada. God hath blessed our labours and hath given unto us fair wheat, rye, barley, oats, peas, beans, hemp, turnips and garden herbs, and this so plentifully that the rye was as high as the tallest man that may be seen."

The Sieur de Poutrincourt refused to leave until after the harvest and when the others sailed, late in July, he, with some labourers, remained eleven days longer, harvested the grain, prepared samples to take to France and resowed part of the crop with the optimistic feeling that they would return. Then with his samples of grain, he, too, sailed for France, seemingly the first man to have sown and harvested grain on his own land in Canada. He was the Seigneur of Port Royal, and he sought and won a prize for both himself and Governor de Monts through the products of his soil. Lescarbot tells the story in his own quaint way in Chapter XVIII of *Nova Francia*:

"Being at Paris, the said Monsieur de Poutrincourt presented the King with the fruits of the land from whence he came, and especially the corn, wheat, rye, barley and oats, as

being the most precious thing that may be brought from what country so ever. It had been very fit to vow these first fruits to God, and to place them in some church among the monuments of triumph, with more just cause than the ancient Romans, who presented to their country Gods and Goddesses — the first-fruits of their tillage.

"Upon the fair show of the fruits of the said country, the King did confirm to Monsieur de Monts the privilege for the trade of beavers with the savages, to the end to give him means to establish his colonies in New France. And by this occasion he sent thither in March last, families, there to begin Christian and French commonwealths which God vouchsafe to bless and increase."

According to Lescarbot, the vessel sent out in 1608 was commanded by Champdoré, who, on his return to France, reported on the beauty of the grain sown by Poutrincourt the previous autumn. Six or more barrels of this were harvested and Membertou, the Indian chief, had a barrel of it for Poutrincourt on his return to Port Royal in 1610.

In the spring of 1608, also, a new and successful attempt was made to colonize on the St. Lawrence, Champlain sailing under the direction of Sieur de Monts and taking with him seeds and implements of various kinds, and fruit trees to plant at the site of Quebec. From this we may date the beginning of successful agriculture on the St. Lawrence, although, unfortunately, we have little information concerning the details of the first few years.

In Acadia, the Sieur de Poutrincourt added to his Port Royal seigniory more colonists with agricultural equipment in 1610. Farm animals for labour and ploughs to break up the soil were amongst the improvements made at this time; also new and large grist-mill equipment. Louis Hébert, the apothecary and botanist, took charge of the gardens

and tried the land in different locations. He was at this time third ranking officer in the colony, and fort commander in the absence of Poutrincourt and his son, Biencourt. It was probably Hébert's lot, also, to receive the first summons for the surrender of the fort to the English under Sir Samuel Argall in 1613, marking the beginning of the long struggle for possession of Canada. Argall destroyed what he could and sent a force up the stream two leagues to the pasture lands, where they took "some horses, colts and a goodly number of pigs"; but fearing to be stranded in the receding of the tide, they did not destroy the barns, mill or farm crops.

Some of the colonists abandoned Port Royal following this disaster, amongst them Louis Hébert, who made his way to France, but soon returned to Canada to engage in agriculture again at Quebec. His experience at Port Royal had been so favourable that he decided to acquire land and to undertake the support of his family by tillage of the soil, thus becoming the first independent farmer of Quebec.

During the next three-quarters of a century Port Royal changed ownership many times but agriculture persisted in spite of the numerous sieges. Crops were grown and the grist-mill kept in operation. Indeed, local tradition has it that a mill has operated every harvest season from 1610 to the present day.

The feudal tenure of farm land appears in the records of the settlement at La Have on the southern shore of Nova Scotia in 1632. Four vessels landed immigrants at that harbour under the direction of Isaac de Razilly, who allotted to them implements and farm animals and land to be held under feudal tenure. In the same year, Charles de La Tour undertook colonization on the St. John River in what is now New Brunswick, and, according to Rameau, had published in Rochelle the first printed notice of Canadian farm lands open for settlement.

Another who took a lead in the establishment of agriculture in Acadia was Sieur Nicolas Denys, who, at his different fishing posts — St. Peters-Cape Breton, Canso, Isle St. Jean and Nepisiguit — tried various farm crops, animals and fruit. He left the record that at Nepisiguit, near the present town of Bathurst, N.B., apples, plums, and pears grew better than at other places where he had tried them.

On the St. Lawrence, the almost constant fighting with the Iroquois retarded agriculture so that its progress, while steady, was somewhat slow. We read that horses were first brought to Quebec for military purposes by the commander of the regiment, Carignan Salières, in 1665 and caused great wonderment to the natives.

At the seed-time a little more than three centuries ago, the acres planted could be counted on the fingers of one hand. Six or seven barrels sufficed to store the Canadian grain crop of 1608. How many million-bushel elevators will be needed this year?

Of particular interest in connection with modern agriculture is the historic record that practically all who pioneered in this field, first learned the principles of Canadian tillage and sowed the seed of which we now reap the harvest, were men of superior education and ability. It seems a fitting thing that their names should be preserved and recorded as the founders of Canadian agriculture:

Jacques Cartier; Jean Francois de La Roche, Sieur de Roberval; Timothée Pierre du Guast, Sieur de Monts; Samuel de Champlain; Jean de Biencourt, Sieur de Poutrincourt, Baron de St. Just; Marc Lescarbot; Louis Hébert; Charles de La Tour; Isaac de Razilly; Nicolas Denys.

"United Empire Loyalists Drawing Lots for Land, 1784."

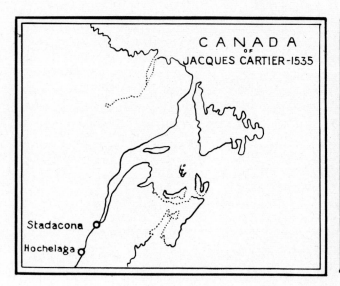

CANADA
OF
JACQUES CARTIER - 1535

Stadacona

Hochelaga

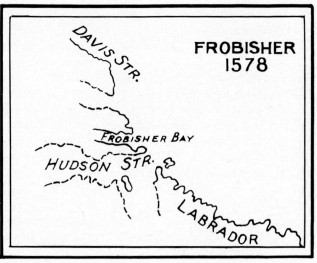

FROBISHER
1578

DAVIS STR.

Frobisher Bay

HUDSON STR.

LABRADOR

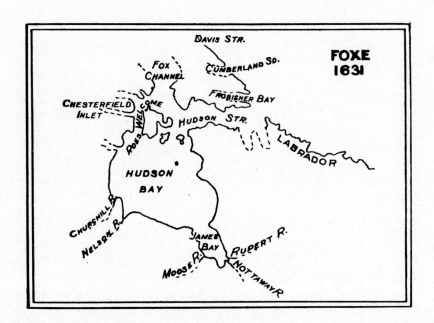

FOXE
1631

DAVIS STR.

CUMBERLAND SD.

FOX CHANNEL

Frobisher Bay

CHESTERFIELD INLET

HUDSON STR.

ROES WELCOME

LABRADOR

HUDSON BAY

CHURCHILL

NELSON R.

JAMES BAY

RUPERT R.

MOOSE R.

NOTTAWAY R.

CANADA
OF
LA VERENDRYE - 1743

HUDSON BAY

Ft Pasquia
Ft Bourbon
Ft Maurepas
Ft Dauphin
Ft La Reine
Ft St Charles
Ft St Pierre superior
Kamanistikwia
Michilimackinac
Detroit
Lake Erie
L. Ontario
Ft Frontenac
Montreal
Three Rivers
Quebec
Sorel
Louisbourg
Annapolis Royal

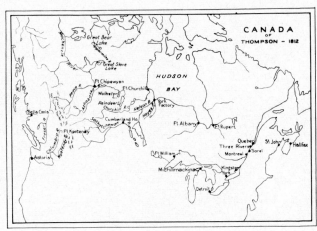

CANADA
OF
THOMPSON - 1812

Great Bear Lake

Great Slave Lake

Mackenzie River

Ft Chipewyan

Wollaston
Reindeer L.

HUDSON BAY

Ft Churchill

Churchill R.

Nelson R.

York Factory

Bella Coola

Ft Kootenay

Saskatchewan

Cumberland Ho.

Ft Albany

Ft Rupert

Astoria

Ft William

Michilimackinac

Quebec
Three Rivers
Montreal
Sorel

St John

Halifax

Kingston

Detroit

SPREADING OUT THE PATTERN

The first settlements, clinging precariously to the St. Lawrence river and dependent on yearly supplies from France, could not contain the more venturesome settlers. The Indians were friendly, new land was there to be discovered, and activity in the infant colony was so restricted by Church and State that life in the bush presented an irresistible challenge. Volunteers were not lacking for official parties of exploration; others defied authority and roamed the country at will.

When Champlain sent Etienne Brulé to check the Indian stories of an inland sea he still hoped to discover a westward route to China. This hope faded, but the fur trade promised wealth to those who controlled it and that control could only be exercised effectively in the fur country. The Great Lakes-St. Lawrence system provided the highway to the west; there was no similar route south of it. To control this route and the waterways to the north would keep the fur flowing to Montreal and Quebec rather than being diverted to New England. Unlike Brulé, La Vérendrye was a fur trader, interesting in developing the wealth of Canada rather than seeking the spice and silks of the Orient.

Meanwhile England was exploiting her sea-power to obtain directly from the north through Hudson Bay the fur that was blocked off from England by the French. York Factory was in the heart of the fur country and was the tide-water terminus of water routes traversing the northwestern sector of the continent through the Hayes, Nelson, Saskatchewan, Athabaska and Mackenzie river systems. It was from Fort Prince of Wales at the mouth of the Churchill River that Samuel Hearne set out on the trip that led him to the Coppermine River and the Arctic Ocean.

Following the battle on the Plains of Abraham national rivalry for the northern fur trade ceased but commercial rivalry between the Hudson's Bay Company and the new Northwest Company based at Montreal produced the funds and equipment that led the fur trader-explorers farther West and North. Mackenzie was disappointed when the great river he travelled bore him to the Arctic Ocean instead of to the Pacific; Fraser thought that the river which was carrying him to the Pacific was the Columbia and did not discover his error until he reached tide-water. Both names are inscribed imperishably on the map of Canada.

In honouring these five men we remember also the others, many of whose names are well-known, who filled in the gaps of knowledge and made their exploits possible.

Thus the pattern was spread out as a series of threads of discovery covering the country. So long as fur was the goal there was little pressure to build settled communities — in fact the fur traders wished to keep the country in its wild state as a huge beaver farm. The framework was established and known, but the vision of a Nation of the North had not yet seized the imagination of the settlers in the East and was not to do so until confederation brought responsibility and challenge to the maturing eastern colonies.

33

La Nation des Puans.

Isle ou il y a vne
miae de cuure.

33

Grand lac.

Sault

Mer douce

Descouuertures de ce grand la
depuis le sault S. Louis p
années 1614. et 161

Grande riuiere qui vient du
midy.

Les gens de
affistagueronons

feu

Nation ou il y a quantité de beufflea

Carte de la nouuelle france, augmentée depuis la
derniere, seruant a la nauigation faicte en son vray
Meridien, par le s.: de Champlain Capitaine pour le Roy
en la Marine; lequel depuis l'an 1603 jusques en l'année
1629; a descouuert plusieurs costes, terres, lacs, riuieres,
et Nations de sauuages, par cy deuant incognuës, comme
il se voit en ses relations quil a faict Imprimer en 1632.
ou il se voit cette marque F ce sont habitations
quont faict les françois.

*Part of Champlain's map of 1632, showing Lakes Superior (Grand Lac) and Huron (Mer douce) with the Sault (Ste. Marie)
between them. The Winnebagoes (Puans) are shown near a non-existent lake where there was said to be a copper mine.*

ÉTIENNE BRULÉ
AND THE GREAT LAKES

by CLIFFORD P. WILSON

In THE TRUE sense of the word, the Great Lakes were never discovered. The French explorers who were the first white men to see them, already knew of their existence through Indian reports, and this may explain why such important achievements were not given the attention they seem to deserve. The voyageur in his frail canoe looked on them, not as a boon and a blessing to man, as we do, but as large, dangerous bodies of water which as a medium of transportation were infinitely less desirable than the rivers and small lakes.

By Cartier and Champlain they were regarded either as links in the westward waterway to the South Sea of the explorers' dreams, or as arms of the South Sea itself. Cartier first heard of them through the Indians as "two or three large, very broad lakes" beyond which was "a freshwater sea (Huron) of which there is no mention of anyone having seen the bounds." Champlain's hopes of finding the ocean which would bear him to China were raised even higher than Cartier's by the Indian report that the sea beyond the lakes was not fresh, but salt. The water of the first lake (Ontario) they said, was brackish; that of the second (Erie) more brackish; while that of the third (Huron) was as salt as the sea.

No opportunity of proving the Indian reports occurred until seven years later, and by that time the route by way of Lakes Ontario and Erie had

Champlain found that his duties as Governor of the young colony restricted severely his keen desire to explore the country. How Brulé, as his agent, discovered the Great Lakes is told in these extracts from an article that appeared in the April, 1932, issue of the Canadian Geographical Journal.

Memorial to Brulé and Grenolle erected near the Canadian lock at Sault Ste. Marie.

been closed by Iroquois hostilities. But in the meantime Champlain had met some Hurons who told him of the great lake on the shores of which they dwelt.

We find him, then, in 1610, still obsessed by the desire to know more about this vast expanse of water. Was it the salt South Sea, or was it fresh? And if fresh, did its waters

flow westward, or eventually find their way into the St. Lawrence, or both. Indian reports were always so confusing, and with them one never knew where fact ended and fiction began. The only sure way to find out, since he could not go himself, was to send a Frenchman into the Huron country.

For this important mission he chose an adventurous youth named Étienne Brulé. The decision to send him was made just after the battle with the Iroquois near what is now the town of Sorel, at the mouth of the Richelieu River. The Hurons and Algonquins were about to return up the Ottawa to their respective domains, and Champlain seized this golden opportunity to send with them the young Étienne. The chief to whom he entrusted this youth was, judging from Champlain's chronicles, a man of character and commanding personality, the Algonquin Iroquet. In the summer he lived in the Ottawa Valley, apparently in the neighbourhood of Pembroke; but in the winter he roamed the country of the Hurons, probably because there the trapping was better. Champlain thus knew that if Brulé stayed with Iroquet he would not only be in the best possible hands, but would have a chance to learn both languages, see both countries, and above all see the great lake.

So about the end of June, 1610, the returning Hurons and Algonquins with Brulé in their care left the mouth

of the Richelieu, paddled probably up the Rivière des Prairies at the back of the Island of Montreal, so as to avoid the Lachine Rapids, and through the Lake of Two Mountains up the Ottawa River. At the Chaudière Falls they stopped to portage and to make their customary offering of tobacco to the local Manitou, so that Brulé was the first white man to see the site of the future capital.

Unfortunately Champlain never set down in writing the information imparted to him by Brulé. The young adventurer's discoveries are recorded only on his master's maps. For this reason we have no definite proof that Brulé went into the land of the Hurons, in 1610, but the evidence that he did so is so strong that eminent geographical historians like Burpee and Dawson have stated plainly that such was the case.

We can picture him, then, setting out in the fall of that year with Iroquet and his Algonquins, paddling and portaging up the Ottawa River to its junction with the Mattawa, following this stream to its headwaters near North Bay, and launching his canoe on the waters of Lake Nipissing. Here dwelt the Nebicerini, or Nation of Sorcerers, a people who, like Iroquet's men, left their own country in the winter for that of the Hurons. Crossing the lake, the Algonquins and Brulé entered the turbulent French River, and at its mouth the boy adventurer, first of the white race, gazed out with wonder over the broad expanse of Lake Huron.

The Indians apparently told him that the lake was 300 leagues (750 miles) long and that its waters flowed eventually into the St. Lawrence, for

on Champlain's map of 1612 are shown the beginnings of a lake 300 leagues long, discharging into another about 100 leagues long, which discharges into the St. Lawrence. It must be remembered that the Indians measured distances by days of travel, which Champlain converted into leagues, and that in reckoning the length of a lake they always referred to the distance along its shores, since they could not venture out into the open water.

Five years later Brulé was to help Champlain discover more about this lake 100 leagues long. It will be remembered that the French governor had promised to help the Hurons and Algonquins in their wars against the Iroquois. This year (1615) a great war party headed by Champlain gathered on the shores of Lake Simcoe with the object of marching on an Onondaga stronghold in the heart of the Iroquois confederacy, not far from the present town of Syracuse, New York.

To reinforce the Algonquins and Hurons, their allies the Carantouannais who lived three days south of the Onondaga fort had promised to send 500 warriors, and in order that both armies might arrive at the same time, someone had to be dispatched to warn the Carantouannais that the northern party was on the war path.

Twelve of the most stalwart braves were chosen for this dangerous errand; but Brulé, scenting adventure, begged to be allowed to go with them. As they took two canoes, it is evident that they went up the Holland River, portaged across into the Humber, and glided down this stream to the place where Toronto now stands.

Thus was the second of the Great Lakes discovered. A few days later Champlain and the great war-party emerged from the Trent River onto the Bay of Quinté and crossed the lake to Stoney Point; but by that time Brulé and the twelve savages would have paddled around the western end and been well on their way overland towards Carantouan, thus avoiding the direct route through the Iroquois country.

The story of the battle of the Onondaga fort is well known—how Brulé and the 500 men from the south arrived too late, and how Champlain was forced to retire. Brulé's subsequent discovery of the Susquehanna River takes us too far from the Great Lakes, so we will pass over the tale of his capture and torture by the Iroquois, and his miraculous escape, and meet him again eight years later at the mouth of the French River, outward bound for the unknown west.

What did he expect to find? "As to the more westerly parts," Champlain had written after his visit to the

37

Champlain discovers Georgian Bay, 1615. From the painting by C. W. Jefferys.

Huron country in 1616, "we cannot quite know the lie of them, because the tribes have no knowledge of them, except for 200 or 300 leagues more to the west, whence flows the said great river (St. Lawrence) which passes, amongst other places, through a lake nearly 30 days canoe journey in extent, namely that which we have called the Freshwater Sea, having regard to its great size, for it is nearly 400 leagues long."

So the savages had reported; but when they spoke of a great body of water thirty days long, they probably included Lake Superior as well as Lake Huron. In spite of this report, a petition presented to the King three

years later (1619) over Champlain's name, stated that this body of water was "a lake about 300 leagues long, from which lake flows a river that issues into the South Sea," and went on to describe the enormous "customs duties on the merchandise that would come from China and from the Indies."

Brulé, then, may still have expected to find the South Sea not far away. Setting out westwards from the French River with a Frenchman named Grenolle and some Indians, he found his way along the rocky shores of the North Channel, paddled up the lovely St. Mary's River, and probably taking the old channel by

way of Lake George, rounded the bend now occupied by the park at the Canadian Sault to come in sight of the mile-long stretch of rapids foaming white across the river.

On the shores were gathered in great numbers the round-topped lodges of the Ojibwas, since the rapids, on account of the abundance of game and whitefish, was a famous meeting-place for the tribes. The travellers would not stay long, however, in this earthly paradise, for the great lake above the rapids—the fabled Gitche Gumee with its copper mines and unknown tribes, which might lead them to the South Sea— lay waiting to be explored.

Party of Indians travelling across the plains, with horse and dog travois. From a painting by Paul Kane.

Étienne Brulé at the mouth of the Humber River in 1615.

So in due course Brulé and Grenolle embarked above the rapids and headed westwards up the river, until rounding Pointe aux Pins, they came upon the largest body of fresh water in the world—Lake Superior.

Thus in the space of thirteen years, three of the great inland seas in the heart of aboriginal America had been discovered by one man. Yet now, because he left no written records, his name is barely known. To be sure, proof has not until now been brought forward that he did discover Lake Superior; but with the help of the Recollet Brother Sagard, who travelled down the Ottawa with Brulé the following year (1624), and of the Ontario Department of Mines, that fact has now been established beyond reasonable doubt.

Friar Sagard relates how Brulé showed him a piece of native copper from a mine he had visited on his westward trip; and Mr. T. W. Gibson, Deputy Minister of Mines for Ontario, states that in the region of the Great Lakes, native copper is to be found only on the shores and islands of Lake Superior. There is only one conclusion—that Brulé visited a copper mine on Lake Superior.

LA VÉRENDRYE–

Pathfinder of the West

by LAWRENCE J. BURPEE

OF ALL that gallant company of adventurers who helped, each in his time and degree, to unroll the map of Canada, one alone was native born—La Vérendrye. Pierre Gaultier de Varennes, Sieur de la Vérendrye, —to give him his full, high-sounding name—was born in the town of Three Rivers, on the St. Lawrence, in November, 1685. As his name suggests, he was of gentle birth, his father being Governor of the district of which Three Rivers was the capital. His mother was a daughter of Pierre Boucher, a former Governor of the same district.

With La Vérendrye's early years we are not concerned here. It was not, in fact, until he had reached well into the forties that he began the course of western exploration which was to engage all his thought and energy for the remainder of his life, and bring him abundant fame, though not in his own lifetime or for many years afterwards. Without doubt La Vérendrye had dreamed and planned schemes of western discovery long before there was any possibility of turning them into realities. He had served in the army, both in America and Europe, had been seriously wounded at the battle of Malplaquet, had afterwards married and settled down for a time on the St. Maurice, and in 1726 had been put in command of an important trading post on Lake Nipigon, north of Lake Superior.

Here there came to him one day an Indian named Ochagach, who told

* * *

Lawrence J. Burpee, who was the first Chairman of the Editorial Committee of the Society, wrote a series of articles on the explorers of Canada for the Canadian Geographical Journal. *This one appeared in the April 1933 issue. La Vérendrye was the first to move west from Lake Superior and reach the prairie.*

* * *

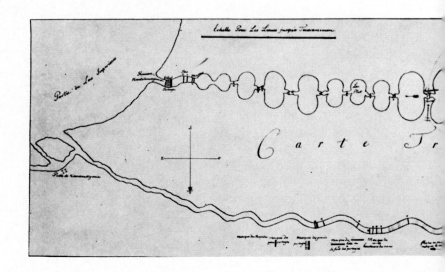

An early map done in France based on the map prepared by Ochagach for La Vérendrye. Note that this map is drawn according to the old convention of looking from north to south, so that Lake Superior in the east appears at the extreme left, and the Mississippi River appears at the top.

him that he had travelled far towards the setting sun until he came to a great lake, out of which a river flowed to the westward. He had descended this river, he said, until he reached a point where the water ebbed and flowed. He had not been able to go down to its mouth because of hostile tribes, but had been told that the river emptied into a great salt lake or sea.

La Vérendrye's imagination, already filled with pictures of the unknown land beyond Lake Superior, took fire, and he determined at all costs to seek for and find that Western Sea which had been the elusive goal of all the explorers of New France. Resigning his Nipigon command he returned to Quebec, taking with him a curious map drawn by Ochagach. The then Governor General, the Marquis de Beauharnois, was a man of broad views, keenly interested in the cause of western discovery. He entered warmly into the plans of La Vérendrye, and wrote Louis XV urging that the explorer should be given the command of a hundred men and sufficient supplies and equipment to carry his project to a successful conclusion. The King, however, was at that time deeply engaged in European wars, and all that he would agree to was that La Vérendrye should be given a monop-

oly of the fur trade in the country beyond Lake Superior. That is to say, he was permitted to build trading posts and trade with the Indians, and might use the profits to cover the cost of his discoveries towards the Western Sea.

Not a very promising scheme from any point of view, and one that at the best must necessarily mean very slow progress in exploration. Any man less enthusiastic and determined would have thrown the matter up in disgust. La Vérendrye, however, set to work at once, put his own little fortune into the project, and, not without difficulty, persuaded some of the Montreal merchants to go into partnership with him, on the understanding that they would provide equipment and supplies and pay the men, and in

return get all the profits of the fur trade.

In the early summer of 1731, therefore, we find the expedition setting forth from Montreal, in a brigade of birchbark canoes. With La Vérendrye went three sons, his nephew La Jemeraye, and a party of canoemen, hunters and soldiers—a very much smaller party than that contemplated by the Governor, but the best that La Vérendrye could manage with his limited resources.

Their way lay up the Ottawa, the waterway which had been the recognized route to the west since its discovery by Champlain. They ascended the river past the Long Sault, scene of the heroic exploit of Daulac and his young comrades; past the Chaudière, sacred to generations of In-

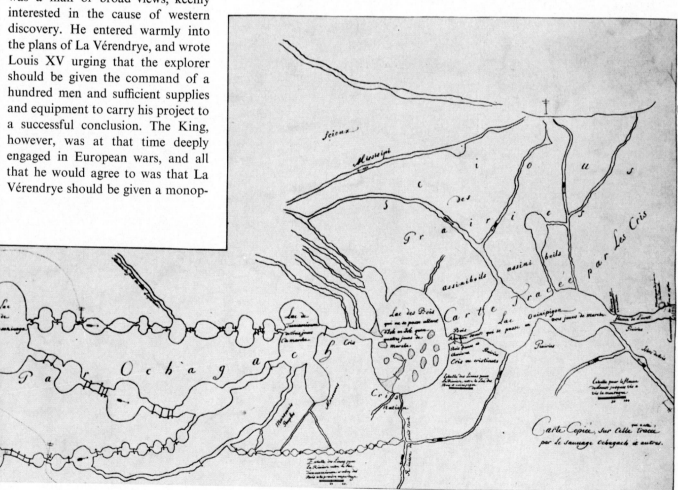

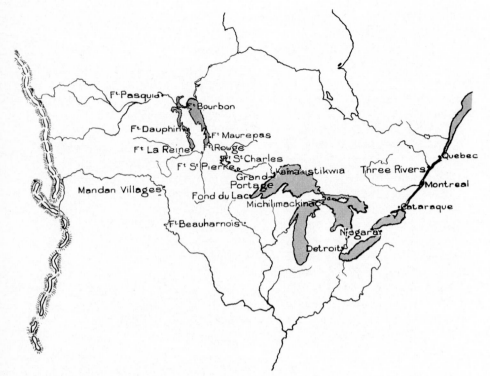

Sketch map showing the various forts established by La Vérendrye during his western explorations.

This became La Vérendrye's headquarters for several years, while he did his best to bring peace to the warring tribes, and matured his plans for further exploration. The site of Fort St. Charles was discovered a few years ago by a party of historical investigators from St. Boniface College, Manitoba.

His eldest son Jean was sent forward, with several men and an Indian guide, in 1733, to find what might be true of the stories of Ochagach and others as to rivers and lakes and strange tribes to the westward. Jean made his way down a small stream known to-day as the Roseau, to the Red River, and descended that river to Lake Winnipeg. Returning up Red River a short distance, he built a third post, which he named Fort Maurepas, after the Minister of the Colonies in France.

The years that followed were filled with sorrow and discouragement for

dians; past Allumette Island, where the Algonquin chief Tessouat had contemptuously denounced Vignau to Champlain; over the swampy height of land to Lake Nipissing; and down French River to Georgian Bay. From there they followed the north shore of Lake Huron and St. Mary's River to Sault Ste. Marie, where there had been a Jesuit Mission and a trading post for many years; and skirted the shore of Lake Superior until they came to what was afterwards to become famous as Grand Portage—one of three recognized water routes from Lake Superior to the west.

To La Vérendrye's indignation and disgust, the voyageurs who had followed him so far, now took it into their stupid heads to mutiny. They refused to accompany him into the unknown country that lay beyond. Finding it impossible to do anything with them, at any rate for the time being, the explorer sent La Jemeraye forward with a small party of picked

men to build an advanced post, while he himself took the malcontents north to the mouth of the Kaministikwia, to spend the winter. La Jemeraye made his way from Grand Portage over the water route that other explorers and fur traders were to use for a hundred years, and that to-day forms the international boundary between Canada and the United States. When he reached the point where Rainy River flows out of the lake of the same name, he thought it prudent to go no farther. He and his men set to work to build a small fort, which they named Fort St. Pierre. It stood in or near the present town of Fort Frances.

In the spring of 1732 La Vérendrye and his party followed the same route to Fort St. Pierre and, leaving a few men in charge, paddled down Rainy River to the Lake of the Woods. On the west side of that lake, in what was afterwards to become famous in diplomatic history as the North West Angle, they built Fort St. Charles.

A chief of the Mandans, from a drawing by George Catlin.

42

La Vérendrye. La Jemeraye died from exposure during the severe winter of 1735, and the following year the explorer's son was murdered by the Sioux on an island in the Lake of the Woods. The Montreal merchants, on whom he had to rely for supplies, refused to send La Vérendrye any more goods, and he was compelled more than once to make the long journey down to Montreal to coax them into a more friendly frame of mind. His enemies in Quebec were industriously poisoning the mind of the King's representatives against the explorer. And to crown his misfortunes the bitter antagonism between the Sioux and the tribes friendly to La Vérendrye made it very difficult for him to make any progress with his western discoveries.

Nevertheless he stuck doggedly to his task. In 1736 he made his way west to the forks of the Red and Assiniboine Rivers and built a temporary post there which he named Fort Rouge. The name is to-day commemorated in a section of the city of Winnipeg. About this time Fort Maurepas was moved from the Red River to the foot of the Winnipeg River. From Fort Rouge La Vérendrye and his men ascended the Assiniboine to a point in or near the present city of Portage la Prairie, where he built Fort La Reine, named after the French Queen. His explorations, hampered though they were by the parsimony of the King, had now covered a large part of southern Manitoba, and at Fort La Reine he held a strategic position for further discoveries. A short portage would take him to Lake Manitoba, Lake Winnipegosis and the Saskatchewan, while in the other direction a journey over the plains would bring him to the Missouri. At this time, of course, he knew nothing, except what he may have learned from the Indians, of either of these great waterways, both of which led to the Rocky Mountains, but his mind was steadily set on the discovery of the Western Sea, and

Interior of one of the tribal lodges of the Mandans. From a drawing by George Catlin.

A Mandan village on the banks of the Missouri, showing the curious circular lodges described by La Vérendrye. From a drawing by George Catlin.

before he was through attempts would be made in both directions.

From Fort La Reine, he made a journey across the plains to the Mandan villages on the Missouri, being the first white man to visit this remarkable tribe. He had been hearing such extraordinary stories about the Mandans from the Chippewa and Cree that he was convinced he would find them to be some race of white people, from whom he could obtain reliable information as to the way to reach the Western Ocean. He was correspondingly disappointed to discover that they were merely Indians,

43

La Vérendrye was the first explorer to enter the prairies westward from the Great Lakes. In 1743, two of his sons, depicted here, sighted the foothills of the Rocky Mountains.

though Indians who had developed a civilization of their own, lived in walled towns and cultivated maize, pumpkins and tobacco.

Nevertheless, a few years later, being unable to leave Fort La Reine himself, he sent two of his sons on an ambitious attempt to find the sea somewhere beyond the Missouri. The sons went to the Mandan villages, and from there set off toward the south-west. After visiting many hitherto unknown tribes, and experiencing many adventures, they finally became involved in a warlike expedition by friendly Indians against the Snakes or Cheyennes. They reluctantly accompanied the war-party because they had been assured that when the Snakes had been overcome, the way would be clear for them to the sea, which they were told was not very distant. This of course was very far from being the truth, as they were then, as far as it is possible to trace their journey, somewhere in the present state of Wyoming, in any event still a very long way from the Pacific. They were bitterly disappointed when the war party, filled with a sudden

panic, abandoned their expedition and turned back, with the mountains, beyond which the explorers had hoped to find the long-sought sea, full in view.

On the return journey to the Mandan villages and Fort La Reine, the La Vérendryes buried a lead plate with an inscription taking possession of the country in the name of Louis XV. It had long been hoped by historians that this plate might be found, as it would fix at least one point in the expedition of 1742-43. In 1913, one hundred and seventy years after it was deposited, the plate was picked up by some school children playing about a sand-hill in the neighbourhood of Pierre, South Dakota.

Having failed to reach the sea toward the south-west, La Vérendrye tried the north-west. In 1741 he had built Fort Dauphin, near the southern end of Lake Winnipegosis; and some time afterward Fort Bourbon at the northern end of the same lake, and Fort Pasquia on the lower Saskatchewan. With these as his bases, he purposed making his way up the Saskatchewan, and did actually get as far as the Forks, but misfortunes were now crowding thick and fast upon him. He was forced to

Plate buried by La Vérendrye on the banks of the Missouri in 1743, and found by school children in 1913, at Pierre, South Dakota.

Indian camp on the shore of Lake Huron. From a painting by Paul Kane.

return to Quebec, and died there in 1749. His sons begged to be allowed to continue their father's explorations, but were curtly refused.

La Vérendrye failed in the definite object he had set before himself—the discovery of an overland route to the Pacific Ocean; but he accomplished something much more important. He was in a real sense the discoverer of Western Canada; first to descend the Winnipeg river; first to see Lake Winnipeg; first on the Red and the Assiniboine and the Saskatchewan, if we except the somewhat indefinite journey of Henry Kelsey; first to cross the great plains to the Missouri. Many years afterward English-speaking explorers were to reach the sea he had vainly sought, both by the Missouri and the Saskatchewan.

Insert: Portage routes from Lake Superior westward.
Below: One of La Vérendrye's maps, prepared after 1740, showing the Missouri River as well as the Assiniboine, Fort La Reine, and other posts.

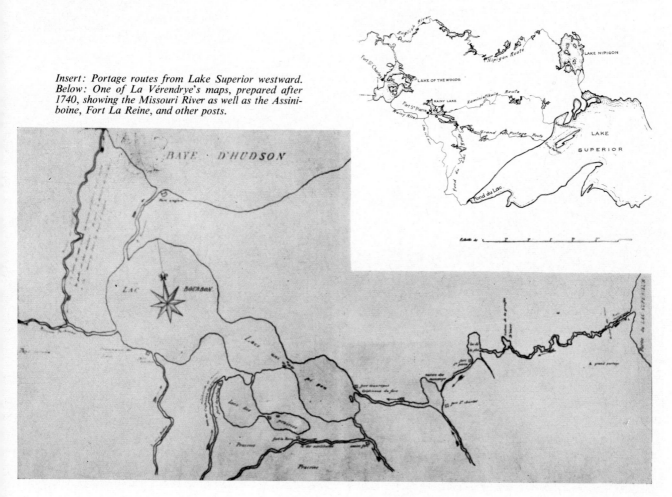

A Canot de Maître, or Montreal Canoe, shooting rapids. This oil painting by Mrs. E. M. Hopkins is in the Public Archives of Canada.

Shooting Parisien Rapid on the French River. The voyageurs would portage past this only going upstream.

VOYAGEURS' HIGHWAY:

The Geography and Logistics of the Canadian Fur Trade

by ERIC W. MORSE

Eric W. Morse, now national director of the Association of Canadian Clubs, is an historian by training and a canoeist and student of the fur trade by avocation. He has himself travelled by canoe the routes described in this article, which is abridged from a series of three in the May, July and August, 1961, issues of the Canadian Geographical Journal.

TWO HUNDRED YEARS AGO, as today, the ice broke up on the Ottawa River around the first of May. In the heyday of the Montreal fur trade, the half century from 1770 to 1820, the first of May saw great activity at Lachine, eight miles above Montreal. "Brigades" of big Montreal canoes, or "canots de maître", each craft paddled by ten or a dozen colourfully dressed voyageurs, and carrying up to three tons of cargo, were loaded and began to move off for the "pays d'en haut".

They went straight west up the Ottawa River to Mattawa, where the Ottawa ends its big swing down from the north. Here they headed up the Mattawa River, and paddled and portaged forty miles to its source in Trout Lake, at North Bay. Three portages over a rough divide led them into Lake Nipissing, from where it was easy going down the French River to Georgian Bay. After following the North Channel above Manitoulin Island, they portaged past Sault Ste. Marie and headed out around the treacherous 450-mile passage of the North Shore of Lake Superior.

About the end of June, after eight weeks of long days, great hazards and unremitting toil, they found themselves at their objective, Grand Portage. This was the great central entrepôt of the Canadian fur trade,

A small rapid on the Churchill River just below Stanley. A canoe is coming through at the left.

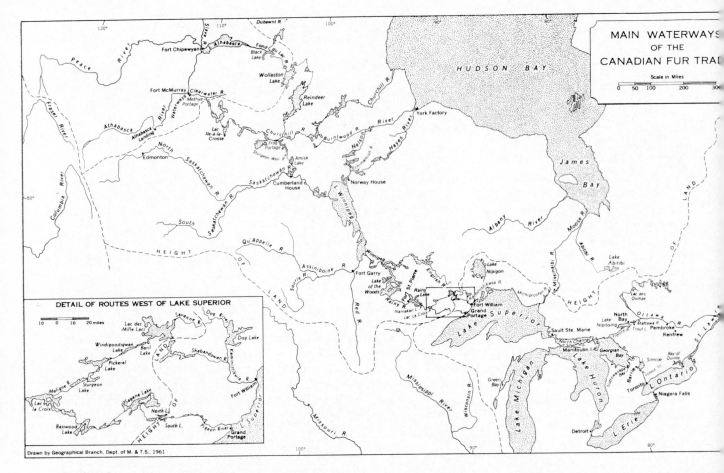

DETAIL OF ROUTES WEST OF LAKE SUPERIOR

10 0 10 20 miles

Drawn by Geographical Branch, Dept. of M. & T.S., 1961

situated on a shallow bay of Lake Superior ten miles south of the mouth of the Pigeon River, the present international border. (Grand Portage was abandoned when the Americans made good their claim to the new boundary, and from about 1803 its place was taken by Fort William.)

Grand Portage was the objective of the big "canots de maître" from Montreal, and a rendezvous. But it was not the end of the line. The other end of the "Voyageurs' Highway" was Fort Chipewyan on Lake Athabasca. The ice in that latitude did not break up quite as soon as on the Ottawa. Though the big northern lakes often were still iced over in June, the turbulent Athabasca River usually burst winter's bonds around May 15. Fort Chipewyan about then became a scene similar to Lachine a fortnight earlier. And while the Montreal canoes were paddling westward, the Athabasca Brigade was

paddling eastward to meet the "canots de maître" at Grand Portage.

The waters west of Lake Superior on the whole were smaller, and two continental divides had to be crossed. The craft used here was the North canoe — high-ended, half the capacity, and paddled by six or eight men. On the trip east they carried, not trading goods, but bales of fur. Up the Athabasca River they paddled for 200 miles, leaving it at Fort McMurray (Waterways) to ascend the swift Clearwater. This stream they left after 80 miles, to cross the gruelling thirteen-mile Methye (La Loche) Portage, which brought them to the headwaters of the Churchill River. The Churchill was followed for some 400 miles to a point north of Cumberland House where Frog Portage led them over to the Sturgeon-weir River which (for its wicked rapids) the voyageurs called the Maligne. This carried them down to the

Saskatchewan River, which they then followed to its mouth in Lake Winnipeg.

Most of this journey from Fort Chipewyan was downstream. There followed the passage of storm-tossed, shallow Lake Winnipeg, and then the laborious ascent of the Winnipeg River and its tributary the Rainy along the border-lakes chain. This led them to the divide, and over it to either Grand Portage or Fort William, the two routes separating at Lake La Croix a little to the east of Rainy Lake.

Along the way, the Athabasca Brigade would sometimes be joined by other less distant Brigades — those from Ile à la Crosse, Cumberland House, or Red River. Actually, because of the greater distance, the Athabasca Brigade usually got only as far as Fort St. Pierre at the foot of Rainy Lake, where they were met by a special detachment from Grand

Portage in mid-July and were allowed to get away on their two-months' home journey before the first of August. Otherwise, the reforwarding of some of their return cargo of trading goods from Fort Chipewyan to the outlying posts in the Mackenzie District could not be accomplished before freeze-up.

All this is of necessity a sketch and a simplification, taking no account of the fur trade's vicissitudes and the later modifications of the route. Nor does it attempt to bring in the avenue used by Canada's other fur-trading enterprise, the Hudson's Bay Company. Staked out here, however, is a water route, Canada's first and main through way, which has probably done more to shape Canada's history and development than any other of its avenues of communication. The coureurs de bois, the voyageurs and early explorers who first used this route are symbols of Canada's heroic or epic age; and few nations have so colourful and romantic a past. Many Canadians seem to be aware of the historical associations of this highway, without realizing that the actual route still lies hardly changed today: the scenery, the conditions of wind and current, nearly all the actual portages have scarcely altered in the three centuries since the first fur-seekers headed out from Quebec and Montreal for the "pays d'en haut".

* * *

It is a staggering statistic that half of all the fresh water in the world is to be found in Canada. Put into other words, there are as many miles of inland waterways in Canada as in all the other nations of the world combined. And, for a craft adapted to the conditions, these waterways are navigable. It is still possible to put a canoe into the water in practically any Canadian city, and paddle from the Atlantic to the Pacific, or from the Arctic Ocean to the Gulf of Mexico.

The water from three-quarters of continental Canada drains off through three outlets: the Gulf of St. Lawrence (10%), Hudson Strait (43%), and the mouth of the Mackenzie (22%). Furs were gathered, of course, from the other quarter of the country, but the heavy transportation of furs and goods operated almost entirely within these three drainage areas.

While it is usual to speak of drainage basins, for this story it would be more accurate to refer to these three areas as drainage *saucers*. This helps to underscore the low elevation of the rims, in relation to the vast areas encompassed. Twelve hundred miles from tidewater up the Great Lakes to Fort William is a rise of just 600 feet. Between the drainage areas, at no point is an interconnecting portage more than about 1500 feet above sea level; and the same holds for the several connecting gateways to the Mississippi Basin.

The combination of these three facts of Canadian geography explains much regarding the fur trade routes. Three quarters of Canada east of the Rockies presented no serious barrier to canoe travel.

This in turn is recognizably related to the presence of the worn down Precambrian Shield, covering half of Canada. The Shield with its countless systems of lakes and rivers — quite apart from its birch trees — is canoe country.

The presence of so many big lakes — Great Bear, Great Slave, Athabasca, Winnipeg, Lake of the Woods, Superior, and Huron — strung along the Shield's border, is another key to east-west canoe travel. These lakes all have one side (or end) in granite, and the other in sand or limestone. Nothing bears out better the newer concept of the Shield, not as a divisive wedge, but as a cohesive core to Canada.

The Voyageurs' Highway, however, was a trunk route; and Canadian geography in its bounty has provided more — an extraordinary system of branch routes, grouped around three well-defined hubs. The hubs are *Lakes*

Superior, *Winnipeg*, and *Athabasca*, each no higher than six or seven hundred feet above sea level. The accompanying diagrams illustrate the cardinal importance of the part that these play.

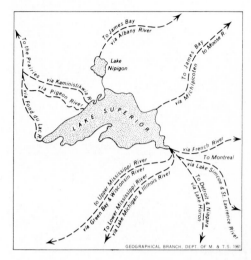

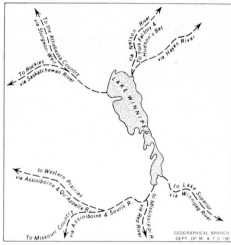

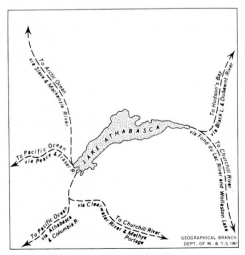

Set of crude stone steps and rock causeway built by the voyageurs on the Second Chaudière portage, across the river from Ottawa.

would prefer to have one Canadian voyageur to three of any other breed. The voyageurs were recruited on the banks of the St. Lawrence, particularly around Trois Rivières and Montreal. In a dull, authoritarian society, yet where men were reared on the traditions and tall tales of the "pays d'en haut", the fur companies had no trouble in recruiting all the "engagés" they required. The voyageurs made no money; the lure was adventure and escape.

These were usually small men (their Scots masters had an eye to every extra pound of furs that could be squeezed into the canoe). Every Canadian is familiar with the tough, gay, insouciant picture the voyageur presented, with a feather stuck in his cap and a bright sash or "ceinture fléchée". The French *chansons* to which they paddled, "A la Claire Fontaine", "C'est l'Aviron", "En Roulant ma Boule", "Youpe Youpe

sur la Rivière", etc., gave rhythm and momentum to their stroke, the sort of function played by sea-shanties for seamen in the sailing age. The voyageur, in fact, was sometimes paid a bonus for his singing voice.

* * *

The principal obstacles along the Voyageurs' Highway, then as now, can be classified as: *rapids or waterfalls*, *watersheds*, and *very big lakes*.

Rapids, however, vary — in drop, in kind, in volume, and from season to season — so there is no single technique to employ. Attacking a rapid upstream, the voyageurs would (in ascending order of necessity) paddle the canoe "demi-chargé", line or pole the canoe, make a "décharge", or portage. Coming downstream they would, depending on its degree of danger or difficulty, run the rapid, make a "décharge", or portage.

Where the rapid was too strong to battle in a fully-loaded canoe, too deep for poling, yet did not call for portaging, the voyageurs sometimes took out half the load, paddled madly up the rapid, unloaded, and returned

Beaver dam on the La Vase tributary, making this streamlet navigable for the "canots de maître". Looking north from the upper end of the middle portage.

A search of the map of Canada fails to show any practicable alternative to this main route. There were (sometimes transitory) short-cuts; but, squeezed between the Shield to the north and the United States border, there was simply no other main artery. This canoe route was used for war, trade, or hunting, each section of it by its own group of Indian tribes, centuries before they guided the white man over it.

* * *

The outboard motor for the fur canoe was the Canadian voyageur, without whom the fur trade would have been patently impossible. He was incredibly durable, always cheerful and tractable. Jacob Astor said he

for the second half. This was termed paddling "demi-chargé".

At a "décharge" the empty canoe was left in the water and lined up or down, but the cargo was portaged. In fact, except for those voyageurs specially designated to carry the canoe, it was no different from a portage. The place for a "décharge" was a very shallow rapid, or a dangerous ledge under the water which would break the back of the canoe when loaded.

The most dramatic, exciting, and least strenuous way to pass a rapid going downstream, of course, was to run it. White water was the icing on the voyageurs' cake. The two main hazards in running a rapid are rocks below and turbulence above; the one can puncture the canoe and the other swamp it. A big "canot de maître", being made of birch bark, was very vulnerable to rocks; and it was usually so heavily laden as to allow very little freeboard for keeping out the waves. Rapids varied in depth in the spring and fall. High water increased the turbulence, but covered the rocks — which of course also worked conversely.

To offset the disadvantage of a frighteningly vulnerable craft, the voyageurs had the advantages of skill and experience. In charge of a "brigade" was the "Guide". He stood in the bow of the leading canoe; he had gone over and over the course to take for each rapid, as he had risen over the years from common voyageur or "milieu", through the ranks to his present position. The top man in each canoe, the "Avant", stood in the bow; the "Gouvernail" stood in the stern and steered with his long "sweep" paddle.

Finally, there was *portaging*. In passing obstructions, the voyageurs regarded portaging as a last and inescapable extremity — for whenever they left the water, the canoe itself and everything in it had to be carried on the men's backs and necks, and sometimes over a rough, steep or boggy path. A "canot de maître" weighed about 600 pounds; a North canoe, about 300. Each voyageur carried over the portage 540 pounds in three 180-pound loads. This understandably coloured the voyageur's whole approach to portaging, and in some cases to the route he took.

A brigade of canoes arriving at a portage was a scene of great activity. The loaded birch bark canoe must not touch land for fear of damage to its skin. As they approached, out leapt the voyageurs up to their waists in water and speedily unloaded the canoe. All the trading goods and the furs had been made up into "pièces", each weighing about ninety pounds. A voyageur quickly slung one of these on his back, with a tumpline over his forehead pulling his head back. Into the hollow thus formed he tossed a second ninety-pound pack which pushed his head forward. Recognizing this as an unhappy condition to be terminated as soon as possible, the voyageurs half-ran, not walked — and many an earlier traveller recorded his own inability, unloaded, to keep up with them.

It is important to stress that the fur-traders did not *make* the portages. These paths went back perhaps 10,000 years, to the end of the last Ice Age and the coming of the Indians to this latitude. In a land without road or rail, obstructions to travel abound. But around every unnavigable obstruction there was a path. Perhaps

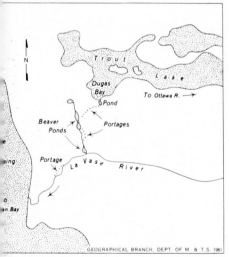

GEOGRAPHICAL BRANCH, DEPT. OF M. & T.S. 1961

The La Vase portage on the North Bay Divide *is one of the most interesting on the continent.*

"The big canoes ran down the winding creek just wide enough to take their six-foot beam." The main La Vase where it is joined by its tributary stream from the north.

51

A York boat under sail. This type of boat, handled by Orkneymen, was developed by the Hudson's Bay Company for travel between Lake Winnipeg and York Factory. Later, it replaced the canoe on many western routes.

A canoe being lined up a shallow rapid on the Hayes River. This river was much more suitable than the Nelson for the small boats used in the fur trade.

the first one made was not the best. One day, a brighter brave, a more purposeful squaw would cut off a corner, and the path would be changed. Refined in this way to its ultimate, it became established centuries ago.

* * *

The exploration of Canada, and the fact that the nation today does not terminate at Windsor — or Lakehead, or Winnipeg, or Calgary — are almost entirely by-products of the fur-trade. A quaint Victorian assumption colours some of our earlier history books, equating the exploration of Canada somehow with the spread of the Empire or the spread of the gospel; but this hardly deserves serious notice today. Canadian exploration has been sometimes represented also as a romantic "search for the western sea"; and this may have confused generations of Canadian school-children into thinking of Canada's mainland explorers in terms of

The beaver by its defencelessness contributed to its own early extermination in nearer areas, and by its value led men ever westward and northward. The fur trade unrolled the map of Canada.

The fur trade, early in Canadian history, established east-west thinking. The Voyageurs' Highway was the certain precursor of the "bands of steel" which later bound Canada as

Superior to Lake of the Woods is defined in the treaty simply as the "customary waterway" of the voyageurs. The fur trade determined also the international boundary from the crest of the Rockies to the Pacific.

The fishing industry was responsible for discovering Canada. Lumbering and mining dominate our modern economy. But in the formative years from 1600 to 1800, spanning both the

W. H. Bartlett print, "The Burial Place of the Voyageurs". Neither the canoes nor the men's hats are at all accurately depicted, but the terrain is portrayed so well that the spot is almost certainly recognizable as being the Des Chats Portage looking down the Ottawa.

Balboa or the searchers for the Northwest Passage, always looking for something, not at hand, but beyond. This approach among most historians seems fortunately at last to have given way to a purely economic interpretation, that Canadian exploration and the fur trade are practically one and the same thing.

a nation. The fur trade thus stopped "Manifest Destiny" at the border; and long before confederation, it ensured that the foundations of Canada as a nation had been securely laid.

The fur trade played a principal role in various negotiations determining Canada's boundaries. The international boundary from Lake

French and early English regimes, Canada's principal moulding influence was the fur trade. Some other nations owe their development to diamonds, or gold, or teak. Canada is a nation built on fur. The beaver, with reason, holds a place just below the crown in our national symbolism and heraldry.

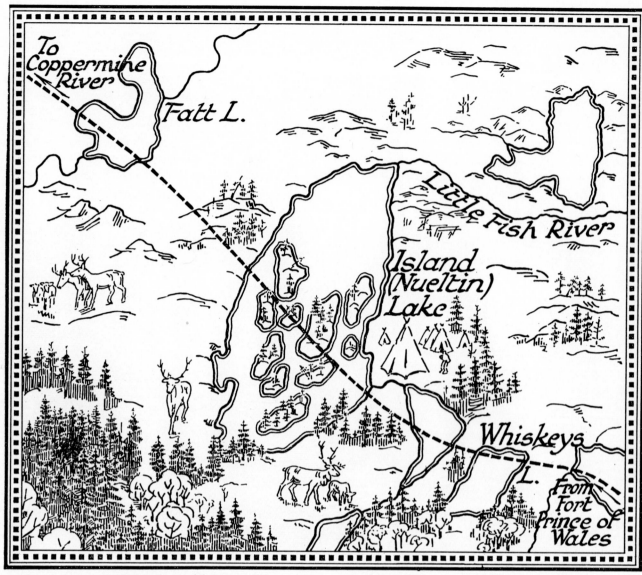

Animated map of the country around Island Lake where Samuel Hearne spent a very dull Christmas.

CHRISTMAS WITH SAMUEL HEARNE

By CHARLES W. JEFFERYS

Samuel Hearne is probably the least known of the explorers of Canada. His discovery of the Coppermine River and his arrival at the Arctic Ocean, overland from the mouth of the Churchill River, had no immediate practical application in the life of his time. Thus his achievement tends to be passed by. It deserves to be remembered.

On Christmas Day, 1770, a party of Indians, accompanied by a single white man, was plodding across the barren lands to the north west of Fort Prince of Wales, at Churchill on Hudson Bay. The white man was Samuel Hearne, on an expedition to the Northern Ocean, or, as his Instructions put it, "in quest of a North West Passage, Copper Mines, or any

other thing that may be serviceable to the British Nation in general or the Hudson's Bay Company in particular."

A young Englishman of twenty-four, Hearne had then been in the service of the Company for the last four or five years, employed, for the most part, in trading along the west coast of Hudson Bay. Rumors of mines of copper in the far north had reached the Company from time to time through Indians who brought specimens of the ore to the Fort. Acting under the orders of the London Committee, Hearne had already made two attempts to explore the interior of the country to the north of Churchill. Both ventures fell short of their objective, owing to the desertion and insubordination of his Indian guides. Undaunted by the hardships and dangers of the journey and undiscouraged by failure, he volunteered to try again. Twelve days after his return from his second attempt, Hearne set out from the Fort once more.

This time he took with him as leader of his party, a Chipewyan Indian, Matonabbee, to whose intelligence and experience the eventual success of the expedition was due. Hearne, in his account of the journey, gives a vivid and intimate picture of the conditions of northern travel, and of the life of the Indians of those days.

To readers of the present age of scientifically equipped exploration, perhaps the most striking feature of the narratives of these early expeditions is the fact that it was taken for granted that they should depend for their subsistence mainly upon the game and fish of the country through which they journeyed. We realize something of the precarious nature of these undertakings when we find that in less than three weeks from the time that Hearne's party had set out they were in danger of starvation. This, it is true, was partly due to the circumstance that a store of provisions which had been laid up by his Indians on their way to the Fort had been robbed by some of their countrymen who had left Churchill a few days before them. "This loss was the more severely felt," says Hearne, "as there was a total want of every kind of game; and the Indians, not expect-

ing to meet so great a disappointment, had not used that economy in the expenditure of the oatmeal and other provisions which they had received at the Fort, as they probably would have done, had they not relied firmly on finding a supply at this place."

But, apart from accidents such as this, the impossibility of transporting sufficient provisions for extended inland journeys is apparent in every account of these early travels. Hunger

stalks through their pages. La Hontan, writing in 1684, describing the difficulties of supplying Fort Frontenac, then the western outpost of French Canada, says, "we might march five or six hundred men by land to guard the canows that carry the provisions; but 'tis to be considered, that before they arriv'd at the fort, they would consume more provisions than the canows can carry". Food, its supply, or its failure,

The Desolation and the Glory of the Barren Lands, through which Samuel Hearne travelled in 1770-72.

C.W. JEFFERYS

This drawing made by Samuel Hearne in 1771, and titled simply "A winter view in the Athapuskow Lake", portrays well the feeling of desolation and isolation he must have felt on his journeyings.

bulks largely in the various Jesuit Relations, in the stories of Hennepin and La Salle, even in the reports of later and more highly organized expeditions such as those of Franklin and Palliser and Hector. Our admiration for the fortitude of these earlier explorers is increased by their matter-of-fact acceptance of famine conditions, and the almost casual way in which they speak of their privations. Characteristic is the apologetic manner in which Palliser, in his Re-

port "presented to both Houses of Parliament by command of Her Majesty," refers to an occasion when he and his party fell upon some game which they had killed and devoured it raw. One can almost see the blush of Victorian shame on his handsome face as he penned the degrading lines. They were a robust-minded race, to whom self-pity was a stranger, and it is only now and then that we get a hint as to their feelings.

But, on that Christmas Day of

1770, young Hearne, moved by the associations of the season, permits himself to indulge in a few reflections upon his lonely and distressing situation.

"On the nineteenth, we pursued our course in the North West quarter; and . . . traversed nothing, but barren ground, with empty bellies, till the twenty-seventh . . . For many days we had been in great want, and for the last three days had not tasted a morsel of any thing, except a pipe of

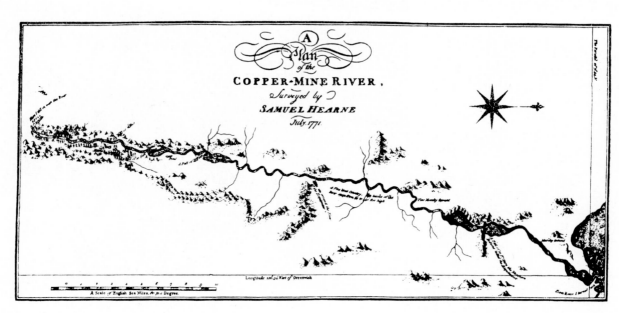

tobacco and a drink of snow water; and as we walked daily from morning till night, and were all heavily laden, our strength began to fail. I must confess that I never spent so dull a Christmas; and when I recollected the merry season which was then passing, and reflected upon the immense quantities, and great variety of delicacies which were then expending in every past of Christendom, and that with a profusion bordering upon waste, I could not refrain from wishing myself again in Europe, if it has been only to have had an opportunity of alleviating the extreme hunger which I suffered with the refuse of the table of any one of my acquaintance."

Two days later they feasted on four deer which the Indians had killed.

Next year Hearne spent his Christmas on the north shore of Great Slave Lake, or, as he calls it, Lake Athapuskow, on his return journey from the mouth of Coppermine River. He makes no mention of the season; but the ever-present subject of food recurs. Quotation from his narrative reveals the usual alternations of feast and famine.

"On the thirteenth (December) one of the Indians killed two deer, which were the first that we had seen since the twentieth of October. So that during a period of nearly two months we had lived on the dried meat that we had prepared and a few fish. It is true, we also caught a few rabbits, and at times the wood-partridges were so plentiful, that the Indians killed considerable numbers of them with their bows and arrows . . . In our way we saw many Indian deer", (as he calls the woodland Caribou) "and beaver were very plentiful, many of which the Indians killed."

Evidently, however, he remembered other things in connection with that second Christmas. He speaks of the brilliancy of the Aurora Borealis and of the stars, which, he says, frequently made it possible for him to read very small print at night. He also avers that he *heard* the Northern Lights. "I can positively affirm, that in still nights I have frequently heard them make a rustling and crackling noise, like the waving of a large flag in a fresh gale of wind . . . It is, however, very probable that these lights are sometimes much nearer the Earth than they are at others, according to the state of the atmosphere, and this may have a great effect on the sound — but the truth or falsehood of this conjecture I leave to the determination of those who are better skilled in natural philosophy than I can pretend to be."

He soon comes back again to the subject of food, and sings the praises of Northern Caribou meat. "But though I own that the flesh of the large southern deer is very good, I must confess that the flesh of the small northern deer, whether buck or doe, in their proper season, is by far more delicious and the finest I have ever eaten, either in this country or any other, and is of that peculiar quality that it never cloys. I can affirm this from my own experience, for after living on it entirely, as it may be said, for twelve or eighteen months successively, I scarcely ever wished for a change of food; though when fish or fowl came in my way, it was very agreeable." Beaver, too, he praises as delicious.

Six months later he was back at Fort Prince of Wales, after a journey of eighteen months and twenty-three days. Doubtless, often in after years, while the Port went round the candle-lit table, he told of the tobacco and snow water, the caribou meat and beaver tail and the Aurora Borealis of those two other Christmas Days in the northern wilderness.

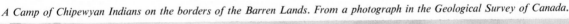

A Camp of Chipewyan Indians on the borders of the Barren Lands. From a photograph in the Geological Survey of Canada.

FRASER RIDES THE FRASER

by LAWRENCE J. BURPEE

The descent of the Fraser River completed the "framework" of exploration of the mainland of Canada, but the western Cordillera discouraged the development of freight routes from the prairies to the Pacific Ocean. East of the Rocky Mountains, trade continued to flow to the St. Lawrence and Hudson Bay.

Sɪᴍᴏɴ ꜰʀᴀꜱᴇʀ, like so many of the pathfinders of Canada, was both fur-trader and explorer. He was born in 1776 at Bennington in New York. As a boy he was brought to Cornwall, on the upper St. Lawrence, and the neighbourhood must have taken a strong hold upon his affections, for more than thirty years later, when he returned from the fur trade, he settled at St. Andrews, near Cornwall, and spent the rest of his life there.

Fraser was apprenticed to the North West Company in 1792, and in 1801 became a partner. For some years he was employed in the Athabaska Department, and in 1805 was put in charge of the Company's operations in New Caledonia, west of the Rocky Mountains. Three years later he made the daring and important journey that gave him an assured place in the story of Canadian discovery.

Fifteen years before, another adventurous Scot, Alexander Mackenzie, had gone down the big river on which Fort George stood to a place later known as Alexandria, but had then turned back. In 1808 the greater part of the river was unknown to white men, and it was supposed to be the Columbia; Fraser made up his mind to follow it down to the sea. On a May day in 1808, he set out, with John Stuart, Jules Maurice Quesnel,

Simon Fraser 1776-1862

nineteen voyageurs, and two Indian guides, to explore the wild, tumultuous river that was later to be known as the Fraser.

As he travelled downstream, Fraser came in contact with strange Indians, members of tribes known as Atnahs and Tahowtins, who arrived on horseback. They were friendly, but warned him that the river was very difficult — a succession of waterfalls and rapids rushing down between steep, impassable cliffs. However, as there seemed to be no way of travelling overland, Fraser decided to make the attempt.

"I ordered the five best men out of the crews into a canoe lightly loaded", he says, "and the canoe was in a moment under way. After passing the first cascade, she lost her course and was drawn into the eddy where she was whirled about for a considerable time, seemingly in suspense whether to sink or swim, the men having no

power over her. However, she took a favourable turn and by degrees was led from this dangerous vortex again into the stream. In this manner she continued, flying from one danger to another until the last cascade but one, where, in spite of every effort, the whirlpools forced her against a low projecting rock. Upon this the men debarked, saved their own lives and contrived to save the property, but the greatest difficulty was still ahead, and to continue by water would be the way to certain destruction.

"During this distressing scene, we were on shore looking on and anxiously concerned. Seeing our poor fellows once more safe afforded us as much satisfaction as to themselves, and we hastened to their assistance, but their situation rendered our approach perilous and difficult. The bank was extremely high and steep, and we had to plunge our daggers at intervals into the ground to check our speed, as otherwise we were exposed to slide into the river. We cut steps in the declivity, fastened a line to the front of the canoe, with which some of the men ascended in order to haul it up, while the others supported it upon their arms. In this manner our situation was most precarious, our lives hung, as it were, upon a thread, as the failure of the line or a false step of one of the men might have hurled the whole of us into Eternity. However, we fortunately cleared the bank before dark."

The Indians again urged Fraser to give up the idea of travelling down the river. By going on horseback, they told him, his party would, in four or five days, reach another large river (the Thompson), whose navigation was much easier than that of the Fraser, and which emptied into it farther down. However, he was determined at all costs to explore the Fraser. That was what he had set out to do, and that was what he would do. He still thought he was on the Columbia, and it was not until he actually reached the mouth of the river that he found, somewhat to his disgust, that this was an entirely different stream, much farther north than the mouth of the Columbia, which had been discovered some time before.

So the party struggled down the Fraser, sometimes on its turbulent surface, sometimes scrambling along its rocky banks. Early in June they came to a rapid that far surpassed all they had previously encountered. "Here", says Fraser, "the channel contracts to about forty yards, and is enclosed by two precipices of immense height which, bending towards each other, make it narrower above than below. The water which rolls down this extraordinary passage in tumultuous waves and with great velocity had a frightful appearance. However, it being absolutely impossible to carry the canoes by land, all hands without hesitation embarked as it were *à corps perdu* upon the mercy of this awful tide. Once engaged the die was cast. One great difficulty consisted in keeping the canoes within the medium or *fil d'eau*; that is, clear of the precipice on one side and from the gulfs formed by the waves on the other. Thus skimming along as fast as lightning, the crews, cool and determined, followed each other in awful silence, and when we arrived at the end, we stood gazing at each other in silent congratulation at our narrow escape from total destruction."

So went the story, from day to day,

of a journey of almost constant danger and anxiety. Fraser was descending the river at the most difficult season of the year, when even the Indians, magnificent canoemen, did not venture upon it. However, he got through, without losing any of his men, and finally came to where the stream divided into several channels. He landed at an Indian village named Misquaime, not far from the present city of New Westminster, almost

within sight of the sea, where he had much the same experience as Alexander Mackenzie. As his party went downstream, the Indians became more hostile, and in the end Fraser, like Mackenzie, had to turn back before he had quite completed his journey to the sea.

The return trip, fortunately, was comparatively uneventful, and early in August Fraser and his men were again at Fort George.

Taken from a colour drawing "The Descent of the Fraser River, 1808" by C. W. Jefferys.

Sir Leonard Tilley   Sir Georges-Etienne Cartier

The Great Seal of Canada and some of the Fathers of Confederation.

Hon. George Brown   Sir John A. Macdonald

PATTERN OF A NATION

What was this Canada which emerged in 1867 as a federal union of four provinces, and which was in due time to include half of North America? Its dominion was not yet from sea to sea, but reached only from the Atlantic seaboard to Lake Superior, and settlement had not yet spread out fully along the tributaries of the Great Lakes-St. Lawrence system. From Lake Superior to the Rocky Mountains and north to the Arctic Ocean fur was still king, but the beginnings of an agricultural economy were being made along the Red River. Men realized the potential of the prairies, but the growth of farming had to await the railroad which would haul the grain to market. Beyond the Rockies, settlement was beginning on Vancouver Island and at the mouth of the Fraser River. Coal and timber were being shipped from West Coast ports across the oceans of the world, but the Rocky Mountains effectively prevented east-west continental trade.

Halifax, Quebec, and Montreal were the old cities, but Toronto was growing rapidly as the commercial centre for the rich farm land of southwestern Ontario. Ottawa was in the throes of transition from lumber town to nation's capital. Winnipeg had not yet been incorporated as a city and Vancouver was still just Hasting's sawmill on Burrard Inlet.

In the East, produce of the forests, farms, and fisheries were the principal exports, in that order of importance by value. Quebec was the centre of the timber trade, the destination of great rafts which came down the Ottawa and St. Lawrence rivers, and the point of departure for the timber ships. The furs of the northwest were shipped out of York Factory on Hudson Bay or were sent to Montreal by way of St. Paul, Minnesota, the nearest rail-head to Winnipeg, the western hub. The second Welland Canal, with a nine-foot depth, was in use but, as yet, there was no Canadian canal at Sault Ste. Marie. This lack was to add an extra difficulty for the Wolsey expedition to Red River a few years later; the United States would not allow transit facilities for Canadian armed forces through the American canal.

Transportation was to be the key to the further development of Canada. The promise of a transcontinental railroad was the deciding factor which brought British Columbia into the confederation in 1871. That promise was fulfilled fifteen years later and the great era of growth on the prairie began. The railroad had replaced the canoe, the York boat, and the Red River cart.

Thus was the original pattern of the nation formed. It was founded on timber, agriculture, fish and fur, and was in two parts: the old provinces of the east and the new provinces of the west, joined by a railroad which ran through a thousand miles of the rugged rocks of the Canadian Shield. So it was to grow, in two sections, until geologists and prospectors would discover the mineral wealth of the Shield and this apparently non-productive wilderness would begin to yield its riches and flourishing communities would begin to fill this void.

THE GEOGRAPHICAL CIRCUMSTANCES
OF CONFEDERATION

by W. L. MORTON

G EOGRAPHY, in one sense at least, is man's concept of his environment at any given time. This essay is first an attempt to sketch how the people of British North America understood the geography of the northern half of the continent in the period 1857 to 1871, and what they anticipated might be made of it.

It is at once necessary, in such an attempt, to point out that in the British North American colonies as a whole, from Newfoundland to Vancouver Island, the factors making for regionalism and disunity had long prevailed, as they continued to prevail down to 1867, over the factors making for unity. Each separate colony,

dominated by its Fundy and North Shore ports, and, paradoxically, Prince Edward Island. The latter was an island, of course, and profoundly insular in spirit, an insularity increased by the winter's practical separation from the continent by the ice of Northumberland Strait. But its fertile soil, its preoccupation with agriculture, and its dependence on the markets of the continent for the sale of its produce, tied it to the continent despite its insularity. Nova Scotia, on the contrary, although a peninsula geographically, was an island in spirit, looking to and living in the main by shipping and by fishing. This tie with the Atlantic world was strengthened greatly by the naval base of Halifax, which kept the province orientated to England when all the others since 1846 and the end of the old commercial system had tended more and more towards the continent, its markets and even its customs and institutions. And Newfoundland, until 1834 regarded as a fishery rather than a colony of settlement, had even fewer connections with the continent. It lived by its fishing on the Grand Banks and by sealing along the waste of Labrador and in the Gulf of St. Lawrence. It was more maritime than its Maritime sisters; nothing really attracted it to the rest of British North America, except the passing thought that its sister colonies might perhaps do more for it than England would in dealing with the difficulties of the French Shore, the source of endless difficulty with France, or with those of maintaining order and abating poverty in the outports.

In Canada East (Quebec) the story, except for the fisheries in the Gulf, was quite different. The settled part of this subdivision of the Canadian Union, and it was now fully settled, consisted of the St. Lawrence Valley

and also the two parts of the Canadian Union of 1840, had its own geographical views and preoccupations. It will be best to begin by noting these, in order from east to west.

The Atlantic Provinces of Newfoundland, Nova Scotia, New Brunswick and Prince Edward Island, as we now know them as a group, were maritime rather than continental in their situation and outlook, as they had always been, and as they were to continue to be. Two were more continental in nature than the others. These were New Brunswick, actually a part of the continental mass, if

between the edge, marked by the Laurentian Mountains, of the Precambrian Shield to the northwest, and the end of the Appalachian system, marked by the Notre Dame Mountain to the southeast. This trough, consisting of forested land of both high and low fertility, had now been settled and cleared back to, and indeed over, the margin of fertile land at the foot of each mountain limit. It was a farming country, most of which had been farmed for several generations, some for over a hundred years. It had for the most part passed through the inevitable frontier crisis of passing from staple agriculture — in Canada, wheat-farming — to a more diversified and more stable economy. A good deal of the lumber industry of course continued, on sandy lands, on the mountain fringes, and in the form of furniture making and, at Quebec City, of shipbuilding. But it was mostly a region of farms and small villages and market towns serving a population French for the most part, except in the Eastern Townships, which, however, was now both English and French, with the French increasing. Land had to be found for farmers' sons. But the great river that flowed through the midst of this agricultural region was only a scant part of its economic life. The river served the trade and commerce of the city of Montreal, largely supplied and stimulated by the western district of the Union, Canada West, or Upper Canada.

That area, still popularly called Upper Canada in 1857, and Canada West officially, was Canada above the rapids of the St. Lawrence and north of the Great Lakes. It was itself made up of a number of interior regions. It was in its settled parts south of the Ottawa River and the edge of the Shield divided into two regions. One was the immediate hinterland of Montreal. This ran as far west as the Trent River and consisted of the rugged country of the north shore of the St. Lawrence and

Ottawa, drawn by E. Whitfield. The city was chosen as capital of Canada by Queen Victoria in 1857 and was confirmed in this status by the British North America Act of 1867. Construction of the Parliament Buildings on the hill in the immediate foreground was begun in December 1859.

Lake Ontario — basically, when not actually, Shield country — as far as Whitby — and the Ottawa valley's southern and western half, itself partly an intrusion into the Shield, and partly modified Shield country in land and forest. This was "central" Canada, in the usage of the day.

West of it — there was no sharp border — one entered "peninsular" Ontario, again in the usage of the day. The climate was warmer, the land not broken by rock and more fertile. It was indeed the area of the orchards and rich wheatlands of Canada, a farmer's elysium. It tended, moreover, to look to the Erie canal and its parallel railways and the port of New York, as at least an alternative to the St. Lawrence route and the port of Montreal. Hence it was regarded as being somewhat "American" in sympathy; but the habit was one Canadians were prone to, as westerners were later to reveal in their demand for the Hudson Bay railway as an alternative to the St. Lawrence outlet for their grain.

These areas of Upper Canada had for the most part been settled for at least a generation, and much longer of course along the great river and the lakes. The first easy returns of frontier farming on virgin soils had ended. The midge, the weevil, and the Hessian fly, in part at least the result of soils exhausted of their virgin constituents, had come to plague the farmer and begin that maturing of agricultural science and practice that was to be so rapid and so fruitful in Ontario in the next generation.

Upper Canada still had its frontier — in the Ottawa valley above Pembroke, in the counties across the edge of the Shield, Lanark, Hastings, Lennox and Addington, Haliburton, Peterborough, and in new counties such as Muskoka. Government in the late fifties, here as in Lower Canada, was cutting colonization roads into these districts, and beginning the policy of free land grants to provide lands for farmers' sons and immigrants who would otherwise go, as many were, to the prairie lands of Illinois, Wisconsin and Minnesota. But the effort and expenditures were misdirected. The acid soils of the Shield yielded, at best, crops of oats and hay for sale to the lumber camps and railway construction gangs. They were incapable of supporting a vigorous and diversified agriculture. Abandoned farmsteads, or worse, shanty farmsteads now the concern of ARDA (the Agricultural Rehabilitation and Development Agency), marked the highwater mark of agricultural settlement in the Canadas.

This Canadian impingement on the Shield was typical of the rural and agricultural Canada that had become dominant, at least socially, in the course of the century up to Confederation. It was, of course, not the only one. Since the Napoleonic wars the great Canadian industry had been the timber trade. Much Canadian wood and wood products, such as potash, had of course come from the clearing of the hardwood forests. But its great pineries stood on the sandy lands of the terraces that paralleled the Lakes and the St. Lawrence, or were the outwash of the Shield. By the late fifties the lumber camps were thrusting up the valleys of the Shield like the Saguenay, the Gatineau, the Mississippi, the Mattawa, the Ottawa itself, both for the square timber for rafting to the timber ships from Britain at Quebec, or for the mills that sent sawn lumber by rail to the booming cities across the border.

This was a natural development, an ever deeper penetration of the Canadian forest of the St. Lawrence Lowlands leading up into the Shield.

Rather different was the search for minerals. The splendid reconnaissance geology of William (later Sir William) Logan had revealed the southern edge, and the most dramatic traits, of the Precambrian Shield, the erosion of its primitive mountains, the rugged nature of its terrain. It had also opened up the possibility of mineral finds. A search began that followed the southern edge of the Shield. It had led to some small mining ventures — gold at Madoc, copper at Bruce Mines — and now in the

Company and that fact indicates one factor in the Canadian approach to the Shield and the Northwest. Not only were Canadians profoundly ignorant of both vast areas; they resented, not without some reason, those regions being the preserves of the Hudson's Bay Company. This rivalry between the Company approaching its second centenary and the province of Canada, bursting at the seams of its Laurentian existence,

down from the northern height of land upon Laurentian Canada. It indeed quite literally did so, because some of its posts were well south of the watershed it claimed as boundary — the King's Posts on the St. Lawrence, Temiskaming on the headwaters of the Ottawa, Fort Coulonge lower down, Sault Ste. Marie, Michipicoten, Fort William. It is true that, as J. S. Galbraith details in his excellent *The Hudson's Bay Company As*

Burrard Inlet, British Columbia, 1861, from a water colour by W. G. B. Willis. In 1862 the first white settlers established themselves in the area, and later, Vancouver grew along the Inlet's shore.

fifties the quest was pushed into Lake Superior itself, as in Allan Macdonell's venture at Michipicoten.

Macdonell had trouble both with the Indians and the Hudson's Bay

was to be one of the main themes of the narrative of Confederation.

In geographical terms, it was inevitably so. In terms of the Company's own claims, Rupert's Land looked

An Imperial Factor, that this overlapping of Canadian and Company territory was ending. The King's Posts were sold to Canada in 1858, duties were collected on goods com-

65

ing over the watershed to Timiskaming in 1858. Sault Ste. Marie, Michipicoten, Fort William were all being agitated by incoming, Canadian settlers and traders.

This was true even of Red River beyond Fort William. In 1857 George Brown's *Globe* began an agitation for the acquisition of the Northwest by Canada. The *Globe* spoke for the business interests of Toronto, who hoped to win a share of the profitable trade St. Paul already had with Red River. Some notable results followed this agitation. One was the creation of an interest among Upper Canadian farmers in the lands of Red River. Another was the assertion in Canada — not by the Canadian government — of the old French claim to all the Northwest as far as the Rockies. This was followed by the dispatch of the Red River Exploring Expedition which in its second and third years was to make the lands of the Red and the Assiniboine favourably — all too favourably — known. Still another was the movement of Canadian adventurers to Red River, traders like Henry McKenny and John Schultz, farmers like Alexander Mclean at Portage la Prairie, the two newspapermen, late of the *Globe*, William Buckingham and William Coldwell, who founded *The Nor'wester*, the first newspaper in Red River. Henceforth there was to be a "Canadian" party in Red River, a party which attacked the continued, if largely ineffective, monopoly of the Hudson's Bay Company, and which demanded annexation to Canada.

More striking than this guerilla warfare by certain Canadians against the Company was the profound ignorance of the generality of Canadians of the Shield and the Northwest. The ignorance was not absolute, of course, nor was it to continue. But it was general and profound. The extent and nature of the territory beyond the blue rim of the Shield seem not to have been known by Canadians. Canadian lumbermen did indeed ex-

The Honourable George Brown, editor of the Globe, *began the agitation for acquisition of the Hudson's Bay Company territories in the Northwest by Canada. Considerable interest in the west resulted.*

ploit the forest resources of the southern Shield, and were developing the technique of lumbering in the winter northern forest. Canadian sportsmen kept alive the use of the canoe and the snowshoe and seasonally penetrated the rivers and woodlands of the south-

Sir John Schultz, typical of the men who built Manitoba, practised medicine at Fort Garry, was federal M.P. 1871-82, Senator 1882-88, and appointed Lieutenant-Governor of Manitoba in 1888.

ern Shield. But this vast, overhanging wilderness to the north was no part of Canadian consciousness. It was not

thought of as a potential asset; it was not thought of as a barrier to the Northwest. As railwayman J. J. Ross's testimony before the Select Committee on the Hudson's Bay Company in 1857 indicates, it was ignored. The water route by the Lakes and the old waterway from Fort William to Fort Garry, improved if necessary, were thought to be a means of turning the Shield. What was alien and incomprehensible was therefore ignored, which perhaps was just as well. Without this wilful disregard of the obvious, so dourly underlined by Alexander Monro in his *The United States and Canada* in 1879, Canada would perhaps never have succeeded in making, to use Wreford Watson's fine perception, a second class route to the Northwest serve in first class fashion its national purpose to expand.

Even less, because they were more remote, was Canadian knowledge and awareness of the northwest territory of the Mackenzie and Yukon river basins, and of the Pacific slope, until the Fraser River gold rush of 1857 caught Canadian as well as world attention. Then, as to Red River, there began a Canadian migration, one is tempted to write, infiltration to the diggings, and the beginnings of Canadian interest and influence. On the whole Canadians went, not as immigrants to settle and possess the country, but as adventurers and professional men — traders, journalists, lawyers — who sought a career beyond crowded Canada, and sought on new frontiers a livelihood they might not be able to win at home.

Even more remote was the Arctic. That had long been an English and a Hudson's Bay Company interest. As such it was a faintly diplomatic, largely sporting interest, and also a means of keeping an idle naval force in training. The search for Franklin was news in Canada as elsewhere, but neither then nor for many years was there to be any popular Canadian interest in the near or the far North.

The drive to expand was orientated to the prairies of the Red and Saskatchewan and the ports of the Pacific.

The strength, the demographic necessity, of the need of the Canadas to expand in years of Confederation has never, to the writer's knowledge, been adequately studied or expressed. Yet there can be no doubt of its reality as a geographical factor in the circumstances of Confederation. It was the Canadian counterpart of the need of the tobacco and cotton economy of the South to take in new soil, of the Boer to seek new veldts, of the Australian squatter to claim broad miles of the outback. It was a demographic pressure created by physical limits on the extent of fertile soil, by the exploitative nature of frontier and unskilled agriculture, by domestic traits such as large families and the pursuit of agriculture as almost the only way of life above that of the hired man or the lumberjack for the surplus sons of the Victorian household, whether English or French.

If these characteristics require much study for their clear delineation, the statistical results of this expansive growth are revealed in the crude and simple, but cumulative, first two general censuses of Canada in 1851 and 1861. The population of United Canada in 1851 was 1,842,265; in 1861 it was 2,507,677. The decade was one of phenomenal growth and contained the year of greatest rate of increase of any in Canadian history to 1951, that of 1856. The growth was both by natural increase and by immigration, with a very high rate of retention of both natives and immigrants. The decade of 1861-71 was, by contrast, to show a great falling off, despite a general prosperity. But it was in the former decade that the demographic pressure and the outburst of energy that led to Confederation were created.

A gold mine at Stout's Gulch in the Cariboo country of British Columbia. The Fraser River gold rush of the late 1850's and the 1860's did much to stimulate development and settlement in British Columbia.

The Hudson's Bay Company post at Sault Ste. Marie, Ontario, drawn by W. Armstrong in 1853. With the decline of the fur trade, Sault Ste. Marie lost its importance until the building of the ship canal in 1895 and the coming of heavy industry at the turn of the century.

The mineral wealth of the Canadian Shield, in earlier days an unknown quantity to Canadians, is now undergoing considerable exploitation. The Algoma Steel Corporation mine at Wawa, Ontario.

The increase and retention of population were of course a result of great material prosperity. The still unexhausted pineries, the ever-widening wheatfields, the Reciprocity Treaty, the Crimean War, the building of the Grand Trunk Railway, produced the greatest and perhaps the most effective boom of Canadian economic history. (Certainly it ranks with those of 1901-1911 and 1951-1961). It left the Canadas equipped with the full complement of Victorian productivity, canals, railways, factories, and a banking system to finance the crop year, the lumber drive, and the factory run.

Government revenues and expenditures responded. In 1851 revenues were £842,184 5s. 2d. and expenditures were £634,666 6s. 8d.*; in 1861 they were $12,655,581.48 and $14,742,834.28 respectively. In fact expenditures rose to levels from which there could be no retreat to former positions, and government reluctantly carried heavy deficits from 1858 to 1863, much to the scandal of opposition and of the City of London where Canada did its borrowing. But what the deficits really signified was that government was committed, however counter to economic theory, to a creative role in financing of expansion both in territory and in transport. Politics, particularly the politics of the Liberal-Conservative Party in power from 1854 to 1862, were positive and in the usage of the day, nationalist, not negative and cosmopolitan.

The popular forces of expansion could be seen in action then, and may

*In terms of 1861 dollars, approximately $4,090,000 and $3,085,000 respectively.

Newfoundland has lived for most of its life by fishing, and was in former days more insular than the other Maritime Provinces, having few ties to the North American continent. This outport is Trinity Bay.

be traced on a map of historical
geography now, may indeed be noted
by the observant tourist. The towns
in the valleys of the Shickshock
mountains, the villages along the
coasts of Gaspé, the settlements in
the crevices and on the slopes of the
Laurentian Shield, in the counties of
the North Shore of Lower Canada,
Haliburton and Muskoka in Upper
Canada, were for the most part
founded in the 1850's and 1860's. As
the work of ARDA today reveals, as
the abandoned farmsteads still witness, there were farmsteads made and
fields cleared on the margin of agricultural settlement. They could survive,
if they survived at all, only in virtue of
virgin soil and local markets, such as
lumber camps. When these transient
aids ended, the flush of rural prosperity ended also, in removal elsewhere, or in accumulating poverty,
material and spiritual.

Even in old settled districts a related movement occurred, as the
French, perhaps more frugal and
more desperate, moved into the unoccupied land and then took over much
of the occupied land of the Eastern
Townships and of the counties of the
south and Upper Canada shore of
the Ottawa River. Glengarry and
Stormont, Carleton and Renfrew became French and Roman Catholic
settlements where they had once been
British and Protestant. The racial
constitution of Canada was changing
within the provincial limits laid down
in 1791. Lower Canada was creating a
French Canada — and a French
America — beyond Lower Canada.
Upper Canada was ceasing to be
merely British American, and was becoming French American also.

The currents of the expansion of

69

population were not only over-running economic and political limits, they were also beginning to flow towards the Northwest. The north shore of Lake Huron and the Island of Manitoulin, in which the treaty of 1862 was to a degree a forerunner of the trouble in Red River in 1869, were being settled. As a result of this infiltration of settlement the District of Algoma, not a county on the traditional model but the predecessor of

expansion, as is indicated by the appalling poverty of the outports of Newfoundland, the serious revolt of 1861, and the spread of settlement into the French shore. This was part of the northeastern shore and all the western shore of the Island yielded by the treaties of Utrecht and of Paris, 1783, to the French for the purposes of the French fishery. Now Newfoundland settlers, not denied the right to settle by the treaties, were

build railways, fully to serve the interest of the trading communities, but especially to begin capital investment that would make work and win votes. Here was the fertile soil from which the project of the Intercolonial Railway kept springing. Such a railway would give the existing railways system; it would create work for population pressing on the margin of exploitable resources; it would win gratitude and votes for the politicians who could claim to have British and Canadian support for so fruitful an enterprise.

"Camping on the Prairie" from the painting by W. C. Hind, brother of Henry Youle Hind, leader of the exploring expedition to the Red and Assiniboine Rivers. Note the "buffalo chip" fuel.

the Districts of the Northwest Territories, was created in 1858. Canada was organizing its own wilderness frontier, it was preparing to expand into the unorganized, the unknown, Northwest.

This Canadian expansion was not without parallel in the Atlantic Provinces. It is true that for almost a decade — since the outpouring caused by the potato famine in Ireland — those provinces had received relatively little immigration; as a result they were both less expansive than the Canadas, and more native, more American in character. But there was

beginning to move into the coast and live there throughout the year. The result was to be a half century of friction both with England and with France.

In the other provinces the best lands and much of the interior had already been settled. Pressure of population was indicated by the migration of groups of people from Nova Scotia and Prince Edward Island in ships built and manned by themselves to New Zealand and Australia. It was indicated also by the eagerness of politicians in both Nova Scotia and New Brunswick to

If the Canadas and the Atlantic Provinces were, however, to expand a frontier was needed. Such was lacking in the latter, except for Labrador which was not then, as it has become since, a frontier of settlement. For the Canadas, on the other hand, an abounding frontier was available beyond the constricting bulk of the Precambrian Shield. This was the Red River Valley, and the parklands and plains beyond. For a half century and more the belief had been firmly held with some assistance, interested but no doubt reasonably honest, from the officers of the Hudson's Bay Company, that this was a land suitable only for the fur trade. But the acceptance of the Northwest as a frozen wilderness properly to be left as a preserve of fur traders had rapidly been diminishing. The evidence heard before the Select Committee of the Imperial House of Commons on the Hudson's Bay Company in the first half of 1857 had given much ground to the new belief, strongly asserted by the prejudiced *Globe*, informed by anti-company people in Red River, that much if not all of the southern plains of the Northwest were suitable for agriculture.

This assertion, inspired as much by feeling against the great Company as by positive information, was suddenly greatly and in the most substantial manner reinforced by a book of substantial weight. This was the American climatologist, Lorin Blodget's

Building a bridge for the Intercolonial Railway in eastern Canada, from the Sir Sandford Fleming Collection, Public Archives of Canada.

The Hind expedition encamped by the Red River, photographed by H. L. Hime who accompanied the expedition as photographer.

work, *The Climatology of North America*, published in September, 1857. Blodget combined the work of Alexander von Humboldt, of Maury, the report of Perry's expedition of 1854 to Japan, the American transcontinental railway surveys and the journals of the fur trade of the Northwest, to advance the thesis that climate was not bound to latitude, and that in particular in North America the isothermal lines ran, not east and west, but sharply northwesterly and southeasterly in summer. The effect of this was to make the great area of the continent west of Red River suitable for agriculture, settlement and railway construction. The *Globe* of Toronto and the journalists of St. Paul at once seized on this scientific support for a proposition they were advancing for other reasons. Science now supported both commercial enterprise and agrarian need.

The same year 1857 saw the launching of two expeditions which, like Blodget's work, gave considerable scientific support to the pragmatic demand that the Northwest should be open to settlement. One was the Red River Exploring Expedition dispatched by the Canadian government to determine the nature of the route to Red River, and the quality of the lands and climate of the Red and Assiniboine rivers. It came to be headed by the Trinity College scientist, Henry Youle Hind. The other was organized by the Royal Geographical Society with financial assistance from the British Government. It was headed by Captain John Palliser, R.A., a one time hunter on the buffalo plains. He was accompanied by a well qualified and able staff.

Hind's expedition was a reconnaissance, and suffered from the fact that Hind shared the enthusiasm of the Upper Canadian annexationists. In his report the aspects of the soil and climate favourable to agriculture were exaggerated, the unfavourable diminished, or ignored. The reports of the Palliser expedition were more cautious, more scientific, and more reliable. They warned that the construction of a railway from Fort William to Red River would be difficult and costly. They detected and described the difference between the short grass plains of the southwestern prairies (Palliser's Triangle) and those of the northeastern. They pointed out the importance and uncertainty of a frost-free growing period. The two sets of reports gave grounds both for optimism and caution.

Both had no immediate effect. The depression that began in 1857 was severe and was prolonged by the outbreak of the American Civil War. There was neither interest nor means for the annexation of the Northwest by Canada. Its achievement depended on the realization of a greater political and economic complex of which Northwest annexation could only be a part.

A hunter pulls his kill from the water near Frobisher Bay. Until comparatively recently, the Arctic was unknown to the majority of Canadians.

72

Landing supplies and equipment at Craig Harbour, Ellesmere Island. Today, weather stations, R.C.M.P. posts, centres for scientific research and settlements of various kinds are scattered throughout the Arctic, and many Canadians have first hand knowledge of the far North.

In the years preceding the Confederation of 1867 there were, then, abundant reasons arising from their geographical circumstances to inspire the movement towards a wider political union. These, when combined with the desire of liberal Victorian England to be rid of the burden of defending British North America against an ever more powerful United States, and with the emergence of a United States capable not only of maintaining the union of the States but after 1865 the dominant power in the Americas, these circumstances produced what may be called the dynamics of Confederation.

The first and most powerful was the separation of the Canadas. Reunited in 1840 to realize the geographical and economic unity of the St. Lawrence River, they were now separated for all local matters to allow a degree of local self-determination that experience had proved to be necessary. Protestant Upper Canada could no longer resist the incorporation of religious orders, nor Catholic Lower Canada vote to extend the educational privileges of the Roman Catholics of Upper Canada.

The next dynamics were two, inseparably related and each embodied in a particular railway enterprise. One was the acquisition of the Northwest, the other was federal union with the

A village in the Matapedia Valley, Quebec. There is much good farmland along the banks of the Matapedia River, a familiar sight to railway travellers to and from the Maritimes.

Atlantic Provinces. The former required the building of a railway westward, a Pacific railway; the other of a railway eastward, the much debated Intercolonial. Nova Scotia and New Brunswick would not enter Confederation without the Intercolonial, Upper Canada would not support the Intercolonial without the Northwest and the western railway. Thus the ingrained sectionalism of British North America actually operated to promote the geographical expansion which the internal needs of its parts called for.

Next was the need of Pacific ports to ensure traffic to a westward railway. This linked up with British Columbia's desire for a railway to the Atlantic, and with the concept of a transcontinental union to match the United States. Thus the political union envisaged in the movement for Confederation was a geographical unity, each part necessary to this whole, and all designed to make up an economic system as well as a political nationality.

Finally, there was the desire to avoid absorption by the United States. American manifest destiny had seldom really turned northward; access to the Lakes and the St. Lawrence, and the same to the ports of Puget Sound, once achieved, the United States could rest easily with a northern neighbour similar in language and institutions. American policy had only one major design to the north and that was the removal of British military power. This was accomplished by the British withdrawal from the St. Lawrence in 1871. The place of the defending power of Britain, in fact little more than an irritant since the Trent Affair of 1861, was taken by the political union begun in 1867 and largely completed by 1871. The political union of the geographical fragments of British North America, a union that was no conceivable danger to the United States, left that power no cause to intervene in the affairs of a northern neighbour ready and capable of keeping its own house in order.

The geographical effects of Confederation were in accord with the motives realized in Confederation. The withdrawal of British troops from Quebec in 1871, coupled with the grant of free navigation of the St. Lawrence by the Treaty of Washington in the same year, realized practically that geographical unity of North America imposed by the Treaty of Paris in 1763, and ended by the American Revolution in 1783. At the same time the maintenance of the fortress and naval base of Halifax kept Canada still within the orbit of British seapower and attached to the British Empire, political nation though it had become. At the same time the diplomatic unity of the inshore fisheries, when Prince Edward Island came in in 1873, was, except for Newfoundland, effectively though not formally, transferred to the jurisdiction actively concerned with their retention for the people of the Maritime Provinces from New England aggression.

The third geographical effect was the ignoring of the Canadian Shield except as an obstacle between Fort William and Fort Garry. This had two effects. One was that the spirit in which Confederation was conceived was quite unrealistic, as Munro pointed out; it led to such absurdities as the oft repeated claim that Canada was to be a second United States. Second, it meant that the Shield that had yielded much of the produce of the fur trade and timber of Canada in the past, as it was to yield much of the electrical power, wood pulp and minerals of Canada in the future, was set aside for a decade while Canada concentrated on agricultural settlement and production. From this came a certain misdirection of economic policy and of social development, and a certain misplacement of political power. The Shield, not being really habitable to any degree, ought to have been made and kept a federal empire, not without representative democracy where warranted, but controlled from Ottawa with its own department of government.

As it was, the Northwest because of its geography produced new and lasting features of Canadian life. The Canadian militia was given a role to perform from 1869 to 1873, when it was replaced by the North-West Mounted Police. A new Indian regime was created. Governments, provincial and territorial, were established. Land and immigration policies were evolved; a fourth Canada, not Maritime, French, or British, was evolved, to complicate the economic and political balance of the Dominion.

And beyond was a fifth Canada on the Pacific slope. An outlet for the Canada of the St. Lawrence in 1871, it was never to rest until it became an alternate to the great river. It created an internal watershed within Canada, from which the flow westward ever increased and that eastward, relatively that is, steadily decreased. A second and a geographical ambiguity was introduced to go with the English-French one, a continental duality to accompany the racial dualism.

Thus the aspirations of British North America in the decade before Confederation reached a geographical consummation in the four years that followed. It had expanded and it was united. It had escaped the frustrations of racial friction and provincial lack of means by creating a new combination of the various elements of British American life, economic, political and geographic. For almost a hundred years the new frustrations and limitations of that combination were to try, but never threaten, the work of Confederation. The geographical base and the political structure were in sound accord in the original concept of Confederation and in its development into the present century.

Vancouver looking across Burrard Inlet to the Coast Mountains. Incorporated in 1886, Vancouver was the Pacific terminus for the trans-continental Canadian Pacific Railway line, and later became the port for C.P.R. shipping across the Pacific.

THE PEOPLE OF CANADA

by LAWRENCE J. BURPEE
and MARIUS BARBEAU

Written in 1939, this article presents a picture of the diverse backgrounds of the people of Canada searching for a destiny that will fulfil their aspirations in harmony with their varied past. This problem seems as challenging today at this hundredth anniversary of Confederation as it was then.

WHO ARE THE CANADIAN PEOPLE? Whence did they come? What has the land of Canada done to them? What have they done to Canada? Whither are they bound?

The people of Canada cannot be considered a compact nation with uniform characteristics, like the English or the French, but rather a collection of racial groups of diverse origins gradually becoming absorbed by the land of their adoption and held together by their common interests, their love for their country, and their loyalty to the Crown.

To the Canadian people each com-

A view of Montreal from St. Helen's Island, a water colour done in 1762 by Thomas Davies. Davies was one of the first to make sketches of the villages and scenery along the St. Lawrence River.

ponent racial group has contributed something from its former homeland, and has in turn gained a great deal from experience in its new surroundings and also from social contact with its neighbour groups. This interchange of cultural features and heritage tends to enrich the nation and to give it an individual character. The northern climate and the initiative fostered by a growing agricultural and industrial life in a new, vast and often rugged country, has already had a telling effect upon the people. It has imbued them with vigour, courage, self-reliance and a great fondness for open spaces and natural freedom.

Should one wonder who were the first Canadians, the only answer is that they were the natives who were found on our Atlantic coasts by the early European explorers, and one of whose tribes eventually gave its name to the whole country. *Canada* or *Kanata* was the Iroquoian designation for village-dwellers in the St. Lawrence watershed, and Cartier understood it to mean the people he met on his way up the river to Hochelaga.

The name "Canadian" was afterwards applied to the French pioneers, and later extended to British and other settlers.

The first European who set foot on the mainland of North America, and met its inhabitants, was Leif Erickson, and this happened nearly a thousand years ago. As the land he called Vinland may very well have been Nova Scotia, he was, perhaps, the first white man to encounter the native Canadian. Leif not only discovered this continent, but spent a winter with his followers in a region of timber and wild grain and fruits, a land which was, indeed, very different from his Arctic home in Greenland. Thorfinn Karlsefni, another Greenlander, a few years afterwards followed Erickson to Vinland. He came determined to found a colony, bringing with him a number of settlers, cattle and equipment. He remained for several years, but in the end was forced to abandon the attempt because of the unfriendliness of the natives. Thus, in intention at least, Karlsefni and his followers were the first white settlers in Canada.

Kingston, Ontario, a water colour by J. P. Cockburn. Stationed in Canada between 1823 and 1835, he travelled extensively in Upper and Lower Canada.

Excavating the Lachine Canal in 1821, from a sketch by W. Schruer. Excavation was by pick and shovel work and loading into one-horse carts.

No other record has yet been accepted as final proof that other Vikings, in the following centuries, journeyed from Iceland or Greenland to the continent of North America; yet intriguing finds in the region of Lake Nipigon and in Minnesota suggest at least the possibility of such an expedition.

John Cabot, in 1497, planted the flag of Henry VII at a spot which seems to have been on the coast of Cape Breton, and Caspar Corte Real, three years later, sailed down the coast and disappeared leaving behind him a few place-names. In the next quarter of a century the Canadian natives may have met the Portuguese captain Joao Alvares Fagundes, and Giovanni de Verrazano who sailed from France, and Stephen Gomez the Spaniard who searched vainly for a

Lake St. Charles, near Quebec, from the water colour by George Heriot.

78

passage to the South Seas at the head of the Bay of Fundy; also unnamed adventurers of Bristol who sailed out into the West and brought back on their ships "three men out of an Iland farre beyond Ireland, the which were clothed in Beestes skynnes and ate raw fflesh and were rude in their demeanure like Beestes"; and fisher-folk and whale hunters from Brittany, Normandy and the Basque country who yearly plied their calling in the waters around Newfoundland and in the Gulf of St. Lawrence.

None of these, however, can reasonably be called Canadian; even less so, indeed, than Erickson and Karlsefni, for the Northmen at least had looked upon Canada as a desirable land, which they endeavoured to make their own, while Cabot and those who followed him across the Atlantic found North America an obstacle in their path, a barrier which

they must break through to find a passage to Cathay and the Indies, whose jewels and spices beckoned them. Even Jacques Cartier, upon entering the Gulf of St. Lawrence in 1534 and sailing up the great river in 1535, was looking for the North West Passage and was counted a failure because he discovered only savage tribes and brought back no wealth to France.

Sixty years later came Samuel de Champlain, whose fame rests more upon his founding of Quebec and his exploration of Ontario than upon what he accomplished on the Bay of Fundy. With De Monts, Lescarbot and other associates, he laid the foundation of Port Royal, today Annapolis Royal, the first permanent settlement in North America, three years before Jamestown in Virginia and four years before Quebec.

From these small beginnings grew

the French colony of Acadie, which, in the next century and a half, spread around the Bay of Fundy to the valley of the St. John River. Although nearly seven thousand of these early settlers were deported in 1755, there were still, a few years later, at the time of the cession of Canada to England, many Acadians left in this country, and today the estimated French population of Nova Scotia, New Brunswick and Prince Edward Island is about one-quarter of the total people of the Maritimes. Of the other three-quarters, the largest group is not Scottish, even in Nova Scotia, as one might suppose, but English. The Scot comes next, then the Irish, German and Dutch in that order. Oddly enough the next group in size is the Negro, whose forefathers drifted up from the South about the middle of the last century. Some of them went to Cape Breton and, in the next

Fort Garry, Manitoba. A water colour by Henry J. Warre, who like Davies, Cockburn and Heriot served with the British Army in Canada.

this continent; the fur trade, forming part of the schemes of early North American colonization, being the main source of contention. Even before New France had a real start, it was conquered for the English by the Kirke brothers, but later restored to the French crown. An effort was then made to enlarge upon the enterprise, but progress was slow, although the Ursulines, the Hôtel-Dieu, the Recollets and the Jesuits had already established their institutions in Quebec for the benefit of evangelization and the care of the early colonists. Actually the first tillers of the soil were Hébert — a Paris apothecary and botanist — and Giffard, who later became a seignior on the Beaupré coast.

But it was only in the 1660's, more than fifty years after the foundation, that New France assumed the complex features that were to develop into French Canada as we know it. The seigniorial system, as part of prevailing feudalism, took charge of the organization of parishes under

generation, settled among Scottish folk, lost their own peculiar form of English and spoke only Gaelic, just as a number of families with Highland names are found in parts of Quebec speaking only French.

The principal town in each of the Maritime Provinces is a seaport — Halifax, Saint John, Charlottetown— and this is not without historical significance, for the story of the Maritimes is largely one of seafaring. From such ports as Saint John or Yarmouth they sailed out into the Atlantic, and they and their hard-bitten skippers and crews were known throughout the Seven Seas. Fishing craft, of the type of the famous *Bluenose* of Lunenburg, brought into the small ports of the Maritimes rich cargoes of cod, haddock and mackerel, not to mention the oil and other products of the whale fisheries.

Whether it is the influence of the sea, or the mixture of races, or a combination of these and other causes, the men of the Maritimes have made good in many walks of life wherever they have gone. They are found in business, in the professions, in public life, from Joseph Howe to R. B. Bennett, revealing always those qualities of clear thinking and shrewd common sense that characterize their people.

The first settlement of Quebec by Champlain in 1608 was beset by natural and political difficulties. The Indian tribes that peopled the rivers and forests were at war with each other, and ancient rivalries between European nations at once spread to

A British Columbia shepherd and his horse rest at Clinton after the flock is safely corralled.

the ægis of seigniors; and Intendant Talon, on behalf of his King, and Mgr. de Laval, the first bishop of Quebec, boldly took it upon themselves to shape the destinies of their new country.

While a large body of skilled workers, whose vocations fell under at least sixty names, provided the colony with buildings, furniture, equipment, tools and materials, another class soon grew into the largest and most important, that of the settler known under the distinctive name of *habitant*. The habitant was so designated from the first to distinguish him from other free elements that did not, like him, permanently occupy the land, like the craftsmen, the townsfolk, the soldiers, the *coureurs-de-bois* and, later, the *hivernants* or those spending the winter at various remote posts.

The habitant, being a born opportunist, never failed to avail himself of any chance for an adventure in the wilderness and for expansion into novel fields. Growing at a rapid pace, the rural population incessantly overflowed its frontiers — as it is still doing, and was easily lured away from home by new opportunities

elsewhere. Thus, from the earliest moment, the coureurs-de-bois, mostly of habitant extraction, were bold enough to penetrate the wilderness and learn native languages and customs.

A helicopter takes off after delivering supplies to a party of geologists in the northern Peace River area.

The coureurs-de-bois, canoemen and *voyageurs* became indispensable factors in the early penetration of North America. Without them Jolliet, La Salle, Marquette, Duluth, Bienville, could not have travelled far afield and founded remote posts from Detroit to New Orleans; the La Vérendryes — who may be considered the most distinguished among them— could not have crossed the prairies, almost to the foothills of the Rockies, and laid the foundation of the fur trade among the buffalo hunters;

Mackenzie, Thompson, Fraser and Hearne could not have journeyed to the Pacific Coast or to the Arctic; and Charles Frémont could not have crossed prairies and mountains to open up California to settlement.

A much smaller element in French Canada consisted of townsfolk connected with government, public service, education, clergy, trade, militia, and the seigniorial system. Distinct as this higher class was from the habitant, craft and coureurs-de-bois folk, it nevertheless drew from them many recruits, and occasionally some of their own members lapsed into the humble but popular callings. No fast line of demarcation really existed between the classes, under primitive conditions that often produced adversity and readjustments. The government of the country during the French period was largely the concern of the Motherland and at times

Another B.C. shepherd with Jack, a 25-year-old mule who is the favourite of the pack string.

it lacked continuity or clear purpose. But the affairs of the clergy, the missions and monastic corporations were much better managed. The religious institutions all along were the mainstay of racial strength and conservatism in Canada, as also they were the repositories of its culture and knowledge.

In the midst of disturbing changes, French Canada is fast losing its traditional features. It is moving with the rest of Canada, and of North America, towards an uncertain, intriguing future. Everything that used to be considered permanent is now questioned in some quarters; and many an heirloom is hastily thrown overboard as of no value, even though it should not be so lightly renounced. In accepting these changes, however, Quebec is a bit slower than the rest, and its apparent conservatism — which is not as ingrained as it may seem — has of late years brought to it many signs of confidence and esteem from outsiders, which it decidedly lacked in the days when almost every one mistook industries, power and wealth for a guarantee that humanity had entered a new millenium.

At the time of the cession of Canada to England, there were three small French settlements in that part of the country now known as Ontario, at Cataraqui (Kingston), Rouillé (Toronto) and along the east side of the Detroit River. The Ontario French of the present day, particularly up the Ottawa Valley, represent a much later movement of population from the Province of Quebec.

Other elements in the population of Ontario, especially the predominantly British stock, had their beginnings in the early days of Upper Canada. In 1783 and 1784 large numbers of United Empire Loyalists made homes for themselves, under very difficult conditions, on the north side of the upper St. Lawrence and along the shore of Lake Ontario to the Niagara peninsula. The majority of these were people of English descent, with some Scots and Irish, and a number of disbanded German soldiers who had served on the British side in the Revolutionary War. German Mennonites from Pennsylvania settled, a few years later, in what became the county of Waterloo.

As the years went by a gradually increasing stream of immigrants, mainly British in the earlier years, helped to lay the foundations of such towns as Brockville, Peterborough, Hamilton, Niagara, as well as Kingston and York (Toronto), and to push back the frontiers of settlement. Of the hardships endured by these Canadian pioneers, particularly by those of gentle birth who had been accustomed to very different conditions in their former homes, one gets a vivid impression in such books as Susanna Moodie's *Roughing it in the Bush*. Mrs. Moodie and her sister, Catherine Parr Traill, came to the Peterborough district when it consisted of nothing but a few clearings in the forest. They and others like them, from various parts of the British Isles, made good because they had courage and resourcefulness, and a sense of humour that enabled them, after a time, to look back smilingly upon the mistakes they had made in their ignorance of New World conditions. Mrs. Moodie gives us the same authentic pictures of life in Upper Canada a century or more ago, that we get of early colonial life in Nova Scotia from the inimitable sketches of Thomas Chandler Haliburton, and of manners and customs in the Quebec of long ago in the pages of Philippe-Aubert de Gaspé's *Les anciens Canadiens*, translated into English by Sir Charles Roberts as *The Canadians of Old*.

Various conditions, some of them geographical, have hampered the growth of Canada. Not the least of these is the peculiar hour-glass form of the country, Eastern and Western Canada joined together by a narrow, inhospitable and largely unprofitable neck of rock north of Lake Superior. On the other hand, particularly in the early history of the people, another geographical feature was of incalculable value. Probably no other country ever enjoyed so remarkable a system of water-ways, lakes and rivers, natural thoroughfares leading in every direction. For a man can start from Lake Winnipeg, and, with nothing more than an occasional portage, travel in a canoe east to the Atlantic, west to the Pacific, north to the Arctic, northeast to Hudson Bay, or south to the Gulf of Mexico.

These water thoroughfares were the routes of explorers, missionaries and fur traders in the early days of Canada, and it was largely because of them that the Prairie Provinces of Canada were discovered, the fur trade expanded into a gigantic industry, and the beginnings of settlement made possible in what is now Manitoba. The people of the prairies as we know them today look back to 1812, when the first lot of colonists sent out by Lord Selkirk reached the Red River valley. They were Scots, and neither grasshoppers nor drought nor the opposition of fur traders could permanently drive them out. Because they refused to be discouraged, they sowed seeds that have since grown into the great and ambitious city of Winnipeg and the provinces of Manitoba, Saskatchewan and Alberta, and because of them and others like them, Canada has been able to play a very important part in feeding the people of the world.

With the cultivation of wheat the Canadian prairies drew to themselves a flood of immigrants from Eastern Canada, the United States, the British Isles, and half the countries of continental Europe, these new settlers travelling west over the just-completed Canadian Pacific Railway. So Manitoba, Saskatchewan and Alberta developed into a gigantic wheat field, and became, more than any of the other provinces, the home of numerous racial groups, British and American, Scandinavian, German, Dutch, French, Belgian, Russian, Polish, Italian, Ukrainian, Doukhobor. Of their distinctive characteristics John Murray Gibbon has drawn a most interesting picture in his *Canadian Mosaic*, and he has shown some of the things that each group is contributing to the Canadian people.

The wave of settlement from the East for years spent most of its force on the prairies, but some of it broke through the mountains and reached British Columbia. The colonization of that far western province began, however, about the middle of the last century, when Vancouver Island became a Crown colony, and in 1866 was merged in the larger colony of British Columbia. Its early history was closely identified with that of the Hudson's Bay Company. The gold rush of 1858-60 brought a nondescript crowd of adventurers from every quarter, but the real emergence of the province as something to be reckoned with dates from the completion of the Canadian Pacific Railway and the entry of British Columbia into the Dominion. The people of that province have been influenced by its peculiar character, a land of mountain ranges and deep valleys, of timber and minerals and fisheries but little agriculture, of natural wealth but no prospect of a very large population; and also by their remoteness from Eastern Canada.

One question put forward at the beginning still remains, that is, whither bound is the Canadian people? The only basis for an answer lies in the past history of the country. Have the people of the Dominion been moving toward nationhood or away from it? The answer depends upon what we mean by nationhood, or by the nature and extent of Canada's political independence.

Despite other bars to unity, certain natural forces incessantly work towards it. They may be more powerful than those against it, and there is, perhaps, prophetic vision in the lines written by Sir Charles Roberts many years ago as a Collect for Dominion Day:

Father of Nations! Help of the feeble hand,
  Strength of the strong! to whom the nations kneel!
Stay and destroyer, at whose just command
  Earth's kingdoms tremble and her empires reel!
Who dost the low uplift, the small make great,
  And dost abase the ignorantly proud;
Of our scant people mould a mighty state,
  To the strong stern, to Thee in meekness bowed!
Father of unity, make this people one!
  Weld, interfuse them in the patriot's flame, —
Whose forging on Thine anvil was begun
  In blood late shed to purge the common shame,
That so our hearts, the fever of faction done,
  Banish old feuds in our young nation's name.

Bright lights, bands, floats and cheering crowds are all part of the night parade at the Quebec Winter Carnival.

CONFEDERATION CHAMBER PRINCE EDWARD ISLAND

by A. E. ARSENAULT

The bronze tablet on the wall of the Confederation Chamber commemorating the 1864 Conference.

Hon. A. E. Arsenault, retired judge and one-time premier of Prince Edward Island, is a keen student of the history of his native province. A member of the board of directors of the Royal Canadian Geographical Society from 1929 to 1960, he prepared this article for the May, 1953, issue of the Canadian Geographical Journal.

As a colony with separate government, in Canada, Prince Edward Island comes second to Nova Scotia. The first General Legislative Assembly met in 1773, just one hundred years before the Island entered Confederation. During that period the administration sought to solve the problems of government which later confronted the other provinces, and the Island statesmen did what they could to bring about that happy relation between the Colony and the Motherland under which the development of Canada has taken place.

In the year 1864, the first meeting looking towards the Confederation of Canada was held in Charlottetown.

At that time there was no railway connection between New Brunswick and Nova Scotia, nor between New Brunswick and Lower Canada, nor between New Brunswick and the United States. Prince Edward Island had no railway. Both New Brunswick

and Nova Scotia had begun the construction of a railway from Saint John on the one end and from Halifax on the other, designed to connect those two provinces, with the prospect of closer political connections and free trade between the Maritime Provinces. And out of this grew correspondence between the three governments initiated by the Government of Nova Scotia.

As a result of this correspondence, delegates were appointed by the three governments to meet at Charlottetown to consider the terms upon which Nova Scotia, New Brunswick and Prince Edward Island might be united as one province in a legislative union.

The delegates from the mainland provinces and from Prince Edward Island were in each case made up of leading members of the respective governments and opposition.

In the meantime, Upper and Lower Canada were at loggerheads. The union of Upper and Lower Canada had not proved a success. Continual difficulties were arising which the leaders of the day were powerless to solve, and government after government went down to defeat without bringing about any beneficial results.

Sir John Macdonald refers to these when he says: "All were alarmed at

this state of affairs. We had election after election — we had ministry after ministry — with the same results. Parties were so equally balanced that the vote of one member might decide the fate of an administration."

It was hoped that, with a parliament composed of representatives from other provinces as well, the rivalry between Upper and Lower Canada would disappear and that the government of the country would not be subject to such frequent changes. And this was, so far as Quebec and Ontario were concerned, the great incentive to the confederation of the provinces.

While the Maritime Conference had but begun its work, application was made on behalf of the Government of Canada, which was granted, to receive a delegation of that body to propose a larger federal union of all the provinces.

Never before had there been a meeting of so many eminent statesmen in Canada assembled in one place for a common purpose. Never before nor since has there been so notable a gathering within the narrow bounds of Prince Edward Island. As the meeting was held in camera, no minutes were kept and the speakers were not reported and, with the view of further considering the union of the provinces, it was proposed to hold a further conference at Quebec, and this conference was accordingly held on the 10th October following.

In the grand result as seen in the great and progressive Canadian Dominion as it is today, the Charlottetown Conference marked a notable date in the history of the North American section of the British Empire.

The delegates to the number of twenty-five sat in the room now called the Confederation Chamber in the Parliament Building. This room has been preserved intact, with the very table around which the delegates sat and the very chairs on which they were seated.

Prince Edward Island was the Cradle of Confederation, and it was fitting that in 1914, the fiftieth anniversary of this notable meeting, a bronze tablet commemorative of the event should have been erected in the very room where the historic Conference was held.

The tablet is allegorical.

In the foreground are the figures of five of the leading statesmen of the time representing the chief industries of the country.

Sir Leonard Tilley holds a scroll on which appears the word "Dominion", for, according to tradition, whilst in London and our representative there, seeking a name that would signify that status of Canada, Sir Leonard Tilley one night opened the Bible and found before him the words "Thy Dominion shall extend from sea to sea and unto the rivers end". He was so struck with these applicable words that next day he suggested the word Dominion to represent Canada — extending as it did from the Atlantic to the Pacific, and from the St. Lawrence to the MacKenzie.

Sir Georges Cartier holds the torch and the sword of justice, symbolic of the fact that his first professional achievement as a lawyer was the recording of the laws of his native province.

At the feet of Sir John Macdonald, who grasps the caduceus, are a scythe, a sheaf of wheat and a locomotive, which remind us that as the rails were laid Manitoba joined the Union; British Columbia became a province; the great unsettled prairies were populated; the wheat was sown; then came the harvest, followed by development and prosperity.

Gray (Prince Edward Island) holds the fasces, the provinces bound together and consolidated.

Tupper with the symbols of a pick and a fish, represents the mining and fishing industries of the Maritime Provinces.

On the margin of the plaque are inscribed the names of the delegates. To the right is the figure of the herald with a trumpet proclaiming the event. The inscription reads:

IN THE HEARTS AND MINDS OF THE
DELEGATES WHO ASSEMBLED
IN THIS ROOM ON SEPT. 1ST 1864
WAS BORN THE DOMINION OF CANADA

———

PROVIDENCE BEING THEIR GUIDE
THEY BUILDED BETTER THAN THEY
KNEW

The room also contains portraits of all the lieutenant-governors of the province since it became a colony and the pictures of the premiers of Prince Edward Island.

Many interesting relics of Confederation and pre-Confederation days are exhibited in the Chamber, and under glass is a very humorous page from the Visitors' Book in 1889 on which occasion Sir John Macdonald revisited this historic room and was asked to register. After writing his name and being puzzled as to what he should put down as his occupation, he turned to Joseph Pope who accompanied him and asked Joseph "What will I write as my occupation?" And, without waiting for an answer, inscribed "Cabinet Maker".

Although the Island is small and her voice is weak in the Council of the great Dominion, she is proud of having had a large share in bringing about the Confederation of the provinces of Canada which has made Canada the great nation it is today.

Confederation Chamber, formerly the Legislative Council Room, in the Provincial Building, with the table and chairs used at the Charlottetown conference in 1864.

La Grande Salle *of the* Place des Arts, *a theatre complex built to house local and visiting symphony orchestras, ballet, opera and concert groups.*

LA VILLE DE MONTREAL

by KENNEDY CRONE

Kennedy Crone has succeeded in capturing the essential spirit of Montreal, which is unchanged and unchanging. The details of tall buildings and other facts as they appeared in 1931 when this article was written have been omitted below, allowing the timeless character of Montreal to show through.

THE BROMIDES, or hackneyed phrases, supposed to typify the city of Montreal, in whole or part, are many and vivid. She is, for example: the metropolis of Canada; the second city of the Empire; the fifth largest city and the second largest port on the American continent; the second greatest inland port of the world, excelled by London alone; the Paris of America; the Capital of New France; after Paris, the largest of all French-speaking cities; the city of churches, of romance and tradition, of Canadian industrial and commercial supremacy, of two million visitors a year; the melting-pot of Latin and Anglo-Saxon culture; the only genuine world-minded city in the western hemisphere; amongst the first six of the world's most beautiful and charming cities; the shining example of a courteous population; successor of savage Hochelaga and pious Ville Marie; fifty times the possessor of the world's first and greatest, from the biggest structure ever laid stone on stone, to the finest fire brigade in existence.

To Americans she is "Abroad, overnight" and the British city to which thousands of Americans come to celebrate Washington's birthday, and drink to liberty from the tyrant with the tyrant's beer.

Not to be too sweet about it, there are other bromides, too, including those who describe her as a forbidding fortress of the Holy Roman Empire, the bungler of town-planning and traffic control, the home of the natural politician, the bulwark of conservatism under whatever label, and the pinnacle of racial prejudice.

But when all the bromides are assembled, and it is admitted that bromides, like platitudes, contain measures of truth, and occasionally, of course, the reptile half-truth, they utterly fail to express the beating heart of Montreal, or convey to the stranger anything approaching the tout ensemble of the city and its people.

To begin with, Montreal rarely repeats for general consumption any of these things, good or bad, about herself. She does not even show that she is particularly conscious of them. She abhors sloppy sentiment and sterile sloganism. She has no braggadocio and regards it in others with a casual contemptuousness. Outside criticism rarely gets beneath her skin. She is, however, quite self-critical beside her own radiators; the state of mind expressed in the Americanism "Boost, don't knock" is not Montrealesque at all.

The Chateau Champlain, being built by the Canadian Pacific Railway Company, adds an interesting architectural note to the Montreal scene.

Like London, she has a solid, quiet pride in herself, but she does not talk about it. Montreal rather assumes, with a touch of superciliousness, again like London, that the world knows a lot about her and gives her a place in the sun. If some persons do not happen to know or understand her, well, that is too bad, but so far as she is concerned they can go on stewing in their own ignorance. She is busy with other things.

The probable truth is that Montreal feels she is, while mainly Canadian, also partly European, and not ashamed of it; she has gone past the

parochial outlook and status of many communities on this continent and combined within herself the world vision and the best of Canadianism. Montreal is at once the most comprehensive Canadian city, and the Canadian city which neither asks nor cares who you are or where you come from, as long as you play the game. The commerce and other attributes of all nations flow through her in great streams by road and rail and water. She is the neck of the bottle for the world in its dealings with the greater part of Canada, to and fro. These things help to make her cos-

mopolitan, blasé, sophisticated. With her sophistication is an odd streak of naïveté and ingeniousness, inherited, perhaps, from days of French and early British rule just as the unexpected courtesy of the Montreal traffic policeman, or porter, or man-in-the-street, comes from old Brittany, Georgian England, the Scottish associations of exploration days with the North West Company and the Hudson's Bay Company, or maybe by way of the American Colonists who entered the northern wilds rather than deny the flag of their forbears.

Gone long ago is the once-prevalent atmosphere of exploration, In-

dian trading, missionary work, trapping, frontiering, which the occasional stranger, taking his lore from a Hollywood movie, still expects to see, to the surprise of local citizens; in its place a humming city, truly rich in history and tradition, and signs of the days gone by, but in most respects as modernized as any other great city, even to its slums and its rendezvous of the demi-monde.

Apart from figures, Montreal is a city with character and individuality of its own, and hardly comparable to any other large city, not even in Canada. Try to imagine a place in which within an hour or two the rambler can be seen in the Chateau of the

Governor appointed by Louis XIV; see several of the most dignified banking halls of modern times; stand in an old-fashioned garden framed with some of the oldest buildings of the white man on this continent; ride in taxi and tramway services without equal anywhere, or in the bumpiest of mid-Victorian horse cabs; pass through public parks which are le dernier cri in landscape gardening and horticultural art, and, five minutes later, in the centre of the city, enter steep Mount Royal park, deliberately left practically as it was when the Iroquois laid wait behind the trees; see together the greyhounds of the Atlantic and the sturdy little bateaux copied from those of St. Malo nearly 300 years ago; pass a row of houses which suggests Madeira, another which is Park Lane, a square from Edinburgh, suburbs that are Mayfair, Bloomsbury and the Faubourg St. Germain, or apartmented like Boston or New York, street after street of the two-flat and three-flat homes with the outside stairway peculiar to Montreal, a Ghetto, a Chinatown, or the purely French region "east of the Main", or "L'est du Boulevard" (depending on your upbringing); sit in a church which seats 9,120 worshippers, is a copy of Notre Dame, and has a great bell heard for 20 miles, and behind it traverse a wholesale district with the narrow twisting streets of the French regime, and many of the erstwhile drawing-rooms of the haut monde turned into warehouses for all sorts of commodities; visit cafes, tavernes, and salles-à-manger which might just as easily be in Deauville or the Montmarte, cafeterias and "Joe's quick lunches" of Broadway and the Bowery, and which have arising amongst them the latest of giant hotels, with bath, phone and radio for every room; note immense convents and

The superbly trained horses of the Montreal Police are quite at home in the modern city.

monasteries, a great University with the Oxford-St. Andrew's air and another reminiscent of the Sorbonne, a female jail managed by nuns, hospitals of antiquity and hospitals of world-wide repute in research and marvels of treatment and cure, towering grain elevators, impressive office buildings with batteries of automatically-controlled cars, the old-time French homes with high-pitched roofs, an electrically-lit Cross on the hilltop (seen at night for 60 miles) enter the reservation from which the peaceable Iroquois go to work as handymen and structural steel workers on the very sites where their paint-and-feather forefathers used arrow, tomahawk, and knife. A medley of old and new, of diverging and distinguishable ethnic groups, of culture and commerce, the beautiful and the bizarre, of the odours of spice and perfume of older days and the carbon monoxide of automobiles, of public signs and the clamour of voices in two

The Chateau de Ramezay, built in 1705 by the Governor of Montreal bearing the same name, originally served as the Governor's residence but is now the best historical museum in the city.

In Lafontaine Park, a delightful oasis in the East End of Montreal.

89

An ancient cannon on St. Helen's Island and a modern passenger liner passing under the Jacques Cartier Bridge between them represent more than three hundred years of history of the Port of Montreal.

languages, an almost-indescribable medley indeed.

A medley, and a melody, too; a modern, metropolitan melody strung on the chords of a pulsing, picturesque past.

Or look at the Rue St. Catherine ("Katareen", s'il vous plait) the main shopping promenade which cuts a gash across the city on the third of the five hillside terraces the city climbs, and on which flows, almost constantly, broad streams of hu-

manity. It has pictures, line for line, of Bond Street, the Rue de la Paix and Fifth Avenue, and its feminine burden is a seeming mixture of the obvious Englishwoman, the obvious Parisienne, and the obvious New Yorker, with the difference that the seeming Englishwoman is often liable to be French, the seeming Parisienne to be English-Canadian, the seeming New Yorker to be either French or English-Canadian, while the real New Yorker, disguised in tourist garb, has

commonly reached the broader category of "American visitor".

The city of Montreal is the central section of the Island of Montreal. The island is 30½ to 36 miles long and from seven to ten miles wide, and is the largest of a group of islands formed by the merging of the St. Lawrence and Ottawa Rivers. At Montreal's front door are the mingling waters of the two rivers, the currents of the Ottawa still holding identity by their clayish colour against

90

the blue-green masses of the mightier St. Lawrence. The belts of water flowing past the island on both sides vary between a mile to seven miles in width, the greater widths being lake formations.

In the heart of the island, and almost the centre of the city, is Mount Royal, a hill of 575 acres, rising 769 feet above sea level. It is the natural park already referred to, and is now surrounded by the builded city. From the top of this hill it is possible to see the entire city as in a panorama, sloping down to the river boundaries, and visitors have often described the experience as one of the most unusual and entrancing of urban pictures, a feature of which lies in the tens of thousands of trees between the rows of flat-roofed structures.

Jacques Cartier, on his second voyage from St. Malo, in 1535, gave Mount Royal its name. When Cartier paid his brief call there was already a palisaded settlement of 3,500 Huron Indians on the slopes of the hill. The Indians called it the district of Hochelaga, and it has been estimated by historians that this settlement dated back to about the year 1400. At any rate, it is apparent that a few years after the New World was discovered, and exactly thirty-eight years after Cabot had claimed North America for England, the Indian town of Hochelaga was already a mother city of this continent. The campus and buildings of McGill University stand where the chief town of Hochelaga stood.

The geologists say that in unknown spans of time before, the waters of the Atlantic flowed over the site of Montreal, now 870 miles from the nearest entrance to the sea, and point for confirmation to the fossilized sea-shells commonly found in the region. The sea receded. A period of volcanic activity followed, from which Mount Royal and other monteregian hills not far away arose.

On this section of Sherbrooke Street we get a glimpse at the same time of the very old, the modern and the very new.

Then came the glacial period, the glaciers grinding deep erosions in the valleys and leaving only the cores of the volcanoes. To this day a regiment of soldiers in step can vibrate the peak of the old crater which is Mount Royal.

The next outstanding date after the call of Cartier is 1611, when Samuel de Champlain, who had in the name of God and France founded the city of Quebec three years earlier, made a spring and summer trading post at the river-side, which he named Place Royale, a mile or so from the settlement of Hochelaga, which in the meantime had disappeared. Place Royale is still Place Royale, and how well Champlain picked his harbours

is shown by the fact that Place Royale remains today the pivot of Montreal's harbour, now more than eight miles long.

Following Champlain's death, in 1635, the Island of Montreal was granted to the Compagnie de Montréal, a body desirous of developing the island as a missionary and colonization headquarters. Seven years later the first executive officer of the company, Paul Chomedy de Maisonneuve, "devout and valiant gentleman" who consecrated his sword to the church in Canada, "and in whom lived again the spirit of Godfroy de Bouillon, leader of the first Crusade", arrived at the site of Montreal with about sixty persons from France to serve as soldiers and prospective settlers. He chose Place Royale as his site and named the new community Ville Marie, or City of Mary.

Maisonneuve erected a fort and for nearly eleven years, on account of the hostile Iroquois, the activities of the members of his little colony were confined to the fort and to the common just outside it. In 1653, however, he received reinforcements of about 100 colonists, the colony began to be pretty well able to take care of itself, and Ville Marie grew steadily up the hillside terraces towards Mount Royal. Farm concessions were granted, and the land cultivated.

Montreal remained as Ville Marie until about 1703 when it became known by its present name. The totals of population to the end of the French regime were: 1661 — 560; 1701 — 1,500; 1731 — 3,640; 1761 — 5,500.

The first streets were planned in 1672. Eight years later the first parish church was near to completion. The town became the centre of the fur trade and the starting-place of explorations. La Salle, Marquette, Duluth, Cadillac and others outfitted there and departed on their journeys to the Great Lakes, Ohio, and the Mississippi.

Montreal was a stockaded town from 1685 to 1722. In 1723 it was fortified with stone walls which embraced an area of 110 French arpents, the measure still used, or 93 English acres. These walls lasted till about 1814.

During the last days of the French regime, following the capture of Quebec by General Wolfe, the French moved their military headquarters to Montreal, which capitulated to the British forces on September 8th, 1760. Then began the extraordinary alliance of two pioneer races, an alliance surviving the Napoleonic Wars, the American Wars of 1775 and 1812, and the French Revolution.

The famous North West Company was formed at Montreal in 1783, a combination of fur traders, mostly English-speaking, who, amongst other things, built the first Canadian canal at Sault Ste. Marie, got into a series of murderous clashes with their older rivals, "the Governor and Company of Adventurers of England Trading into Hudson's Bay", less grandiloquently known as the Hudson's Bay Company, and were finally, in 1821, absorbed by the older concern.

In 1815 the city, now a mixed assemblage of 15,000 French-Canadians, Scots and Englishmen, with the Scots, ever on the outposts of things, numerically quite strong, was considered a nice town in which farmers and frontiersmen might spend their last leisurely days. Manufacturing had recently begun. Town planning schemes were afoot, under the aegis of a commission which had as one of its members James McGill, the Scott who later founded McGill University.

In 1840 the population had grown to 40,465 and about that time the English-speaking minorities of Scotch and English were added to by a considerable influx of Irish. Montreal was still secondary to Quebec, the old capital city, but was then wresting from her the title of Canadian metropolis.

By 1861, the beginning of American Civil War days, population had grown to 90,323, and ten years later, four years after confederation of Canada, it was 107,223. Incidentally, Montreal sympathies in the Civil War seem to have been curiously divided between admiration for Abraham Lincoln and wish to end slavery, on the one hand, and, on the other hand, hope that the southerners, towards whom they felt a distinct kinship, would not be distressed and humiliated.

Meanwhile much railway development had taken place. In 1859 the first train from Montreal passed over the first bridge to the mainland. The bridge was the Victoria Tubular Bridge, then regarded as the seventh wonder of the world. The Prince of Wales, afterwards Edward VII, drove

Looking south on Peel Street, at the corner of St. Catherine Street, below which it becomes Windsor Street and continues on towards the water front. All day long there is a ceaseless flow east and west across this artery as Montrealers go about the business of the day. Shoppers, students, business men and women and tourists all contribute to the stream.

92

Dominion Square, an oasis in the heart of Montreal, is flanked by the Sun Life Building, a modern structure in the classical tradition completed in 1931. Over its shoulder looms the ultra-modern Place Ville Marie.

the last spike of the two-mile bridge, long since replaced by a larger and more modern Victoria Bridge. In those days were founded the railway links which resulted in Montreal becoming the headquarters of rail transport in the Dominion. Coincidentally, Montreal developed as the transatlantic port, and Scottish Montrealers founded and developed the famous Allan Line, a foundation often credited in error to the city of Glasgow.

Affairs of transportation and associated interests extensively affect the destinies of Montreal and pervade its psychologies to an unusual degree. This is to be expected when it is remembered that the city is headquarters of two immense transcontinental railway systems, the Canadian National Railways and the Canadian Pacific Railway — the only railways in North America that can properly be described as transcontinental — and is the head of

ocean navigation and the transference point for grain and other exports.

It will be seen from these mere sidelights how elusive a city Montreal is to describe and interpret, but perhaps from the written word and the complementary illustrations, there can be drawn something of understanding and appreciation of the melodious medley which is at once amongst the strangest and quaintest of great urban harmonies, and the charming song of La Ville de Montréal.

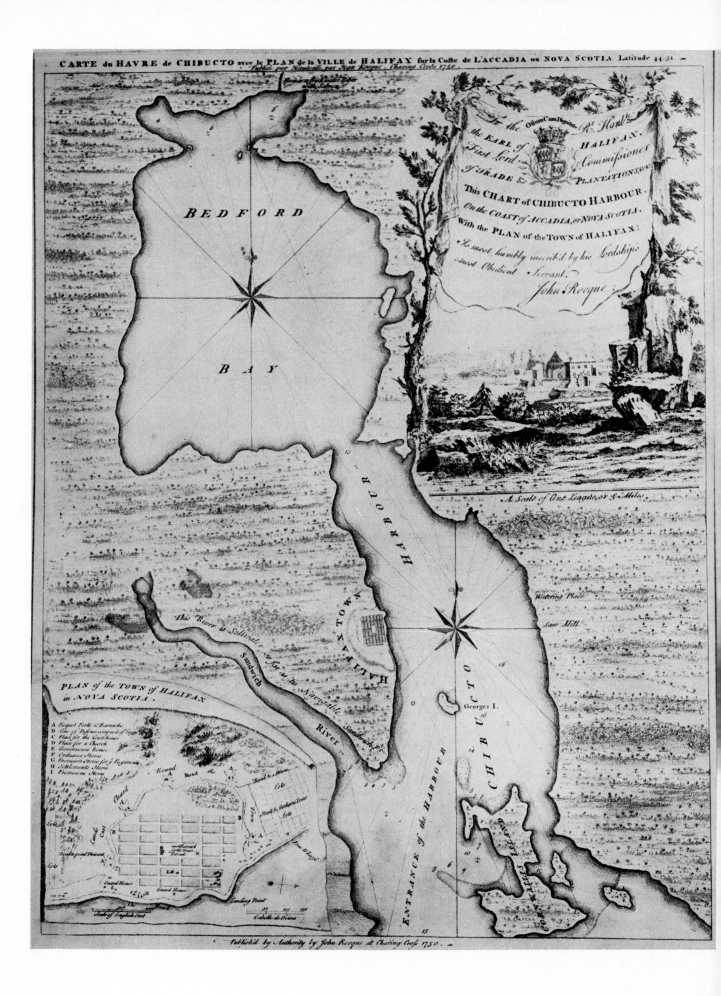

View of Halifax from Dartmouth Cove; from Bouchette's The British Dominions in North America, London, 1832.

HALIFAX

From Founding to Confederation

by D. C. HARVEY

This early story of Halifax is taken from an article in the Canadian Geographical Journal *of January 1949 written to commemorate the bicentenary of the founding of the city.*

FEW CITIES IN CANADA can claim two centuries of recorded history; and none can claim such a magnificent natural harbour whose "liquid history", to borrow a phrase applied to the Thames by the late John Burns, preceded and enriched its recorded history, was enshrined in its original name, and lent wings to the imagination of all who have attempted to describe it.

To the aborigines, this harbour was long known as **Chebucto,** which means the great long harbour. It has been known to written history since the days of Champlain, who visited it in 1607, and described it as "a very safe bay, seven or eight leagues in circumference". It has had something to do with the making of history since 1698, when the Sedentary Fishing Company of Acadia attempted to form an establishment on its shores and brought over a missionary from the Penobscot, whose plan was to induce the Indians to congregate here for trade and settlement. Dièreville

95

visited it in 1699 and found the remains of fish stages that had been erected by this company for drying their cod. He describes it in indifferent verse as follows:

This Harbour is of great extent,
And Nature has, herself, formed there
A splendid Basin, and around about
Green fir-trees, which afford the eye
A pleasant prospect; at its edge
A Building used for drying Cod;

To Delabat, military engineer in Acadia (1702-13) and pupil of Marshal Vauban, who thought that Chebucto meant "large estuary and bay of fire", it was deserving of another name: "for it is one of the best anchorages for all kinds of vessels that one could find. It can hold more than a thousand and they could anchor all the way from the beach B. [McNab's

The clock on the Customs Building has shown "Harbour Time" to many generations of workers on the waterfront.

Island] right into the back of the basin." After recommending fortifications at various strategic points very similar to those later chosen by the English, he asserted that more than thirty mills could be built along the small river [Sackville], from which the Indians made their first portage towards Minas Basin and Port Royal.

It was by this well known Indian route that Governor de Brouillan went from Chebucto to Port Royal in June, 1701. He too described the harbour as "one of the finest that nature could form", although to make it secure would cost rather dear "because its entrance is wide and very easy".

Chebucto Harbour and its potentialities, therefore, were known to the Indians and to French officials long before the British showed any interest in them. During the first half of the eighteenth century it was visited by individuals and families of fishermen; but the events which led to its occupation and fortification in 1749 were the conquest of Louisbourg by New Englanders in 1745, D'Anville's expedition with a view to its recapture in the following year, and the restoration of Louisbourg to the French in 1748.

It was founded on June 21, 1749, by the Hon. Edward Cornwallis, with disbanded soldiers, sailors, their wives, families and servants, essentially as an outpost of New England against the French of Nova Scotia, Cape Breton and Quebec; and from that date until the American War of Independence, Halifax was as much a child of New England as of Old. Lumber and supplies came from Boston, and Boston merchants or their agents flocked here to look after their interests.

Here the famous "cabbage planting" expedition of 1757 congregated

against Louisbourg. For two months in that year some 15,000 officers and men were encamped on the peninsula. Lord Loudoun arrived here on June 30 with men and transports from New York, and Admiral Holburne arrived on July 9 with a fleet and transports from England. Here the men of both armies were encamped and grew vegetables while the officers debated the wisdom of attacking Louisbourg, which was reported to be defended by a stronger fleet and almost as strong a garrison. Finally, towards the end of August, the project was abandoned, Lord Loudoun returned to New York and Admiral Holburne, after twice reconnoitring Louisbourg, returned to England.

In the following year a larger fleet of 23 ships of the line, 18 frigates and over 100 transports, 157 vessels in all, assembled in this harbour under Admiral Boscawen and on May 28 sailed for Louisbourg. They were met by General Amherst at the mouth of the harbour and proceeded on their eventful voyage.

Again, the winter of 1759 saw preparations going on in this harbour for the attack on Quebec, and on May 1 Admiral Saunders and General Wolfe arrived here. From here, on May 3, Admiral Durell was despatched with eight ships of the line and some troops to make soundings on the St. Lawrence, and a few days later Admiral Saunders set out for Quebec with the remainder of his fleet.

Thus, for ten years, from 1749-59, it may be said that this harbour was alive with military and naval forces coming and going on major errands, or going through their manoeuvres on the Grand Parade and in the shadow of Citadel Hill. In this same period the press made a beginning with the **Halifax Gazette** of March 23, 1752, and on October 2, 1758, the first legislative assembly in Canada met, thus completing the constitution under the old royal government.

In this same period the first pri-

Ships in Bedford Basin awaiting convoy, World War II.

vateer set out from Halifax, an incident that was prophetic of a profitable industry in the days of the American Revolution, the French Revolution, and the War of 1812, when this harbour was alive with shipping and this town was agog with the sale of prizes in the Vice-Admiralty Court and the profits that were made for all, official and civilian, by these by-products of wars that were no longer waged upon our soil but in the main across the Atlantic. Between 1777 and 1814, nearly 800 prizes were brought into Halifax harbour by privateers and ships of the navy, and

in the three years 1778-81 alone 900 sea-going craft of all descriptions entered the port of Halifax from colonial ports, New York, the West Indies or the British Isles. This same period saw the feeble beginnings of the Nova Scotian trade with the West Indies, a trade which grew in volume and importance in the early nineteenth century and in time brought Nova Scotia into the domain of international affairs.

So far I have spoken of liquid history in the sense of history that literally flowed with the tides in and out of the harbour. Naturally in time of war

this was more impressive. From 1815 until 1914, with the exception of the Crimean War and the Indian Mutiny and the Boer War, there have been no wars in which Nova Scotians were specifically interested; but during those years, until 1905, this harbour was an imperial military and naval stronghold, and in that time many ships came in relieving the garrisons, and practically every regiment of the British Army lay in barracks here or were manoeuvred on the Grand Parade or the Common.

In the meantime Nova Scotian built ships sailed in and out of the

97

harbour. Here too the first steamers of the Cunard line, a line created by a citizen of Halifax, arrived from Liverpool enroute to Boston; and other lines have made the harbour a port of call ever since. From all this it is clear that this harbour, which the Micmacs received from the hand of Nature and Champlain described as **safe harbour**, has figured in history as one of the great harbours of the world, capable of sheltering and having sheltered some of the largest fleets that have crossed the Atlantic. In the two world wars of this century it has sent out some of the largest convoys that have ever left the shores of America.

But Halifax has been more than a haven of refuge from storm, or a port of call and departure for military, naval and mercantile expeditions. It has been a base of supply since 1749; has had a dockyard since 1757, which even then, according to Captain Knox, had "all the conveniences for the largest first-rate ship to heave down and careen"; has extended hos-

pitality to many generations of officers and men who have visited or been stationed here; and has given many distinguished sons to the Imperial Army and the Royal Navy.

The continued connection of the Imperial Forces with Halifax, until the beginning of the twentieth century, has coloured its entire history.

Generally speaking, there was an average of two regiments of foot in garrison, together with detachments of artillery, engineers, ordnance, commissariat, pay and medical corps; and after 1819, when part of the dockyard establishment was moved to Bermuda, on an average a dozen ships of war, including the flagship of the North American and West Indian squadron, rode at anchor in the harbour each year from May to October. Furnishing supplies and accommodation to these in normal times kept the merchants busy; but there were times when the number of the forces exceeded the population of the town and the problem was acute. In 1749 the population was 3,000,

with an equal number of troops. In 1757, after the Germans and Swiss had been removed to Lunenburg, the population was less than 2,500; and there were 15,000 troops encamped on the Peninsula. During the American Revolution, when General Howe's flotilla arrived, the civilian population was little more than 3,000; and during the War of 1812 it was less than 10,000, while at one period there were as many as 4,000 troops in garrison and the average number of warships in the harbour was more than doubled.

It is to the army that Halifax owes its first theatre, many amateur theatrical performances and much martial music; and to the navy the early regattas, which led to the organization of the Halifax Yacht Club, the ancestor of the present Royal Nova Scotia Yacht Squadron. The introduction of curling is also ascribed to a young naval officer, while that of hockey is credited to the army. Both co-operated in organizing the Turf Club and patronized many other sports according to their season; but the army was more prominent in winter sports since most naval personnel wintered at Bermuda.

Though the City of Halifax in 1849 differed considerably from the town that had been laid out a century earlier, the difference was one of degree rather than of kind and not so marked as the changes which have taken place in the character and extent of the business and residential areas since that time. It was not unnatural that a town established on a tree-covered peninsula should in the first instance be built of wood; but even some of the first settlers found it a novel experience, while later visitors to Halifax found it a matter of surprise that the practice was still continued with satisfactory results.

The original town, as laid off by Mr. Bruce, the engineer, and Mr.

Barrington Street in 1949, looking south, with the spire of St. Mathew's Church in the distance.

98

Halifax Harbour, with its wharves and dockside railway tracks is linked to the city of Dartmouth by the Angus L. Macdonald bridge.

Morris, the surveyor, lay between the harbour on the east and the foot of Citadel Hill on the west. The whole area was surrounded by a strong palisade of pickets, with log forts or blockhouses at suitable intervals for defence against the Indians. The north and south suburbs were extensions of the town along the waterfront, but outside the pickets, and were known as Dutch Town and Irish Town respectively. A number of lots were laid out for fishermen between Freshwater Brook and Point Pleasant.

After 1751 five-acre lots were laid out over a large part of the peninsula, and were known as the north, south and middle divisions. The last was directly west of the Common, which comprised some 240 acres and in turn lay west of Citadel Hill to Robie Street, but extended northward to Cunard and southward to South Street, to use modern nomenclature. The Common of today is only a small part of the original allotment: for the larger southern area, chiefly in the second century of the city's history, was called upon to provide sites for the public gardens, a public cemetery, several hospitals and educational institutions, a cathedral and a number of private residences.

The thickly settled areas of the city did not expand greatly during its first century but some of the finest public buildings and private residences were built in that period, and those which have survived are still a source of pride to Haligonians, as evidence of the faith of their forefathers in the great future of their city and province.

Wright's Mill and Tavern, Chaudiere Falls, 1823. From a picture by Henri du Vernet.

OTTAWA OF YESTERDAY

by EDWIN C. GUILLET

Those who feel that the early history of Canada lacks drama and colour must admit, after reading this account from the January, 1931, issue of the Canadian Geographical Journal, *that Ottawa in its early days was exceptional. Mr. Guillet has concentrated on the "seamy" side of the story, but that was one facet of Canada's growth.*

THE CAPITAL OF CANADA ranks high among the continent's beautiful cities, but its origin was com-

monplace. Professor Goldwin Smith, who had a pronounced opinion on everything and seldom failed to publicize it, called Ottawa "a sub-arctic lumber-village, converted by royal mandate into a political cockpit"; but Anthony Trollope, who saw it about the same time, found his spirit exalted by the "natural grandeur" of its location on a "magnificent" river, and he considered that "Ottawa is the Edinburgh of British North America".

For two centuries after Champlain's journey past the site, in 1613, the region was known only to the traders and *voyageurs* who pressed on by the Rivière des Françaises to the far west. Then, in the late 1790's, an enterprising American, Philemon Wright, pushed laboriously up the Ottawa and investigated the possibilities of lumbering and settlement. He surveyed the scene by climbing a hundred of the tallest trees in Hull Township, and it was obvious to him

Wellington Street and Barrack Hill (now the corner of Wellington and Bank Streets), about 1842. From an oil painting by W. H. Thompson, after Lt. Sedley, R.E.

that there was great wealth in prospect. In February, 1800, he brought in thirty American settlers, well supplied with stock and tools. No pioneer undertaking was more courageous. At the Long Sault, 80 miles from their goal, they met difficulties that would have repulsed lesser men:

"In consequence of the depth of the snow," he wrote, "we were obliged to make a stand, and set one part of our men to alter our teams so as to go singly, and the other part to proceed forward to cut the road. Before dark we cleared away the snow and cut down trees for fire for the whole of the night, the women and children sleeping in covered sleighs, and the men with the blankets around the fire, whilst the cattle were made

fast to standing trees . . . The ice being covered by snow about a foot thick, it was impossible to know whether it was safe without sounding it with the axe. Towards the end of the first day on the ice an Indian volunteered to guide the party without promise of fee or reward. With his small axe he tried the ice every step he went . . . Owing to the deepness of the snow it took us about six days to pass up this river a distance of about 64 miles."

Wright established his settlement on the north shore at Wright Village, or Wrightsville, considering the rocky cliffs across the river an inferior location.

An enterprising employee of Wright's, Nicholas Sparks, saved up

$240 and bought most of the eventual site of Ottawa from John Burrows. W. P. Lett, poet-historian of old Ottawa — without whose writings our records would be much the poorer — has this to say of Sparks, whom he calls "an honest, upright man":

Now first among our old landmarks
Comes Laird of Bytown, Nicholas Sparks,
Who came across in '26*
From Hull, his lucky fate to fix
Upon a bush farm which he bought
For sixty pounds — and little thought,
While grumbling at a price so high,
That Fortune had not passed him by.

Sparks built a log shanty on the southeast corner of Sparks and Bay Streets, where in later years the Wellington Ward Market was located. In after years, like Jesse Ketchum of

*Sparks actually crossed the river several years earlier and had built his log house by 1824.

101

early Toronto, he was noted for generosity in supplying sites for schools, churches, and other public buildings. Meanwhile others, among whom were the Honeywells and the Bellows, had settled in the neighbourhood. In 1819, Caleb Bellows kept a store at Richmond Landing, and a quarter mile west stood Isaac Firth's tavern. Says Lett:

Isaac Firth, an old John Bull,
Of milk of human kindness full,
Of rotund form and smiling face,
Who kept an entertaining place
For travel-worn and weary fellows
Who landed where Caleb T. Bellows
Out on the point his habitation
Built in a pleasant situation.

Apart from these few rude buildings, the site of Ottawa comprised cliffs and cedar swamps, but a notable enterprise was being planned. As early as 1816 a survey had been made for an interior route between Montreal and Kingston which would be safe from interference in case of another war with the United States. Ten years later the site of Ottawa was chosen by the Imperial Government as the terminus of the proposed canal, and Colonel John By arrived to supervise the work. Lett has this to say of the Colonel:

As 'oer the past my vision runs,
Gazing on Bytown's elder sons,
The portly Colonel I behold
Plainly as in days of old,
Conjured before me at this hour
By memory's undying power;
Seated upon his great black steed
Of stately form and noble breed,
A man who knew not how to flinch,
A British soldier every inch:
Courteous alike to low and high,
A gentleman was Colonel By.

Bytown, as the settlement was named, speedily became a bustling place.

"The streets," said a visitor, Joseph Bouchette, "are laid out with much regularity and of a liberal width that will hereafter contribute to the convenience, salubrity, and elegance of the place. The number of houses now built is about 150, most of which are constructed of wood, frequently in a style of neatness and taste that reflects great credit upon the Inhabitants."

But the Irish labourers on the canal lived half underground in:

Two rows of cabins in the swamp
Begirt by ponds and vapours damp
And aromatic cedar trees.

They were:

Adepts at handling the spade,
And bruisers at the wheeling trade,
Lovers of poteen strong and clear,
In preference to rum or beer;
Sons of the sod who'd knock you down
For half a word 'gainst Cork's own town.

Mother McGinty, tavern-keeper, was well able to look after her own interests:

She kept the reckoning, ruled the roost,
And swung an arm of potent might
That few would dare to brave in fight;
Yet she was a good-natured soul
As ever filled the flowing bowl;
In sooth she dealth in goodly cheer
Half pints of whisky, quarts of beer.
And when a man had spent his all
She chalked the balance on the wall;
And woe to him who, soon or late,
His tally did not liquidate.

In 1832, Colonel By bought for £1,200 a piece of land bounded by the present Laurier, Gladstone, and Bronson Avenues and the Rideau River; its value now runs into millions. Earlier he had built his house on the site which is now Major's Hill Park, apparently selected for the view. From that bold eminence rising from Entrance Bay he could see the wild shore opposite with its gleaming church spire, the river's picturesque islands, the canoes, barges, and rafts sailing among them, and a succession of varied bridges. Most impressive of all were the wild falls of the Great and the Little Chaudière, hurling a great volume of water with terrific force into the abyss below.

Life in old Bytown, however, was far too active to leave much time for gazing at beautiful vistas. It was indeed a stirring period. Some forty stores or tradesmen's shops served the community, but a brewery and nine bars dispensed liquor in profusion, and brawls were frequent and bitter. Raftsmen, lumbermen, canal labourers, and old soldiers intensely disliked one another and took pleasure in showing their feelings. On St. Patrick's Day, 1828, a mob of one hundred and fifty labourers from the Hog's Back Rapids paraded through

Early days of the Rideau Canal.

Bytown carrying the inevitable green flag. A contemporary account says that:

"In a free and violent series of fights with sticks and clubs and fists Thomas Ford was killed by a blow from the limb of a tree . . . The Flag was carried to *illuminate* St. Patrick's Day . . . They were all Roman Catholics, so there could be no party complaints . . . Abe Dow said he saw a number of men amusing themselves fighting . . . All were drunk, dancing and fighting."

And it is characteristic that when one McKibbon was tried for murder it was a case of Hog's Back *versus* Bytown, and the jury found him not guilty.

In July 1829 Bytown held its first fair. But:

Twas not to buy or sell they came—
They all assembled, wild and free,
To have a ranting, roaring spree.

The fair ended in a wild horse race (as late as the 'forties these were held in the streets) and a pitched battle between "grangers" (lumbermen) and Irish "shiners", so the event was withdrawn for some years. When it recommenced, its chief purpose was the trade in oxen for the lumber camps of the Gatineau and beyond.

For a few years Bytown was little more than a suburb of the older Hull. Mathew Connell was appointed first postmaster of Bytown in 1829, before that date all mail being delivered in Hull. Until 1828 Hull was, too, the graveyard of Bytown, the dead being ferried over; but there were so many deaths among the canal workers that a cemetery enclosed by a ten-foot cedar-post stockade was inaugurated in Bytown. No religious denomination would countenance common burial places, so separate lots were set aside for Presbyterian, Roman Catholic, and Church of England, while Methodist and lesser sects were

apparently completely beyond the pale of polite burial and the Kingdom of Heaven!

Upon completion of work on the canal in 1832 some of the more turbulent citizens left the community, but quarrelsomeness persisted in Bytown for many a year. In private brawls eye-gouging and forms of mutilation were not uncommon. Perhaps the most notable public row was related to that major Canadian sport — politics. Known in local history as Bytown's Stoney Monday riot of 1849, the occasion of the trouble was the proposed visit of Lord Elgin to Bytown, just after he had signed the debatable Rebellion Losses Bill. Those who supported his course of action called a meeting to arrange a suitable reception; but Tory opponents, augmented by wagon-loads of farmers who opposed Bytowners

from force of habit, also congregated at North Ward Market. Each faction of the mob sought to elect a chairman of its own political colour, and such an uproar ensued that no one could restore order.

"Props under the platform were pulled over," says an account, "and the speakers were precipitated to the ground . . . Angry words soon led to blows, and in about three minutes every loose stone on the market square was hurtling through the air. In the midst of the mêlée a shot was fired, and a general run for arms took place. The farmers were plentifully supplied from a store on Rideau Street, and the inhabitants of Bytown supplied themselves as best they could."

One man was killed and twenty wounded before two companies of rifles ended the disturbance. The same

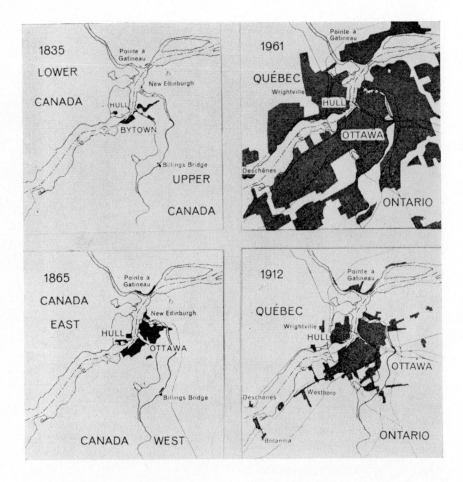

On January 20, 1847, the Mechanics' Institute was organized, and it long provided the only effort to advance education and culture among industrial and commercial workers; for half a century and more, in fact, the Institute's library was almost alone in supplying books to the citizens. In the same year Bytown was incorporated as a town, the population having increased from 2,400 to 6,000 in thirteen years. In 1854 Bytown became the City of Ottawa, with John B. Lewis as first mayor.

The entire region assumed much greater importance when Queen Victoria selected Ottawa as the future capital of Canada. On December 20, 1859, the first sod for the erection of the Parliament Buildings was turned on old Barrack Hill — site of the barracks in Colonel By's day. On September 1, 1860, the Prince of Wales laid the cornerstone, the materials used in construction being limestone, cream-coloured Nepean sandstone, and marble quarried in the vicinity and near picturesque Chats Falls, combined with dressings

force, together with some common sense and good luck, prevented further bloodshed two days later when hundreds of well-armed Tories and Reformers were drawn up in battle array on Barrack Hill and Market Square, respectively.

On quieter days more worthy people were engaged in educating the youth. Perhaps the most long-suffering teacher was James Maloney, who persisted for half a century, from 1827 to 1878:

A fixed star in the teacher's heaven
Since the old days of twenty-seven,
He taught and ne'er forgot the taws:
The handle was just two feet long,
And well he trounced the noisy throng.

Maloney was obviously an enthusiast, for he conducted also a night school in his 'English Mercantile and Mathematical Academy', where: "those of riper years can be carefully and expeditiously instructed in Reading, Writing, Arithemetic in all its various ways, Book-keeping with Double and Single Entry, English Grammar, Geography with the use of the Globes, Geometry, Algebra, Navigation, etc., all according to the precepts of the most modern and approved writers."

In the absence of any state facilities, numerous other more or less private schools were instituted. There was "a School for Boarders and Day Scholars", "a School for Advanced Scholars", "A Seminary for Young Ladies" (stressing the *Ladies*), and one "for Philosophy, Reading, etc." In May 1843, the Dalhousie Grammar School commenced in rented rooms, but not until 1871 were girls permitted to attend. In 1848 the French Roman Catholics established the "College of Bytown". In 1861, it became the College of Ottawa, and subsequently was granted university status.

Sussex Street around 1896.

of Ohio freestone and Potsdam sandstone. The colours were most effective, and the perfection of Gothic towers and the graceful beauty of the Parliamentary Library have earned encomiums from the most discriminating world travellers.

Among shades of political opinion in old Ottawa were numerous Irish Fenians. One of them, who moved up from Montreal for a purpose, was Patrick Whelan, and in the early morning of April 7, 1868, he effected that purpose when he shot the great orator and statesman, Thomas D'Arcy McGee, just as he was entering his hotel the Toronto House, after delivering an anti-Fenian address in the House of Commons.

As a result of clever detective work Whelan was caught, the bullet traced to the revolver found on his person, and his threats and other activities clearly associated with the murder of McGee. At his trial he was capably defended by the Grand Master of the Orange Lodge, John Hillyard Cameron, whose life was threatened by Orangemen as a consequence. Whe-

Russell House at the corner of Sparks and Elgin Streets, about 1860.

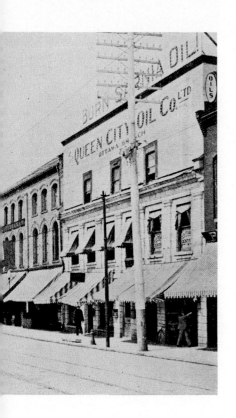

lan was convicted and sentenced to death. Every string that could be pulled to prevent his execution, every appeal that could be taken, was ineffectual, though his death on the gallows was delayed two months.

His public execution on February 11, 1869, provided a scene unparalleled in Canada. Below, on the streets, were 8,000 excessively turbulent citizens, hooting and howling in barbarous fashion; above, on the wall, was Whelan, surrounded by priests engaged in earnest prayer and at the same time hard pressed to prevent the fanatical Irishman from making an impassioned harangue from the scaffold. In dramatic intensity this scene most resembled an episode in the Spanish Inquisition or the burning of some seventeenth century witch.

There have been many memorable occasions in the life of the Canadian parliament. One occurred in the autumn of 1873 when Donald Smith (later Lord Strathcona) precipitated the defeat of Sir John Macdonald's administration by withdrawing his support in the "Pacific Scandal" is-

sue; another on March 14, 1879, when Sir Leonard Tilley introduced the "National Policy" of protective tariffs upon which Macdonald had swept back to power. The great statesmen of the past have on innumerable occasions risen to the heights in debate, in strategy, in repartee; there have been days of intense sadness when national leaders were mourned by men of all parties; and days when declarations of war have been fraught with both patriotism and tragedy for the entire nation.

For three-quarters of a century Ottawa evolved with little system — a queer combination of French and English, old and new, polished and primitive, noble and tawdry. But in 1899 a belated start toward planning was made with the creation of the Ottawa Improvement Commission. This commission, representative of the federal government and the city, had permanent control of government improvements and was authorized to own property. The turn of the century, therefore, brought a new phase in the development of Canada's capital.

Vancouver Harbour as seen from the North Shore. The second narrows bridge can be seen upper left, and beyond it is Burnaby Mountain, the site of the new Simon Fraser University.

THE PORT OF VANCOUVER

by TOM MacINNES

This account appeared in the April 1931, issue of the Canadian Geographical Journal. *Mr. MacInnes proved an accurate prophet of how his adopted city would grow in importance and beauty. Some idea of that growth and that beauty may be obtained from the pictures, which have been chosen to show parts of Vancouver as they are today.*

BECAUSE OF NEAR-AT-HAND and varied beauty of its mountain and forest scenery, and pleasant summers to be enjoyed along its several sea-fronts, Vancouver is in the way of becoming a great tourist resort. Even through its winters of salt winds and rain, it is not without unique attractions for such as come to it from the northern United States and central Canada. Vancouver, be-

fore long, may hold its own as a pleasure city with any other on the continent. But in that is not its destiny.

Vancouver as a city and Vancouver as a port are two different affairs. As a port, it cannot be interfered with by provincial or municipal authorities, being entirely under the administration and direction of the Dominion Government, acting through the Harbour Commission. The citizens of Saskatchewan and Alberta have an equal interest with the Pacific coast in Vancouver as a port.

It is the port which makes the city. Its strategic commercial position, linking all western Canada so economically with the Orient and with Europe; the advent of transcontinental railways; the work of the farmers of Saskatchewan and Alberta; and the manner in which harbour and terminal facilities have been developed and administered by the Vancouver Harbour Commission; all combined have gone far to justify the opinion of Roger W. Babson, American economist, expressed to a gathering of business men in 1929, that before this century ends, one port on the Pacific coast of America will be the trade leader of the Pacific, as New York leads the trade of the Atlantic, and that port may be Vancouver.

The port of Vancouver includes all of Burrard Inlet, together with the outlying waters from Point Atkinson to Point Grey. Before British Columbia entered Confederation there were two saw-mills established on Burrard Inlet, the first on the north shore and the second on the south shore, about two miles across from each other. The city grew around and from the saw-mill site on the south shore, the site where now the Vancouver Harbour Commission has its headquarters.

Burrard Inlet was discovered by the Spanish navigator, Jose Maria Narvaez, in August, 1791, and named by him "Boca de Florida Blanca". Narvaez was in command of the schooner *Saturnina* at that time, having been sent forward by his superior officer, Lieut. Francisca Eliza, after the latter's entry on an exploring expedition through the Straits of Juan de Fuca in May of the same year. Narvaez also discovered Nanaimo, naming it, jointly with Departure Bay, "Bocas de Winthuysen"; Howe Sound, naming it "Boca de Carmelo";

A part of the vast salmon fishing fleet on a quiet Sunday at Fisherman's Wharf in Vancouver Harbour. On the skyline beyond are "The Lions".

Canberra *in the port of Vancouver, "Canada's Gateway to the Pacific". Giant liners from every country of the world visit this busy port handling more cargo than Seattle, Portland, San Francisco and Los Angeles combined.*

and Fraser River, naming it "Rio Blanco".

Burrard Inlet was entered by Captain George Vancouver the following year, but he gave it scanty attention because of having, as he wrote at the time, "a grander object in contemplation"; that is to say "Fretum Anian", or "Northwest Passage". Vancouver rowed into the inlet in the afternoon of June 13th, 1792, and rowed out again at four o'clock the next morning, naming the place Burrard's Channel, and showing it on his chart as Burrard's canal. As to this locality Vancouver's chart is quite inaccurate, except for the North Arm and Port Moody, branches of the inlet, into which he did not enter, but whose proper contours and proportions he obtained from the findings of Cayetano Valdes, who examined them under direction of Galiano a few days after Vancouver left. It is peculiar that Captain Vancouver, usually accurate in such matters, should have been so inaccurate about the one place from which his name was eventually to be made familiar to all the ports of the seven seas.

About 60 years passed before any Europeans again came to bother the peace of the inlet.

From 1857 to 1863 Captain George Henry Richards and Mr. Daniel Pender, R.N., in the paddle-sloops *Plumper* and *Hecate*, made a complete survey of the British Columbia coasts and tidal waters. Included in the early part of their work in 1859 was a survey of Burrard Inlet; the first since the tracing made by Valdes in June, 1792.

Following the first shipload of coal out of Nanaimo, and down to Victoria on the *Cadboro* in September, 1852, both Hudson's Bay men and independent prospectors were on the look-out for more coal-mines on the sea-front. In time, reports were received from Indians that the same combustible black rock was to be found at a certain part of Burrard Inlet. In 1859 a private syndicate sank a few shafts on that part of the south shore of the Inlet which came to be known generally as Coal Harbour. The syndicate included the late Walter Moberly, who earlier in that year, as Superintendent of Public Works, had begun clearing the site and erecting the first official buildings for the new mainland capital, founded by Col. Moody of the Royal Engineers and Sappers, called Queensborough, and later New Westminster. The coal

The West End of Vancouver has been rebu is Stanley Park, wl

seams uncovered at Coal Harbour by Moberly and his associates were too narrow to be worth mining, and the syndicate project was abandoned.

In June, 1862, a young Englishman, John Morton, recently arrived from the Old Country, noticed a sample of coal in Tom Cunningham's hardware store in New Westminster. Morton had come from a family of potters, and he made inquiries concerning the sample, not because he wanted coal but because at home he had always associated the best potter's clay with coal seams, and he thought the same rule might apply in the new land. He had in mind to acquire a fine holding of clay for

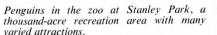

Penguins in the zoo at Stanley Park, a thousand-acre recreation area with many varied attractions.

...partment houses, and the shoreline of English Bay cleared of buildings and landscaped for public enjoyment. To the left, out of this picture, ...rows bridge leads across to the north shore. The inner harbour is always busy with shipping.

himself. Cunningham put him in touch with an Indian who had brought the coal over from Burrard Inlet. Morton and the Indian took the trail, which later became the Old Douglas Road, through the dense primeval forest to the inlet, camped for the night where the well known hotel of Maxime Michaud was built in after years, and proceeded next morning by canoe to Coal Harbour. Morton did not find the clay he expected. But he liked the lay of the land, and became the first settler, acquiring title to much of what is now the west end of the city of Vancouver. With his cousin, Sam Brighouse, he finally extended his holdings clear through to Lulu Island in the Fraser Delta. It was this occupation of land, coming to the ears of

lumbermen operating at Alberni, which led to the establishment in 1863 of the first saw-mill on Burrard Inlet; the hamlet which grew around the mill being called after its subsequent owner, Sue Moody, Moodyville. Two years later another mill was established on the south shore, about opposite Moodyville, and that place was called Hastings, after Admiral Hastings.

Then to the inlet came sailing ships from the Orient, South America and Europe. As many as 14 would be loading lumber at one time from the two mills. The inlet became lively with well-paid loggers, and with sailors ashore. But it was not until 1883 that the general public had any inkling of the great city which was to be founded between Hastings and Coal Harbour.

In that year, the directors of the Canadian Pacific Railway Company let it be surmised, with authority, that the line would be extended down the inlet from Port Moody, which then was, and still remains officially, the western terminus.

It took one Dutch Van with another to convey eventually the right name to the new city which was to be incorporated and have its centre somewhere west of Hastings. Captain George Vancouver was an Englishman of Dutch descent; and Sir William Van Horne, President of the Canadian Pacific Railway, was an American of Dutch descent. It was Van Horne who first advocated the name of Vancouver for the new city; and the first instance of the name as such appearing in print may be found

Twin peaks, "The Lions", overlook Vancouver from the north shore. Vancouver lies at the foot of Coast Range mountains which provide excellent snow for skiing in the winter when the temperature in the city is well above freezing.

in *The West Shore*, a magazine at that time published in Portland, Oregon. In the issue of September, 1884, page 304, appears an article on Coal Harbour, over the signature of an enterprising young firm of real estate dealers in those days, Messrs. Gravelly and Innes. It followed the desire of Van Horne, and I quote this from it:

"It is only once in a lifetime that the public have such a chance as the present, and we would recommend those who have money to invest to investigate the merits of Vancouver, on Coal Harbour, before making other investments."

The City of Vancouver was incorporated April 6th, 1886. Two months later, June 13th, the quickly built wooden town of 2,000 inhabitants was entirely destroyed by fire, with the exception of a few buildings around the Hastings sawmill. On May 23rd of the following year, the first transcontinental train came down from Port Moody to Vancouver.

Naturally, during its first two decades, the Canadian Pacific Railway Company mothered and moulded the new city, which thus had all the inaugural advantages and disadvantages of a place under control of one powerful private company. Among the immediate advantages, apart from those involved in the fact of being made a transcontinental railway terminus, was the establishment of a magnificent fleet of freight and passenger ships to the Orient, Australia and New Zealand; and the erection of a first-class hotel and opera-house, both under the efficient management of the company. The disadvantages need not now be detailed. They were removed when, after much official obstruction, entry was provided in 1906 for the Great Northern and Northern Pacific Railways; and later by the entry of the Canadian National Railways, with new terminals, new steamships, and the promise of a metropolitan hotel on a par with any on the continent.

Owing to the small-town spirit prevailing during the time of the Klondike gold rush, much of the out-fitting trade which should have gone to Vancouver, because of tariff advantages in its favour, went to Seattle. From 1906, however, to 1913, there were seven years of fast growth for both the city and port of Vancouver. Then came the war.

During those anxious four years Vancouver came much to the front, not only by sending more fighting men to France in proportion to its population than any other city in Canada, but also by supplying materials and food. Shipyards were built, and, outside of Great Britain, Vancouver became during this period the greatest shipbuilding port for steel ships in the British Empire. Larger ships were built, and at less cost, than could be done at any other port in Canada.

Towards the end of 1924, the prophesy of outside observers, made variously for more than two decades, about Vancouver becoming one of the great grain ports of the world, began to be believed even by the local inhabitants. The farmers of Alberta

West end apartment towers and the mountains beyond form a spectacular backdrop for sun worshippers on Vancouver's Kitsilano Beach.

and the Harbour Commissioners of Vancouver have worked hand in hand to that end.

The bulk of exports from Vancouver consists of wheat, flour, lumber, copper, lead, zinc, paper, pulp, apples, salt and canned fish. The imports are chiefly iron and steel, silks, wool, meat, butter, salt, tea, glass and oriental goods. Except for butter, all these are likely to increase greatly in quantity; and raw silk may in time be manufactured here into the finished products.

If the present artistic scheme of town-planning to meet the growth of the city be carried into effect, and the present wise policy of the Harbour Commissioners be maintained and extended, Vancouver will equal Liverpool for business, and Atlantic City for pleasure, and become more mature and inviting than ever in her cool, green beauty!

Most photographed Vancouver scene is this view from Little Mountain, a park in the heart of the city's residential area.

111

"In winter the mail was brought in by dog-team."

"Then came the duck hunt in the fall."

MY HOME TOWN

by CHARLES CAMSELL

Dr. Camsell, first president of the Royal Canadian Geographical Society, wrote this account for the September, 1940, issue of the Canadian Geographical Journal.

STATISTICIANS tell us that there are eleven million people in the Dominion of Canada; but I venture to say that very few of these eleven millions ever even heard of the small fur-trading post of Fort Liard, situated in northwestern Canada, very near to the point where the boundary between the Yukon and the Northwest Territories cuts the northern boundary of British Columbia.

This might be called my home town, for I was born there. At that time, it was nothing more than a group of half a dozen log houses, with a population of some eight or ten persons. It was one of the most isolated posts of the Hudson's Bay Company.

To-day, the modern person with the radio, the motor-car, and the aeroplane, does not know what isolation is. At Fort Liard, when I was born, our next door neighbours were at Fort Simpson, 180 miles away to the northeast, and at Fort Nelson, some 150 miles to the southwest, perhaps twenty people in all. To the north, west, south and east, were hundreds of miles of densely forested wilderness, of mountain or plain, occupied only by a few roving families of Indians. The nearest doctor was 1,500 miles away, and it would have taken six months to get him. Sickness or accident had to be treated by the most simple and primitive methods. I remember when Bishop Bompas cut off David Villeneuve's leg with a carpenter's saw and a butcher knife, while David smoked his pipe

and stoically watched him do it. Contact with our neighbours, and through them with the outside world, was made only twice a year: once in summer, when the York boat brigade came in with supplies of trading goods and provisions; and again in winter, when the mail was brought in by dog-team. Otherwise, the year was unbroken by visits, except for the arrival from time to time, of a few Indians who came to trade their furs for tea, tobacco, or ammunition.

However, I am not inclined to think of Fort Liard as "my home town" and I remember very little of it — because, when I was about four years old, my father moved to Fort Simpson, the trading headquarters, to take charge of the whole Mackenzie river district.

Before leaving Fort Liard, I should like to tell of an incident of my last visit to that place, about five years ago. It illustrates the point that the expression 'town" for Fort Liard is quite in order.

I had come across the mountains from the Pacific Coast by aeroplane, looking for the mythical tropical valley. Although it was thirty-five years since I had last seen Fort Liard, there was no mistaking it, for it had changed very little. From the plane, the collection of log houses in the small clearing was only a scar in the interminable forest, but it was a very welcome sight indeed. My arrival was more than a home-coming to me, for it was the end of a somewhat hazardous flight across several hundred miles of unexplored mountains; and we were nearly out of gas.

On arrival, we stopped at the Mission House, at the upper end of the settlement. At the other end, a third of a mile away, through the bush,

was the Hudson's Bay Company's establishment, with some four or five more log houses. Some time after supper, I asked the priest where my companion, Dan McLean was. "Oh", he said, "I guess he's gone down town". meaning to the Hudson's Bay Company house. Dan was spending the night in my old home town with the Hudson's Bay manager, actually in the house in which I was born.

Fort Simpson is situated on an island in the Mackenzie River, at the mouth of Liard River. I prefer to think of it as my home town, because I lived there for four years, and, in fact, until I left the North to go to school.

Life at Simpson was not very different to that at Liard, except that there was more of it. Being the fur trading headquarters of the whole Mackenzie River district, it had, perhaps, a dozen more people.

At either end of the clearing were the Missions, Anglican and Roman Catholic. In the middle was the Hudson's Bay fort, enclosed by a high picket fence; inside which were the officers' quarters, storehouses, office buildings, and the inevitable flagstaff. Behind, and up against the forest, were the servants' and other men's houses. On either side of the fort were the cultivated fields. Surrounding the whole on two sides and the back was the dense northern forest; while in front was the broad sweep of the Mackenzie River, here almost exactly a mile wide.

Fort Simpson was then the most important post between Lake Athabasca and the Arctic Ocean, and it occupied a very commanding site, with a view of several miles of the Mackenzie River.

Life at Fort Simpson in the early

eighties of the last century was primitive; but, as I see it now, not unpleasant. Spring and fall were the busy seasons. In the spring, gardens had to be planted and boats built or repaired for the York boat trip to the

vided the only light, were made in the fall from moose or deer fat.

To live in the Far North with any degree of comfort, one must have resourcefulness and initiative. More important, however, in the time I

for delivery in the fall of the following year, sixteen or eighteen months later.

Very little food was imported into the North in those days. A post manager was allowed a hundred pounds of flour, twenty pounds of tea, and twenty pounds of sugar for the year. The rest of his requirements had to be obtained from the country — fish, rabbits, ducks and geese, and moose and caribou meat. Frequently, there was hardship, and sometimes death among the Indians from starvation, particularly when rabbits were scarce.

Our diversions and amusements were simple. Every man had a line of traps or rabbit snares which he visited once a week throughout the winter. Indoors we had, occasionally, dances to the music of the fiddle, and played card games, chess and checkers. Simpson was unique in that it had a billiard table imported by my father from England. There was also an excellent library of several hundred volumes. The houses were heated by wood stoves or fireplaces and light was provided by candles.

"We left Simpson with the fur brigade consisting of a number of York boats."

Long Portage. Spring also was the time for making birch syrup and soap from wood ash and grease. In the fall, fuel and fish and other food had to be put up for the winter, and snowshoes and toboggans and other winter gear overhauled. Candles, which pro-

speak of, and even to-day, is the need for foresight, because one had to anticipate and provide for his needs months ahead. For example, requisitions for goods and other supplies required from the outside were made out in the early spring of one year

While there was a very definite daily and annual routine to the life at Simpson, as at every other trading post, there were certain events that stood out in high relief. There was the departure of the York boat brigade for the Long Portage early in June and its return three months later. A voyageur was only considered to have reached manhood when he had made this journey. At the end of the warm lazy summer came the fall duck hunt, and the fishery at Great Slave Lake, which produced some fifty or sixty thousand white fish for winter use. Then came the freeze-up of the river; the return of the caribou hunters with the first sled loads of meat; and the luxury of marrow bones sneaked from these sleds and cooked in the ashes of the fireplace. The short winter days began to lengthen, followed almost immediately by the New Year's Day celebrations when the flag went up, guns were fired, everybody went visiting, and there was a grand ball and fast in the evening. The arrival of the March packet, with news of the outside world, was the next great event; and finally, the arrival of spring and the break-up of the river.

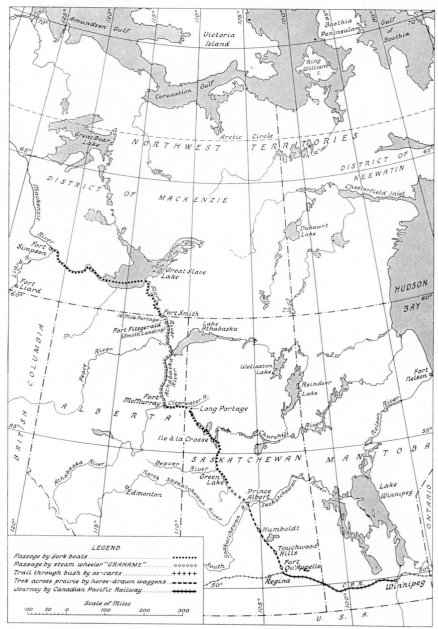

LEGEND
Passage by york boats .... ••••••••
Passage by steam wheeler "GRAHAME" .... ○○○○○○
Trail through bush by ox-carts .... +++++
Trek across prairie by horse-drawn waggons ... ------
Journey by Canadian Pacific Railway .... ++++++

Scale of Miles
100 50 0   100   200   300

These were the high points of the year.

No one who has not lived in a northern climate and has not endured the long cold winter, can fully appreciate the meaning of spring. Even after an interval of forty years, the

memories of spring-time are the most vivid of all my northern experiences. To pass from winter to spring is like entering a new world and a renewal of one's youth.

At every post from the Saskatchewan River to the Arctic Ocean, there is recorded in every post journal — which the manager is obliged to keep — first of all, the arrival of the first goose and, second, the break-up of the river. No other events in the whole yearly calendar are so eagerly

awaited or so significant.

Educational facilities at Simpson were very limited. What we had was provided by that saintly old man, Bishop Bompas; but he was away a great part of the time, carrying the gospel to the natives in their camps. So, as we grew up, the boys of my family were sent to school at Winnipeg, and my sisters to England.

When I was eight years of age, my turn came to go away to school and the long journey of over three months to Winnipeg had to be made.

We left Simpson about June 10th with the fur brigade, consisting of a number of York boats, each manned by ten voyageurs: for these were the days after the passing of the freighting canoe, and before the coming of the steamboat.

The York boat is an open craft, about forty feet long, built on the lines of a Viking ship and propelled by eight oars. The Indian crew towed the boat with a line to the shore. Only in dead water did they row with the long, sixteen-foot oars.

We travelled as much as sixteen hours a day, and camped every night on the beach — usually without shelter, but always under a mosquito net. There were my father and mother and five children, of whom I was the eldest. I have always considered that, in my mother's long, active and eventful life, her greatest accomplishment was the care and handling of those five children on that long journey. One died on the way and was buried at Ile à la Crosse.

As we proceeded southward, the brigade was joined at each post by other boats until it numbered well over one hundred voyageurs. It was a stirring sight, particularly at camping time, and even more so in the morning when one crew vied with the other for the honour of being first away.

The route of the brigade lay up the Mackenzie River and across Great Slave Lake, then up the Slave River to Fort Smith. Here, the sixteen-mile

"The route of the brigade lay up the Mackenzie River and across Great Slave Lake, then up the Slave River to Fort Smith."

portage was made in ox carts — all of us except my father and me, who rode across the portage in style on a horse. From Fitzgerald, or Smith Landing as it was then called, the newly-built, stern-wheel steamer *Grahame* took us up to Athabasca Lake and up the Athabasca River to McMurray. From there, we again used York boats on Clearwater River to the Long Portage, which constituted the great divide between the Mackenzie River and Hudson Bay waters. Here, the fur brigades from the North met those from the South; and for days their crews were engaged in transporting goods or fur packs across the twelve miles of the portage. Each man carried a 200-pound load on his back and made one trip across each day. From this point, after exchanging its fur packs for trading goods, the Mackenzie River brigade returned north and we transferred to the southern brigade.

Beyond the Long Portage, travel was continued by York boat past Ile à la Crosse, and up the Beaver River to the head of Green Lake where navigation ended. Thence we travelled in ox-carts over a newly cut bush trail which led from there to Prince Albert, then a thriving village of one street.

By the more modern and comfortable methods of horses and waggons we crossed the prairies to Fort Qu'Appelle, passing Humboldt and Touchwood Hills, the only settlements on the way. The Canadian Pacific Railway then brought us to Winnipeg about the middle of September, Thus, in three months, we completed a journey which can now be made easily in two days.

Few of the incidents or characters of that journey now remain in my memory. But I cannot forget an Indian by the name of Friday.

Friday was a Simpson Indian who acted as our personal servant on the long journey. According to the white man's code, he was a criminal, for he had been compelled, through starvation, to resort to cannibalism during the previous winter and he had been sentenced to a term at the Mounted Police headquarters in Regina. According to the Indian code, however his misdemeanour was merely an expression of one of the primitive instincts of human nature. I distinctly recall my interest in seeing that Friday got his meals regularly in case he should again feel inclined to indulge this instinct.

He was not kept long in Regina before he was sent back home. When next I saw Friday, he had appointed himself a judge of his own band and held court regularly once a week, as he had seen it done in Regina. He was a good fellow and turned out to be a useful person in his community.

I stayed in Winnipeg through school and college and it was ten years before I saw the home town again. The change in the character of the place was even then beginning, and it was starting to lose some of the atmosphere of the fur-trading post, which it has now almost completely lost. Simpson to-day enjoys the luxury of the radio, aeroplanes, electric light, central heating, and even unemployment relief. Romance has gone from the old town!

"We made the trip up the Athabasca River on the Grahame.*"*

"We travelled in ox-carts from Green Lake to Prince Albert."

The easterly end of Long Sault Island shows through the mist of early morning from the upstream end of a raft section, or dram.

Drams separated out opposite Coteau Landing, preparatory to running Coteau, Cedars, Split Rock, and Cascades Rapids — a twelve-mile run.

RAFTING ON THE ST. LAWRENCE

By D. D. CALVIN

THE last raft of square timber went down the St. Lawrence, running the rapids, in 1911. Rafts had gone down the great river, from ice to ice, every year before this from the earliest days when hewn timber could be "made" close at hand and hauled to its shores. Gradually the supply receded up the tributary rivers, and westward to Lake Ontario and the rivers flowing into it. But "the lake," even in summer, was soon found to be no place for a raft, and schooners began to bring the timber into the headwaters of the St. Lawrence.

As the country along the Great Lakes was settled, the timber was made further and further back from their shores. The tributaries of Lake Erie, Lake St. Clair (much fine oak came down Bear Creek, now the Sydenham River), then Lake Michigan, Lake Huron (particularly Georgian Bay) and finally Lake Superior were in turn invaded by timber vessels, at first schooners then steamers and tow-barges. The timber was loaded off-shore as the vessels lay at anchor or from booms in the bays and river mouths.

At a later period, but while this purely water route was still in full use, timber began to come into various lake ports by rail. Toronto and Hamilton used to handle considerable quantities of pine and hardwood from the western peninsula of Ontario. This rail and water business developed until finally pine came into Duluth from as far west as Idaho and oak into Toledo from as far south as West Virginia, Kentucky and Tennessee.

Lumbering was second only to the fur trade in penetrating the Canadian wilderness and in providing a "cash crop" for export. The great St. Lawrence rafts brought to Quebec the timber from the area drained by the Great Lakes. Smaller rafts brought white pine from the drainage basin of the Ottawa. This account first appeared in the Canadian Geographical Journal *in October 1931.*

General view of a raft, looking forward. The tug can be glimpsed in front of the sail on the right. By 1908, when this picture was taken, canvas tents had replaced the wooden cabins used earlier.

All of this timber was carried down the lakes in vessels to the bases of the rafting industry in the neighbourhood of Kingston and there "rafted up" to go down the St. Lawrence to Quebec for export to Great Britain.

The Ottawa River man, if he has read so far, will be saying that when the Ottawa rafts joined in, via the "Back River," below Montreal Island, these upper St. Lawrence rafts were not the whole of the timber which was going to Quebec. True;

but the Ottawa raft was a different species, built for different conditions. Most of the Ottawa rapids were passed by slides, and the Ottawa "cribs" which went down them could not safely have run the St. Lawrence rapids. The "drams" of the St. Lawrence rafts were of a much sturdier construction. It may be that this

stronger type of raft was evolved in dealing with sinking timber like oak, for all the Ottawa timber was pine.

Nor was rafting on the Ottawa a distinct trade, as it was on the St. Lawrence. An Ottawa raft was usually one man's timber and remained in his hands from the bush right through to Quebec; on the St. Lawrence, especially in later years, rafting was a forwarding business for various owners of timber in widely separated places.

Unloading pine timber from the "ports" of a lake vessel.

And now we come to describe the St. Lawrence raft itself as it was known for so long to the men who built and navigated it. These men, in later years at any rate, were chiefly French-Canadians from the Coteau Landing area, with some Indians and halfbreeds from the reserves at St. Regis and Caughnawaga. A nucleus of the best men was employed full time, but in the main it was a seasonal employment. A rowdy lot the raftsmen were when they arrived each spring, but they soon sobered up and may be seen, in the photographs, at their work.

The photographs were taken in different seasons from 1898 to 1908, but are correct, in the main, for earlier years. The timber was unloaded from the lake vessels by steamwinches ashore, and kept in the boom until it was rafted. The "dram" or unit of the St. Lawrence raft consisted of three tiers; bottom, cross-tier and top-tier. The bottom was made up from the smaller-girthed and longer-lengthed pieces, the cross-tier of the shorter pieces, and the top-tier of the biggest-girthed timber whether long or short. The framework into which the timber was stowed consisted of three pieces longitudinally, jointed each 40 feet, with cross ties (traverses) every 10 feet. The longitudinal pieces were 42 feet long and six inches in diameter at the top, flatted two sides to about seven inches thickness; the traverses were 30 feet long and three inches at the top, not flatted. It should be said in passing that the getting out of these "raft trimmings" was a separate subsidiary of the rafting business.

Stowing pine timber to form bottom tier of dram. In the background, men have begun "withing".

This is also true of the withes and toggles which will be mentioned presently. Each intersection of this framework was fastened with a round hardwood pin or "picket" driven home and wedged. When a bottom was completed the next step was "withing"; each piece of timber in the "bottom" and the traverse as it passed above it were tied together by a withe (a small white birch sapling softened between power-rollers) twisted up tight by a lever or "toggle." The small end of the withe was made into a twisted loop which was laid against the butt of the withe; the toggle was put through this loop and used as a lever by a man who walked round and round the point of fastening.

The joint being snug, the toggle was forced along the traverse and included, to hold it, in the next joint. Rows of these fastenings can be seen in the photographs; there would be about 600 to 700 of them in an average dram. From the tough elastic nature of the withes and their being evenly and snugly tied, a really extraordinary strength was developed in the whole fabric of the bottom of the dram. The cross-tier was next put on using a steam winch to drag the timbers across. Then the top-tier was loaded similarly. The top-tier was sometimes a full tier, sometimes not. The finished three-tier pine dram was a floating island of wood able to resist great shocks and even greater strains.

Oak timber could be rafted only one tier deep, for it had to have pine with it to keep it reasonably afloat; in other words, only a strongly buoyant bottom, of pine or elm, could carry additional tiers.

A specification of each dram was made out as it was assembled, each piece of timber having its length, girth and cubic contents recorded, and the whole totalled up. An average pine dram would contain some 600 pieces, or about 25,000 cubic feet. All drams were 60 feet wide, their length varied from 225 feet to 300 feet, so that a raft of six or eight drams covered quite an area — big enough, in narrow waters.

One dram, usually the first to be finished, became the leading or "cabin dram," so named because the foreman's cabin was on it. These cabins were for many years built wholly of lumber, but latterly, to save expense, they were covered with canvas. The

Withing up. The lever is called a "toggle".

A finished dram. The small building is on a floating pontoon and houses the machinery used for loading the cross-tier and top tier.

foreman's cabin was divided into two parts, one with two bunks and a table opposite them, the other with two more bunks (on the table side) and the cookstove opposite. There was a door in each end, and a gap in the dividing partition, so that the cabin could be quite airy, or, alternatively, very hot indeed. The cook and his "boy" were the cabin builders, and great experts they were at producing liveable quarters with the simplest materials and tools. The second dram had the men's cabin built on it, a simpler structure with eight bunks.

The "raft kit" was a very varied lot of gear; the kit proper was that part of the equipment which at Quebec was stripped off and brought back on the towing steamer to Garden Island to be re-used. Two and even three kits were in use in busy seasons. Each consisted of a couple of medium-sized anchors and their chains, a wooden windlass, sails, 150 to 200 oars 30 feet long (cut from traverses) for use in the rapids, chain of various sizes, light and heavy rope, pikepoles, axes, cant-hooks, carpenter's tools, augers, crowbars, lanterns, a boat to carry 15 or 20 men, a lighter boat, pulley blocks, cookstove and the cook's gear packed in special boxes, blankets, straw ticks, tiny windows for the cabins, and a lot of other oddments. Besides the kit there were always put on board spare material for repairs, such as traverses, withes, toggles, pickets and other gear described earlier.

Other preparations for departure from Garden Island were taking out grub, usually in the bigger raftboat, from the company's store — salt pork, hardtack, bread, groceries; making out in the office, for the foreman, his "raft book" with the names of the crew, their dates of hiring and the state of their accounts; getting cash from the Bank in Kingston, some $500 to $800, chiefly to pay the extra men who helped in the rapids. The money was usually shoved into the straw of the foreman's mattress and left there quite unguarded. "Holdups" were unknown.

Given a fine summer day — in retrospect a raft inevitably left on a fine afternoon — it will be understood that the last hours of preparation were a delight to youngsters. The ordered confusion of getting all the gear aboard, the half-guessed secrets of the boxes and bags of grub, the characteristic scents of clean pine timber in the sun, of the raw wood of the cabins, of the fresh straw in the mattresses, combine to make a delightful memory in which the sounds are the shouts in French, the

121

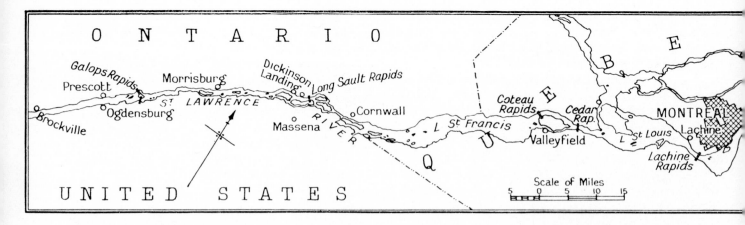

signal gong in the towing steamer's engine room and the wash from her paddle-wheels as she backed to stop alongside the raft.

At last the steamer gave us her tow-line, it tightened, and the raft started "with the stealth of a bad habit." For the first 20 miles, until the current quickened in the narrows above Alexandria Bay, the speed would not be more than three miles an hour. Not much work beyond the necessary setting of lights ("navigation lights" on a raft were merely a lantern at each corner) and seeing that everything was snug, would be done the first evening, but after six o'clock breakfast next morning there was plenty of activity. Masts were put up and sails set. (It should be said here that in the earliest years sails and the river current were the only motive pover, and it sometimes took weeks to get to Quebec.) Then began the fitting up of rowlocks and footholds for the rowers, really steersmen, to use in the rapids. The crew of a raft would be only 6 to 8 men, and since with good luck the Long Sault would be run the second day, there was plenty of work to keep the men busy, getting ready for the rapids.

The raft's usual running time in summer, Kingston to Montreal, was three days. Leaving one evening, Prescott would be reached late the next evening or early the second morning. The Long Sault would be run during the second day and St.

Cooking for the crew. Boards, covered with earth and ashes, prevented damage to the timber.

Zotique at the foot of Lake St. Francis reached that evening. Starting very early the third day, perhaps an hour before daylight, the raft would be through the Coteau run by 9 o'clock, cross Lake St. Louis and run Lachine in the late afternoon, reaching Montreal early in the evening. This ideal schedule presumes fine and moderately calm weather; any other wind than the prevailing south and south-west breeze meant tying up and waiting for a change. This was particularly true for northerly winds on the Coteau run or in

Lachine. It is perhaps not necessary to add that a raft could not navigate at night except in the quiet parts of the river.

For the "passengers," life on the raft in quiet water and in fine weather was a leisurely thing indeed. Perhaps the photographs, especially the general views of the raft under way, will convey the feeling — they do so for the initiate, at any rate. The amusements were simple — fresh air, sun, sleep, food, reading, swimming, watching the raft crew at their work, they were specially handy with the axe. Then, too, there were the visitors who constantly came aboard and went a few miles with us. Sometimes, when the right men were in the crew, there would be singing, and even dancing.

But the great man of the rafts which I knew was Aimé Guérin, "Le Vieux," chief foreman for my grandfather and my father from 1875 to 1909. Strong, capable, forceful, fearless, his relations with his employers were a perfect example of what such relations can be when there is complete loyalty and trust upon both sides. He died at his home in Laprairie very shortly after landing his raft safely in Montreal for perhaps the 500th time. The old man always spoke of "mes cages", and while he was in charge of them they were his rafts, and no mistaking the fact!

The chief reason for occasional guests on the raft was that they might see the rapids. To go down the rapids of the St. Lawrence on a passenger steamer, tourist fashion, is well worth doing; to run them in a smaller vessel would be better; but the raft showed one the real thing. The Indians' canoes never went through the really

Aimé Guérin, "Le Vieux".

wild water, and the steamers as it were go over it, but a dram of pine timber went through, almost literally. The oak timber, rafted one tier deep and awash in quiet water, went through absolutely — a safety platform was built on each oak dram, for the rowers to climb up on. Photographs have not been made from oak timber!

The raft went down the Galops, below Prescott, and Rapide Plat, above Morrisburg, without being

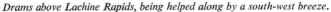

Drams above Lachine Rapids, being helped along by a south-west breeze.

separated into its constituent drams, and with the steamer towing all the time. These two are mild affairs (fast boats can come up them against the current) but even in them the timber bumped about underfoot as the raft bent to follow the waves of the rapids, and the novice got a warning of what the really rough water would be.

Below Rapide Plat the steamer and raft made quick progress in the strong current until above Aultsville the Long Sault pilots and their men, some 50 or so, began to come aboard

the raft. These pilots were English-speaking and lived in and about Aultsville. The men were a mixed lot, Indians from the St. Regis reserve, men from the river farms on both the Canadian and American shores; one well-known figure was "the schoolmaster" who always made the run through the Sault and rowed an oar, when he could. He even "taught" on the raft, if he could find a victim who had not been forewarned. I remember hearing him explaining the composi-

tion of the Milky Way to the Professor of Political Science at Queen's, who was a guest on the raft. This Long Sault crowd understood little French; Richard Dafoe the senior pilot who took down the cabin dram spoke none at all and in his dealings with Aimé Guérin needed an interpreter. One did not always give "Rich" an exact translation of what Aimé said to him when things were not going just right!

The timber drams did not run the north Sault, where the steamers go, but separated out in a long line above

Cat Island, keeping to the south of Long Sault Island, in American water. This was a very pretty and little known channel, full of bends and with beautifully wooded banks. It took expert use of the long oars at bow and stern to make the dram take the turns. At the foot of Long Sault Island and further downstream than the main north Sault rapids, the drams went through the only sharp pitch of the south Sault.

The drams were then re-assembled, the pilots and extra men were paid off and went ashore at Cornwall, the raft went on down through the islands and out on to Lake St. Francis. Opposite Coteau Landing, the raft having received a second lot of pilots and extra men, this time all French-Canadians, the drams were again separated out by dropping them off one at a time, the steamer dropping the last one above the Canadian National Railway (then Canada Atlantic) bridge.

The leading dram soon reached the main pitch of the Coteau Rapid. There is a photograph of a dram just entering it. The raft channel here was again different from the steamer channel, this time nearer the north shore. There was perhaps a clearer feeling of an actual drop, at this point, than in any other rapid. The next pitch is the Cedars, which has some of the roughest water in all the rapids. After another quick mile or two the Split Rock Rapid was passed, then after sharp turns right and left the Cascades, fourth and last rapid of the Coteau run, which is about 12 miles in all. Immediately below the Cascades the first of the brown Ottawa water comes into the St. Lawrence, which from here loses more and more the brilliant colour and clearness so characteristic of its up-

per reaches. At Cascades Point the Coteau pilots and their men left the raft in their own and the raft's boats, landing at the foot of the Soulanges canal.

And so out on to Lake St. Louis, which is smaller and deeper and has more current than Lake St. Francis. With a fair wind steamer and raft in a few hours neared Lachine, by which time the third set of pilots and men would be aboard and assigned to their duties. For Lachine rapids a large proportion of the men were Caughnawaga Indians. The senior pilot, a picturesque veteran called "Michel", was said to be of pure Indian blood; he wore his long black hair coiled in plaits about his head. The drams were again towed clear of one another, beginning above the Canadian Pacific Railway's Lachine bridge — a mile or so below the bridge they would be fully separated out and ready for the quick, sharp and dangerous run through Lachine Rapids. The steamer went on quickly ahead; one saw her, through field glasses, rolling and splashing in the main pitch a mile ahead of us; when she got through and "rounded to" to wait for the drams, one saw only her smoke — there is a really big drop in Lachine. And the entrance to the channel is narrow; in the swift eddy-

ing water above the rapids proper there was often some very expert steering with the 30 foot oars, old "Michel" controlling his men by a wave of his arm.

It would be interesting to know how the technique of guiding the unwieldy drams into the rapids was gradually evolved, for once in them, especially in the crooked channel of Lachine, there was a sense of being in the grip of elemental forces. The water in Lachine is very rough and very fast; the dram, bending in its whole fabric to the great swells of the rapids, and leaving great rocks close on either hand, dashed down the main pitch in a few seconds — it is an unforgettable experience. Small wonder that snapshots convey little idea of it, even the portable movie-camera, had it been invented early enough, could have got only bits of the scene, and could not have reproduced the thudding of the big timber underfoot.

But it was soon over and the day's work went on; the waiting steamer picked up her charges once more, brought them down past the Laprairie shoals, under Victoria Bridge, and through Montreal harbour.

At Montreal the Lachine pilots and their men were landed. "Le Vieux" also left the raft to go back

124

up to "the Island" for the next one; the quieter work below Montreal could be done by lesser souls than "old Aimé."

It took a whole day to tow through the crooked channel down to Sorel, so that unless Lachine happened to have been run in the early morning the raft tied up below Montreal, about where the Vickers plant now stands, and left at daylight the next morning.

The two to four days' run from Montreal to Quebec was a lazy business in fine summer weather when all went well. But if there was bad weather on Lake St. Peter — the "Julie Plante" was not the only floating thing to get into trouble "on wan dark night on Lac St. Pierre". Or if below Batiscan, and especially below Portneuf, there was a heavy east wind with a strong flood tide, then all the skill and experience of

years was called on to decide when and how to fight it out or when and how to "round to" in shelter. There were accidents, of course, both in the rapids and below Montreal, but the vast majority of the rafts were finally swung safely in on the tail of the ebb tide at the timber-cove piers at Sillery Point, five miles west of Quebec.

Not all the drams would be for the same cove, sometimes it took two or three tides (the drams could be moved only at high or low water) to berth them all at their proper coves. The raft crew were then paid off and they headed first for the pubs and later for train or boat to get back home.

The "kit" was taken aboard the steamer; the wood cabins, all loose wood and the framework of the raft, became the prey of the covemen whose work it was to break up the raft and prepare the timber for ship-

ment to Britain. In the great days of the square timber trade, 1850 to 1870, there would be scores of sailing ships loading in the Quebec area, from Cap Rouge down to Indian Cove, opposite Ile d'Orléans. Gradually the quantity of timber decreased, tramp steamers took the place of the timber ships, then even the tramp steamer was replaced by space in regular liners, until now the whole trade, except for small quantities of timber going direct by rail to the ship's side, has become a memory.

Perhaps the timber itself may keep alive the memory of the rafts — at any rate, years after St. Lawrence rafting ceased, one could see, along the southeast coast of England, groynes built of rock-elm timber, and find a link with the great river in deciphering the familiar bushmarks and culler's marks still legible upon their solid sides.

In the main pitch of Lachine. The men's figures give a scale to measure the long swells of the rapid. The rock, middle left, is the spot from which pictures of steamers coming down Lachine were taken.

Survey outfit with Red River carts, 1871.

Main Street, near Portage Avenue, Winnipeg, 1878.

Canadian soldiers swarm ashore from ships of the Royal Canadian Navy, Normandy, June 6, 1944.

A tractor train in Canada's northland.

Bundling cordite in a munitions factory, 1942.

PATTERNS OF GROWTH

When Newfoundland entered the confederation on March 31, 1949, the pattern conceived by the Fathers of Confederation was complete. The Fathers would have been pleased to know that their dream of the whole land united under one parliament was at last a reality but even more satisfying to them would have been the knowledge that in the same period of time Canada had achieved full national stature. Her political maturity was to be proclaimed to the world in the following year, when she accepted the decision of the General Assembly of the United Nations, a decision in which she had played a part, and committed armed forces to battle, under United Nations auspices, in Korea.

Fascinating as is the record of political growth from the first acceptance of national responsibility on July 1, 1867, to maturity in 1950, it is not ours to tell here. We are more concerned with the economic and social changes which occurred within our country as we came to understand the nature of our great inheritance.

The great open space of the western prairie had to be filled, the land brought under the plow, and the crop transported to world markets. The great era of railroad building came first; then the railroads offered special inducements to settlers in order to build freight traffic to make the railroads pay. Land-hungry persons came from the Canadian East, from the United States, from the British Isles, and from Continental Europe. The best and most accessible land was soon taken up but still more settlers came, pushing the cultivated land up into the Peace River country and into the arid regions of southwestern Saskatchewan and southern Alberta.

To transport the grain, huge terminal elevators were built at the lakehead — Port Arthur and Fort William — and the canal system through to Montreal was improved and deepened. The St. Lawrence Seaway, which was to open the Great Lakes to world shipping, was under active discussion and would shortly be built. Grain also flowed out through the West Coast and a third route was built through Churchill on Hudson Bay.

From the outset, the young nation encouraged the processing of raw materials and the further manufacture of a wide variety of items. This activity was stimulated and expanded during the two world wars, so that by 1950 Canada had a firm industrial base and was beginning to compete actively in world markets with manufactured goods as well as primary commodities.

The last great frontier was the north. The gold rush of 1898 brought settlements to the Yukon Territory and the beginning of local territorial administration. In the Northwest Territories and in the Arctic Islands, fur traders, missionaries, and the Royal Canadian Mounted Police were dotted about in small settlements. Prospectors were gradually increasing their activity, oil was being produced at Norman Wells on the Mackenzie River to meet local needs, and the aeroplane had become the common means of transportation throughout the vast area.

With all these developments there had finally emerged a broad general knowledge of the whole half-continent. Details were still lacking but the time had come to sponsor further development in a systematic way in the light of national needs and the needs of world markets.

MEMORIES OF '85

by HOWARD ANGUS KENNEDY

This article, which brings to life part of the action of the Northwest Rebellion, was written fifty years after the event and first appeared in the Canadian Geographical Journal *in August 1935.*

"WE'RE MAKING HISTORY, EH?" The young Mounted Policeman who spoke had been riding beside me in silence for an hour. Few of us were in any mood for conversation, and most of us could hardly keep our eyes open.

The day before, we had set out from Battleford three hundred strong. We had ridden all night to catch the Indians at dawn, asleep in their tents on Cutknife Hill. We had failed. After the most disastrous fight of the campaign we were now in full retreat, carrying waggon-loads of dead and wounded, with little chance for the rest of us if the Indians had followed us unseen to pick us off piecemeal as we threaded a narrow winding trail through the woods.

There is no denying that we "made history" at a painful rate in "the '85", but we made still more Geography — and, for all but the killed and wounded, it was the Geography that hurt. History, with its high spots

128

of battle, murder and sudden death, filled the endless columns of war news in the press, but Geography, with its immensity and variety, filled the endless columns of marching life. The men who went right through that campaign endured far more hardship on the march than in the short, sharp ordeal of actual fight.

The temperature climbed as we went north, from a nightly sub-zero on the southern plateau to 80 or 90 (by guess, for we had no thermometer) when 200 miles nearer the pole.

The water was often too highly flavoured with alkali, till late in the campaign when we got up into the northern woodland with its rushing streams; but we managed to drink it boiled with tea and sugar, — we had no milk, even canned.

The hard tack was severe, and some of it was inhabited; but it was nourishing, and, when we had time to fry it, almost tasty.

The northern muskegs were dangerous to ford, but we managed to circumnavigate them, picking our way, heads down, between wood and water.

The northern mosquitoes were a plague to man and beast, — unspeakable, and, on the march by day, inescapable, though we kept swishing them off our horses and ourselves, with branches plucked from the trees as we rode. At night we could only get sleep by filling the tent with the dense smudge of burning turf, crawling under the smoke when it had risen a foot from the ground, and then pulling the flap shut tight.

Our clothes wore out into rags; but, thanks to motherly foresight, a few of us had brought along needle and thread; many a soldier marched home in stylish pants reconstructed from oat sacks, stencil brand and all.

Feet were less easily accommodated than legs. We had shoemakers as well as tailors among the volunteers, but no leather for them to make shoes with. I suppose our French fellow-citizens have lost the ancestral art of

making sabots; for the gallant 65th of Montreal, after marching north from Calgary to Edmonton, descending the North Saskatchewan, and then striking north again in pursuit of the Frog Lake murderers, were doing sentry-go in bare feet when I found them at last on the banks of Beaver River.

Here, you will please understand, I am not trying to pack into a few pages either a history of that curious campaign or a geography of its arena. I am reproducing some of the impressions made upon my mind in 1885 by the scenes through which I rode and the events as they occurred before my eyes. These impressions are as fresh today as when they were made, for I have checked them carefully with the original detailed reports I wrote at the time under canvas, waggon, or blue sky, — often jogging along in the saddle.

The novelty of that year's experience to most of us can hardly be exaggerated. Few of the citizen soldiers who formed our militia battalions had ever been on active service before, — just a sprinkling of Imperial Army veterans. To most of us Easterners, the West was then an unknown land, and few even of the Winnipeg volunteers had ever been out in the wilderness beyond their own, then, "postage stamp" Province.

The first eastern units despatched got their surprise even before they reached "the West", which was supposed to begin with Manitoba. Fortunately, the building of the Canadian Pacific Railway was far in advance of its contract, or the fire of rebellion might have spread into a conflagration before the troops could arrive to stamp it out. As it was, there were still four gaps in the unfinished line north of Lake Superior. Over the snow and ice of the two shortest gaps, the soldiers marched; over the other

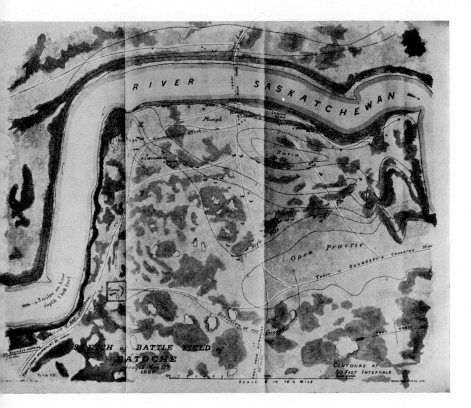

The Batoche battlefield. From a sketch in the
official Report of the Department of Militia,
1886.

129

two, they rode in sleighs provided by the railway company; on the stretches of steel between gaps they were carried in open trucks. The company's promise to rush an army from Toronto and Montreal to Qu'Appelle in eleven days, though received with incredulity by the Government, was fufilled, with three days to spare. But when I saw the troops alighting at Winnipeg they looked as if they had already gone through a campaign. Many of them were frostbitten, and half blind with the glare of the snow.

My own escape was simply due to the fact that I was allowed, as a civilian, to travel through the United States, though our men in uniform were not. From that time on, throughout the campaign, I took pot luck with them, — pot luck and shot luck.

One advantage I had, over the infantry at any rate, — I could ride, while they had to walk, with an occasional lift from a supply waggon. In Winnipeg I bought a cheap saddle — $8, to be exact. Travelling by train to Qu'Appelle, whence the troops under General Middleton were to march north against the Métis in arms at Batoche, I found that another force, under Col. Otter, was going on to Swift Current, for a dash up north against the Indians at Battleford.

Indians on the warpath seemed to

promise a more exciting adventure than their comparatively civilized half-cousins. I climbed into a caboose leaving Qu'Appelle with the first detachment of Otter's force, and presently landed where the city of Swift Current now stands. It then consisted of half a dozen shacks facing the station.

Not a horse was to be had. Presently, I found a man who owned one and offered it to me for $75. But where was it? "Oh", said he, "out there", waving expansively at the prairie, where it had been roaming all winter. The prairie stretched for a thousand miles or so without the vestige of a fence to limit the travels of an enterprising horse. Even if it had not strayed to the Great Lakes or Rocky Mountains, it had probably joined a herd of wild horses. Such herds were common on the prairie then. They were the most independent communities in the world, avoiding humanity and detesting its restraints, — all the more defiant because many of their recruits had escaped from the service of man. My

chance of a mount seemed small.

Days passed, — the army arrived, but no horse. More days passed, — the army went marching off to the north, and still no horse. At last it came, a calcareous bag of bones that might have fetched $7 or $8 in peace time. I paid $75 for him and caught up with the army at its first camping place. Imagine the surprise of that starveling at his first generous feed of army oats!

That was really a notable march to the relief of Battleford, — five days for the hundred and fifty miles from the crossing of the South Saskatchewan, thirty miles north of Swift Current.

The crossing itself had been hard enough. There was a ferry boat, but what was that for the transport of nearly 200 loaded waggons, 600 horses and 500 men? Up at Medicine Hat, however, there was a river steamboat, a stern-wheeler called the *Northcote*, such as "floats in a heavy dew". The water was still low, for the mountain snows had hardly begun to melt, and in any case that river was full of sandbanks, with no charted channel, or soundings, or lights to guide the navigator. Never mind, that steamer had been ordered, first to ferry us across

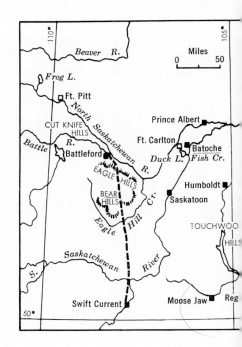

The 90th Winnipeg Rifles leaving Fort Qu'Appelle by the Touchwood Trail, on the march to Batoche under General Middleton.

at Saskatchewan Landing, and then to go down the river with supplies for General Middleton's column, which had started overland from Fort Qu'Appelle for Batoche, the Métis headquarters below Saskatoon.

Such a voyage had never been made before, and it took the *Northcote* nearly a week to reach us, a distance now managed by train in five hours. She was drawing only twenty-six inches of water, but soundings often showed a depth of twenty inches. How did she make it? It sounded like a miracle, till I saw the thing done myself later on. If we stuck on a sand-bank we slipped a cable round a tree on the shore and hauled on the cable with a steam winch. Something had to go — the tree or the cable or the ship. If there was no tree within reach, we stuck a pair of poles down into the river bottom, one on each side, with pulleys and tackle fixed to their tops, and hoisted the steamer up bodily, as if

on stilts, — then full steam ahead, and away she would go into deep water, or on to another sand-bank, as the case might be . . .

How dead the prairie seemed, before the dawn of spring! The thin dead grass of yester-year was sprinkled white with skulls and skeletons of myriad buffalo. The slaughter field of centuries! Twenty years afterwards, when I rode once more the war-trail of '85, the bones had gone — all gathered up by waggonners for U.S. sugar factories, — the first crop yielded by that vast plain, and the first freight carried by the C.P.R. from Western Canada. Though the renascence of the buffalo was still in the future, the prairie was alive with antelope. In '85 the antelope were invisible, scared away doubtless by our march. The only living things we saw were early risers of the gopher tribe, erect and watchful by their holes, a few meadow larks hopping out of our way, and pallid wind-flowers

peeping through the dry brown grass, pioneers of the floral host that soon would glorify the summer plains.

Those first nights, early in April, of the march across the bald-headed prairie from Swift Current to Battleford, the temperature must have been well below zero. At first I accepted the hospitality of Colonel Miller and Major Allen, of the Queen's Own, from Toronto. Two pair of grey blankets, however, and the warmest of clothing, barely kept the frost from my bones. A jug of water by my head was frozen solid. Fortunately I found a private of the Toronto Infantry School who had once been a tailor. He sewed up my blankets into a sleeping sack. That night I chipped in with a tentful of the rank and file. As there were thirteen of us, lying spokewise, our twenty-six feet hob-nobbing around the tent pole, we were as warm as if in our beds. As warm, but not so comfortable. We had no time, even if we had had the spade and

131

pick-axe, to hollow that frozen prairie into harmony with our hips; every night of the march the new camping ground seemed lumpier than the last.

Cold as the nights were, within two hours of the saddle-up my eastern foot would be roasting in the sun, — the western foot still cold in the shade

swallow a mouthful of fried salt pork or Chicago corned beef, gulp down a mug of tea, and stuff his ration of hard tack into his pocket. Before he could throw the saddle on his horse, the column was moving off.

Somewhere among the hundred and ninety waggons was a supply of dried apples, by way of anti-scor-

knew nothing of all that. We had found a treasure, and in a few minutes every unit in the column had secured a share. Until then I had hated curry, — could hardly sit at the same table with it. Now, as long as the curry powder lasted, we curried our corned beef, our sow-belly, even our hard tack, softened by frying in

The looting of the old village of Battleford south of the Battle River. The Mounted Police fort is seen in the background on the high plateau north of the river.

of my cayuse. By noon, the sloughs, if any, were all thawed out, and the boys with both energy and leisure went in swimming. Most of the infantry, cooks excepted, threw themselves down under the waggons and went to sleep. The Cavalry and Artillery wished they could.

So did this war correspondent. He had not only to feed and water his horse but to finish the despatch he had been writing as he rode, on the off-chance of some courier being sent back to the base. Then he would

butic; but our regular diet, thrice a day, was as I have described it, until, nearing our destination, we discovered two carts full of groceries. The owner, a trader named Frank Smart, had passed us several days before, resolved to run them into Battleford if he could. Seeing Indians ahead, and caching the carts in a bluff, he had succeeded in getting through to the town by dark; but later on, riding out in the hope of rounding up stray cattle for the garrison, he had met sudden death from an Indian bullet. We

pork fat; from that day my attitude toward curry has been one of respect verging on affection . . . Of course we meant to pay Frank for his goods. I hope the Government paid double the price to his heir.

We had come west with a vague belief — still held by most outsiders — that the prairie was flat. After the gentle rise from the infant town of Swift Current, we had to cross a thirty-mile bare and level plateau, till we looked down into the deep-sunk valley of the Saskatchewan from the

132

edge of a ruggedly broken precipice. From the northern bank, the prairie stretching a hundred and fifty miles to the Battle River was sometimes heavily and sometimes gently rolling, but never flat. It was wholly bare of trees, except in a patch, the "sixty mile bush", that distance from the Battle River itself. Nearing the river

to Regina. On the outbreak of these troubles all the inhabitants had crossed the river to the new town and taken shelter in the adjacent Mounted Police fort, with its stockade and bastions and guns, on the high plateau in the fork of the Battle and the North Saskatchewan. The neighbouring Indians, under persuasion of

raid. Hence the urgent appeals for rescue, which gave an impression that Battleford was in imminent danger of destruction by an organized and determined enemy. The fact is that even the few Indian tribes who were described as "on the warpath" were not convinced by Riel's claim of Messianic power to win back their coun-

The Battle of Cutknife Creek, where Colonel Otter's force was surrounded. From an imaginary sketch, based on information by various participants, published by the Grip Publishing Company, Toronto. The neat arrangement of waggons, horses and men suggests that the informants were playing a joke on the artist.

we espied the first trace of human habitation, the log huts of an Indian reserve. Even there no sign of life appeared. Under a heap of straw behind his house we found the body of the farmer-instructor, Payne, killed in a tussle with a tribesman whose demand for hunting rations he had refused.

Descending toward the Battle River, we passed through the old original village of Battleford, seat of Government for the Northwest Territories before "Pile of Bones" blossomed in-

Riel's envoys, had gathered into a camp, some distance away to the West. From time to time they would come to the uninhabited village, carry off such articles as tempted them, and make a bon-fire of a deserted house. An outbuilding of old Government House was burned, but not the house itself.

Away across the river from old Battleford, the new town stood secure, — "serene and unafraid" I should like to add, but many of the refugees lived in constant fear of an Indian

try and depose the white man. In Poundmaker's camp the majority allowed the war party of Sioux, or Stoney Indians, to set aside the peaceful chief's authority; but Riel's men could not persuade them to go off and join him in active prosecution of the war.

Let me add, in fairness, that if any tribe has to be singled out for blame it should be the Sioux, not the Cree, that the great chief Poundmaker tried again and again to break away from the camp under the war party's con-

Big Bear, Cree chief at Frog Lake, who tried to prevent the massacre started by Wandering Spirit. From a pastel sketch by Edmund Morris, son of the Lieutenant Governor of the Northwest Territories.

trol, and that on our retreat from Cutknife Hill he checked a pursuit that might have meant our annihilation.

That was a bad time, the worst of the war; for just before our defeat at Cutknife, General Middleton's advance on Riel's headquarters had been abruptly stopped by the human "hornet's nest" in the ravine of Fish Creek.

Middleton's force could afford to wait, without risk of starvation, for their line of communication with the base at Qu'Appelle was unbroken. At Battleford, we were totally isolated. As aeroplanes and automobiles did not yet exist, we had to draw our provisions by waggons over a hundred and eighty miles of unprotected trail from Swift Current. The Indians, encouraged by their success at Cutknife, had started eastward at last, apparently to join forces with Riel. Cutting our line of communication, they captured a whole train of 29 waggons laden with our supplies.

The capture of Riel's headquarters, by one rush at the end of three days skirmishing, came just in time to halt the Indian march. On the 26th of

May, riding out from Battleford, I met their chiefs coming in to surrender. Silent and solemn, they crossed the river, climbed the heights, and squatted in front of General Middleton's tent, to await their doom.

The General, fresh from his victory at Batoche, took his seat on a campstool, and the famous pow-wow began. I still have an old bunch of telegraph forms crowded with my verbatim notes, taken standing beside the General and his trusted interpreter, — big Hourie, himself part Indian, who accompanied his words with a dignified swaying of his body and arms. Poundmaker sat facing the General, a little in advance of the other chiefs. His handsome, strong

Poundmaker, friendly Cree chief whose authority had been set aside by warlike Sioux, defended his camp against Otter but prevented pursuit of our retreating force.

and intelligent face was surmounted by a coonskin, the head overlooking the chief's brow. His black hair, in narrow plaits, bound at intervals with brass wire, hung below his waist. With quiet dignity the chief repelled

every suggestion of responsibility for the wrong-doing of the tribes. The peppery Middleton called him a liar, but the chief kept his temper.

The general demanded the surrender of the murderers, not only of Payne, but of a farmer named Fremont, shot down in cold blood while greasing the wheels of his waggon. The chief said he did not know who they were, but he spoke a few words to the Indian crowd behind him, and the two killers came forward without hesitation.

With the Métis and Indian leaders in gaol, and their disarmed followers sent back to their homes, our soldiers thought it high time to be homeward-bound themselves. Instead of that, the roughest though not the reddest of their adventures lay ahead of them, — to hunt the Northern wilderness for the Wood Crees who had perpetrated the Frog Lake massacre.

We called this episode the pursuit of the "arch-fiend" Big Bear. In reality that poor old chief had tried to prevent the crime. Like Poundmaker, he was set aside by a fanatical group of his followers, — excited by the news of Riel's early success at Duck Lake.

Carrying with them the survivors of the massacre and a score of white folk captured immediately afterwards at Fort Pitt, these Indians were now roaming through a vast labyrinth of forest and muskeg. At one point General Strange caught up and attacked them; they were in a strong position on Frenchman's Butte, but when he went off for fresh ammunition they gave him the slip. A party of scouts caught up with the tail of their procession fording a lake, but again they got away.

Those prisoners had to be rescued, and the whole of our available force was put on the job, — four columns hunting north on different trails.

After the bad lands and bald prairie of the south, the contrasting beauty of that northern park-land was at first delightful, — its infinite variety

of forest and glade, lush meadow, purling brook. Our aesthetic instincts were gratified — but we were conscious of others!

At Frog Lake, a paradise of natural beauty, nothing was visible of the settlement but cellar holes where houses had been burnt. From one of these we dug the headless remains of two men, and identified by a fragment of red shirt the Indian Agent, Tom Quinn, whose refusal to budge when ordered up to the Indian camp gave the signal for the massacre.

Farther north, where the land was mostly water, the trail was impassable until it was covered with makeshift corduroy of pine and poplar branches. When the swamp was too deep for that, we either waded or, if the muddy bottom was too soft for safety, crept around the edge between wood and water.

The hard tack and salt pork never gave out, but sugar did, — and that, when it happened that the only water for our tea was a pool of black mud and crawling life, was — well, that was that! Then the oats gave out, and the waggon teams, needing strong food for hard hauling, began to suffer. The broncos and cayuses, on the other hand, laughed and fattened on the grass.

At last, emerging from dense forest, we found ourselves looking down into the valley of Beaver River.

It was the end of the trail — the world I knew was all behind me. In front, the outer universe, illimitable, dark, unpeopled, and unknown. The great stream under my eyes, beyond the next curve would become a river of dreams, its course conjectural, a dotted line on our only map, until somehow it resumed existence making for the Churchill and Hudson Bay.

Looking across the swirling water to the high forest barrier of the Great Beyond, I felt for the first time the thrill of a discoverer — on the verge of a new world to explore.

Fortune denied me the chance, by letting the captives escape from their peripatetic imprisonment. After that, it was not thought worth while to hunt their captors, the war correspondent's enterprise ended with the war.

The first fight at Duck Lake. Crozier's Mounted Police and Prince Albert Volunteers, going to save stores from capture, were driven back, leaving ten dead on the snow. The news of Riel's victory inflamed Indians at Frog Lake to murder priests and settlers.

Clinton was the first main stopping place beyond Ashcroft, B.C., on the "Poor Man's Trail". The Clinton Hotel, shown here, continued in use from the early days of the Cariboo Trail until it burned down in the 1950's.

THE POOR MAN'S TRAIL

by MARIUS BARBEAU

When this account was written in 1934 there were still many people in northern British Columbia who remembered the days of the Yukon Gold Rush and who told stories of the gold-seekers who had chosen the overland route rather than pay for steamboat passage to Skagway. Most of them were forced to turn back before reaching their objective, some died on the trail, but the hardy remainder, mainly the most experienced and best equipped, reached the goldfields.

MANY YEARS have passed since a malignant fever for placer gold caught thousands of people all over our continent and sent them scurrying over the trails and mountain passes into the gold fields of Alaska. Not a few easterners, from the United States, Ontario and Quebec, succumbed to the epidemic, in spite of distance and expense, and joined the 'stampeders' in a perilous adventure. They fell in with those who had preceded them, the 'sourdoughs' and the 'chee-chakos' — those who knew how to take care of themselves from experience and those who did not; "cheechako" is from an Indian word meaning fresh or "new at the game". Many of them never came back.

Nowhere are those reminiscences better preserved than in the settlements of northern British Columbia, in the Caribou and the Skeena districts. There you meet with live knowledge, along the very trail that bears the brand of the 'stampede'. For

there were two ways of reaching the Klondyke: by water from Seattle or Vancouver to Juneau, and over the Chilkoot Pass; or overland, from Ashcroft, in southern British Columbia, to Whitehorse, in the far north.

Soon after I arrived on the Skeena River, some years ago, I was thrilled again to hear "cheechako" and "sourdough" stories. They were of the "Poor Man's Trail", which struck the Skeena at Hazelton and followed it upwards to the Stikine heights.

"That was a strange year '98," widow Hankin told me, one of my first evenings at Hazelton. "The people here thought that the whole world had gone wrong. Hundreds of stampeders passed on their way to the Klondyke, that summer. They came along the Bulkley River, from the south. Bank clerks, doctors and lawyers, lunatics, remittance men and highway robbers tramped the trail from the Caribou country north to the gold fields, most of them in a pitiful state. Cowboys drove horses, or herds of cattle and little donkeys. There were clergymen and college folk among them; even a circus outfit.

Yes, sir, that happened in '98. Three thousand people were fooled by Seattle merchants, who made them believe that the shortest and cheapest route to the Klondyke was overland.

The 'Poor Man's Trail', as they called it, drew the crowd as honey draws flies. Its head was at Ashcroft, on the Canadian Pacific Railway. A map showed how direct the trail was to the Klondyke: only a few hundred miles. Stampeders purchased horses, grub and supplies, from merchants there; and they made off in a rush, on to the Caribou, through Hazelton, to the north. Not many of the three thousand that started on the trail that year ever reached the Klondyke." So her vivid story went on, most of the evening.

An old officer of the Mounted Police, whom I met in a little barber shop the next day, started to recite a poem about the "Poor Man's Trail",

This is the pan of virgin gold
From the Klondyke River swift and cold
Found by a northern miner bold,
And by him to a steamboard owner sold.

This is the steamboat owner, sly,
Who wanted his boats to the north to ply,
And so bought over the honest (?) P.-.I.
And ran his rates up ever so high.

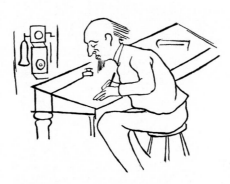

This is the editor, false and cute,
Who said it was proved beyond dispute
By evidence no one could refute
That the best way in was "The Poor
Man's Route."

but he could only remember the first lines. Once this Mounted Police officer had travelled from Hazelton northwards and had seen the poem on a blazed hemlock tree, done with a knife and indelible pencil. Others had seen it too, had learned and

A stage coach near Ashcroft, B.C., on the Cariboo Road. The scenery is still the same today for travellers on the Trans-Canada Highway.

copied it. But no one quite remembered it now. Little drawings filled the space between the stanzas: the Poor Man, a stick in his hand and a pack on his back; the grave — a pile of stone and a wooden cross with the words "Found dead"; and the last words in capital letters: "HELL"!

The spirit in this unusual epitaph made me regret its loss. So I started a search for it among the "old-timers"; not without hope of success, for I heard that Beirnes, the Scotch packer, might have a copy of it in his cabin, at Mission Creek.

Beirnes, some time later, found his copy, and turned it over to me. Here it is reproduced. He had made it a few years after the stampede, while the tree still stood there, way up the Yukon Telegraph trail, at the headwaters of the Skeena.

Little is known in the north about the "steamboat owner", who supposedly bought the P. and I., a newspaper, for his publicity, "and ran his rates up ever so high." Evidently he was a pioneer in this kind of business. And here is his monument, with beaver hat, moustache and glittering diamond!

The newspaper editor "false and cute" gets his share of the blame. He is shown here at his work. Bald as an egg, with a bristly imperial, he pens his "dope" and looks jaded. He is underpaid, but nonetheless treated as an accomplice. For it is he who spread the news abroad that "the best way in was the Poor Man's Route." The Poor Man, "innocent fool" who fell for it, did not forget him in his will.

Before the rush began, the early settlers in the north had wind of the affair. Bishop Riddley preached, in his little church at Hazelton, that "the people of the earth soon would shift as never before." His words sounded like a prophecy. Indians and white people have remembered them to this day. He had foreseen the Klondyke rush.

The Ashcroft "stampeders" began to arrive in June at Hazelton, after covering several hundred miles of a wretched trail. Heading north in a great hurry, they all wanted to arrive there first, to stake the best claims.

John Connon drove past Hazelton with five pack horses and a collie dog, someone still remembers. He camped close to shore, one evening, on the upper Skeena. He crossed the river with his collie, in an Indian dug-out he found there, and discovered that the feed for his horses was better on the other side. Leaving his dog behind, he went back for the horses. They were swimming in line, in front of his canoe, when the dog leaped into the river, to meet them in midstream. The leader, frightened, headed straight down the river, where they were drowned. The canyon was a short distance below.

Poor Connon, in a few minutes, lost all he had. He blazed a tree with his axe and lamented his ill-luck in a letter which he pencilled on the tree, for others to read. It could still be seen years later, just like the epitaph of the "Poor Man's trail". With all he had left tied in a handkerchief, he continued his journey to the Klondyke, he and his dog.

This is the Poor Man, innocent fool,
Who never went to a lying school,
And so was willing to be the tool
Of selfish liars, false and cruel.

This is the grave that the poor man fills,
After he died from fever and chills,
Caught while tramping over the Stikine hills,
Leaving his wife to pay up his bills.

This is the place where those men will go
Who swindled innocent people so,
Robbing them of their hard-earned dough,
And giving them only Mud and Snow.

The natives at Kispayaks village were kept busy taking "stampeders" and their baggage in dug-out canoes across the Skeena. That was at one of the two most dangerous ferries of the whole trail, in the freshets of June and July. Cowboys with herds of horses and cattle for the Klondyke hailed the ferrymen from the far shore, and fixed it with them at so much per head to be taken across. The ferry men made money that way.

Strange animals made their appearance across the river, one bright morning. The Indians, who never had seen them before, thought that they were ghosts. But they were donkeys, "burros" as they were called, two hundred of them, each with an *apparejo* (pack). The whole Indian village came down to the shore and looked at them. They were so much better than horses on the trail, their owner boasted. But their short legs were against them in the deep mud up the river.

A circus was the next thing the Indians marvelled at. Its leader was a tall and slim fellow, who walked around with a long whip. In his troupe was an old man, the owner of the show, and his niece, a pretty girl, a tight rope dancer. The outstanding features in the outfit were a splendid black horse, with a white star in its forehead; two circus dogs; a music box with rolls inside; and a large tent with red stripes and ziz-zag trimmings all around. The tall fellow refused to have his black horse towed across the river like a burro! And he would not pay for him. It was enough for the Indians to have seen him. He could swim across the river like the pack horses, he declared. But the Skeena there is wide and treacherous. The horse, frightened, drifted down to the bend of the river, and was drowned before he could be reached with a dug-out.

Herdsmen and cowboys drove cattle and horses northwards, to be turned to gold at the end of the trail. But they found it difficult to keep their herds steady on the forest trail. The

An old Indian suspension bridge at the Hagwelget canyon, Bulkley River, on the Yukon trail
From a drawing made about the time of the '98 stampede.

two ferries below and above Hazelton gave them much trouble. The mountain trail farther up was mostly forest and canyon. Not a blade of grass much of the way, only leaves, fireweed, skunk cabbage, Indian rhubarb, nettles and the weed at Poison Mountain.

"Our herd had to be rafted across the river at Kaldo, that's where we had endless trouble," Hankin still remembers. "While at the ferry, one end of the rope broke, and the raft swiftly drifted down with our Indian 'captain', Thomy, on it, and some baggage. The river was swollen, during the freshets, and the waterfalls were not far below. Running down along the shore, we could not keep up with the raft in the race.

Soon we lost sight of it. Several times we shouted: 'Thomy, are you dead?' No answer. The worst had happened, we were sure. So we were going back to the herd, repeating, 'Thomy, are you dead?' We stumbled upon him, sitting on the little trail. He was too weak to answer.

The first thing he said was, 'I want to go back home!' We could not persuade him to change his mind, much as we needed him. He had fallen into the water close to shore, and had barely escaped with his life, hanging on to a branch. We gave him food, paid him off, and struggled along without him."

Three "stampeders" with six horses had gone as far as the trail to Telegraph Creek, but they could not reach Telegraph Creek before the heavy snowfalls. They built a cabin on the Spatsezee River and tried to winter their horses. The horses died. Had they gone thirty miles farther down, they would have found enough feed for them. But they did not know, and they were at the end of their wits.

Two of the men went on their way to Dawson. The third died alone in camp and his body was found there by a surveyor named Dawson, who went through that country the following year. The cabin behind which he was buried stood close to the trail. People stopped there and read his name cut with a knife into a log of the cabin. The letters were filled in with heavy red pencil. The date was written under, and Dawson's signature.

The roof of the cabin was still on the first time Angus Beaton, a miner passed there, but the second time it had fallen in. The name carved on the post was that of Henry Wright, from Montana.

Kisgasas (Sea-Gull), Indian village on the Babine River where the "Poor Man's Trail" passed.

139

The centre block of the Parliament Buildings in Ottawa before the fire of 3 February 1916 swept through it. Ret
The Parliament Buildings were first begun in 1860.

CANADA AT THE TURN OF THE CENTURY, 1900

ARTHUR R. M. LOWER

THE NINETEENTH CENTURY lies for us today a lifetime off. In the sixty-five years that have passed, a new world has come into being, a world as different in some respects from those days as they were from the days of the discoveries. Never has the pace of change been so rapid as in this century of ours. It takes, in consequence, historical reconstruction to recapture the days of one's own childhood. The present writer was born in the nineteenth century, remembers a good many public and private events of those days and has watched the scenes about him ever since. Queen Victoria's Jubilee or the Boer War are for him not merely matters recorded in books but warm, living memories. He is therefore both observer and observed, both part of the scene and the reporter. How this affects his qualifications to write about it, the reader must judge.

If we cast back from 1900 as far as the historical clock has since then advanced, sixty-five years, we find ourselves in 1835. Let the reader bring before his mind's eye that earlier Canada of 1835. The term Canada itself had no legal meaning. There were Upper and Lower Canada, the Maritime provinces, the "Hudson's Bay Territories" (whatever they were!), a set of struggling scattered British communities, with little knowledge of each other, whose principal bond was in that first word of their collective title, *British* North America: they were *British*, in contradistinction with *AMERICAN*; monarchists, not republicans.

Two years later, 1837, two of the provinces were torn apart in rebellion, and in one of the others there was serious discontent. All this arose out of bad government, and in Lower Canada out of the racial clash. Three years more and Upper and Lower Canada became The Province of Canada, Great Britain's largest colony and territorially a considerable unit. More and more self-government followed — we Canadians call it Responsible Government — until in their internal affairs these British North American colonies became almost fully autonomous. Growth based on new land, the forest and the maritime life was rapid and the 1850's were to be the most prosperous decade the colonies were to know until the 1900's. Growth brought its own problems. It called for the new modes of transportation then springing up everywhere — canals and railways. These required heavy capitalization. It sharpened up the political situation and brought into existence — through the issues it forced, fitted to the traditions of an earlier day, particularly as determined by the rebellions — the historical parties, which still survive.

Out of all this came Confederation, 1867, four provinces uniting themselves into THE DOMINION OF CANADA. Confederation for us Canadians was as conspicuous an historical mountain top as had been the original English conquest, for it set our feet on the way to national life. In these days, when our national life lies under threat, it cannot be too often recalled that, if Durham had

141

exclaimed in 1839 over the horrid spectacle of "two nations warring in the bosom of a single state", the statesmen of 1867, particularly Macdonald and Cartier, seem to have regarded Confederation as a peace, a burying of hatchets, a recognition that in the new country there were to be neither conquerors or conquered, but all were to be equal — Canadians. Let the reader look into that volume of Thomas Chapais's *Cours d'histoire du Canada* in which he describes the reception of the first Lieutenant-Governor of Quebec, a man of French speech, a descendant of the conquered, now guarded by British troops, their arms at the present in honour. While it would be foolish to imagine that race and languages are clothes that can be changed at will, they yet are hands which may be extended in anger or with the clasp of friendship. Con-

federation changed fists into handshakes, and relatively cordial handshakes, as the fair measure of cooperation marking the subsequent generation "at the summit" was to show.

Confederation, 1867: just thirty-three years before the period of our survey, from birth to early manhood for an individual. In my childhood I must have encountered scores of persons who were born before Confederation and who could have remembered those days. Later, I conceived the idea of collecting those memories, but by that time it was almost too late and I have few of them. All the more excusable, perhaps, does my own exercise in memory become for "Canada at the Turn of the Century".

That generation preceding my own, the post-Confederation generation, did not measure up to the spirit in

which it was born, and the new country almost foundered on the reefs of popular racial and religious intolerance and the surrounding quicksands of economic disabilities. From these, the Canadian ship has not yet got clear. The New Brunswick schools quarrel, the ultramontanism of Quebec extremism, the two Riel disturbances, the Jesuit Estates Act, the Manitoba Schools question; all these were to keep tempers on edge and racial friction prominent. Canada might well have died in infancy but that, as Adam Smith once remarked, "there is a lot of ruin in a nation".

And yet, think of how far by 1900 we had come! Not only a federal state established, but the bounds of that state flung across a continent "from sea to sea". Not only across the continent, but up and down it, so that by 1900 the confines which a few years before had gone only as far

Bonsecours market, one of the oldest in Montreal, photographed about 1900 by William Notman and Sons, with the harbour in the background.

north as the height of land now stretched to the remotest Arctic island. And not only this vast geographic expension, which made our country, on the map the second largest in the world; but the heroic effort to tie it together, which had by some miracle of faith, courage, and that more lowly political oil that makes the great qualities "work", pushed a railroad across from Atlantic to Pacific. In 1900, the Canadian Pacific Railway was completing its fourteenth year of transcontinental service. The writer remembers the red coaches that used to go northward, over the Grand Trunk, through his town to join the main line at North Bay: they did not seem a marvel, then, to the small boy, but part of the order of things. To older persons, those coaches, thundering along mile after mile through northern wilderness, prairies, mountains, till they came down to salt water, probably still retained the atmosphere of the miraculous. No wonder that they drew people out with them, to occupy the intervening stretches and build new Canadas along their empty miles.

Material accomplishments — "progress" in the mind of the average man — may be documented in the dry light of statistics. To do this in the perspective of our "before and after" glance is interesting. In 1965, we have about twenty million people in Canada. In 1835 there were about one million, four hundred thousand (1,400,000). At the half-way point, 1900, we had not quite five million and a half (5,371,000). In the one period of sixty-five years we increased our numbers by about 3.8 times, in the other by just about the same ratio. The long view thus immediately introduces us to a salient point in historical studies: it smoothes out year-by-year inequalities and gives us a wide perspective. It is reasonable to assume that the idea holds good not only for measurable quantities but for more subtle aspects of social evolution.

There is a wide range of statistics available for measuring the trends of society, both before and after 1900. Some of these may be rapidly reviewed.

The vast difference in size at the two ends of the period rests in large part on the settlement of the west. In

Churchgoers at Notre Dame du Portage, Quebec. Religion enjoyed widespread secular influence in Canada at the turn of the century.

1835, this had not even been thought of: in 1900, it was far enough advanced to have given rise to two new provinces, Manitoba and British Columbia, and several administrative divisions whose population entitled them to something close to self-government. The population of all these units was small. While the present great western cities existed as corporate entities, none of them except Winnipeg and Vancouver was more than a small town. Perhaps nothing has been more significant for the period since 1900 than the growth of these western outposts of settlement into the large cities. Not only Vancouver and Winnipeg (these two close to metropolitan stature) but also Edmonton, Calgary, Regina.

But has the rise of western cities

been any more significant than that of those of the east? Admirable as a strong countryside is and much as we owe to the "bold peasantry, its country's pride" which cleared away the forests and brought into being the life-giving fields, and many and hor-

rible as are the blemishes on urban life, countries remain weak in organization and backward in culture unless there arise within them great centres of population. In 1835, these did not exist in Canada: Montreal alone was the only one that was more than a good-sized town. By 1961, everyone knows the situation which had arisen: Montreal and Toronto great semi-metropolitan centres, with a couple of million of people each, Ottawa stretching up to half a million, Quebec and Hamilton not far behind, numerous secondary centres. How was it at the half-way mark, 1901? In that year Montreal had 328,000 people, Toronto, 209,000, Ottawa, 60,000, Winnipeg, 42,000. Montreal and Toronto were thus considerable centres and they had much of the apparatus of metropolitanism — a distinct hinterland which they commanded through devices of transportation, commerce and finance, some industry, a financial structure (banks, etc.), of considerable autonomy and a promising beginning in some of the arts: Toronto's Massey Hall, for example, dates from the early 1890's. They received the visiting musical artists and the plays which any other good-sized provincial town had, such as, say Cincinnati, but neither one had yet much pretension to an original culture.

Canada was, in fact, a simple society, as every piece of data that can be gathered bears out. Take, for example, housing. For the whole country, coast to coast, only 968 buildings are returned in 1901 as housing four families and over; that is, the modern "apartment" which more and more dominates our large cities, was virtually unknown. For 1,070,000 families, there were 1,057,000 houses. This accords with the writer's own memories, for in those days a family which did not have a house for its castle, however humble, was rare indeed.

The country was simple, but it was solid. Its aims were not high, but they were laudable: they were the aims of a society rapidly changing from mere pioneering to the middle class worthiness of the town and small city. Take schooling, for example: the country was already well equipped with elementary and secondary schools: no promising youth need go without an

Granville Street, Vancouver. Along with other western centres, Vancouver grew very rapidly since 1900.

Indians at Calgary during the tour of King George V and Queen Mary as Duke and Duchess of York across Canada in 1901.

The visit of King George V and Queen Mary as Duke and Duchess of York to Ottawa in 1901. Sir Wilfrid Laurier, then Prime Minister, and Mr. W. D. Morris, Mayor of Ottawa, flank Queen Mary, while King George V walks behind the Mayor.

education up to what we today would call Grade XI, or even Grades XII and XIII, particularly in Ontario where the system of Collegiate Institutes, with their "Specialist" teachers, was well-developed and where fees, though charged, were low. The writer when he began to go to his local Collegiate Institute, already a school with considerable tradition and with masters of competence, paid ten dollars a year. Even this small amount was enough to keep the louts and idlers out: teachers had not yet become baby-sitters for young people who should have been earning their own living. These limited numbers in secondary schools reflect a considerably higher rate for illiteracy than is given in modern returns, 17 per cent

of those 5 years and over for the country as a whole, a little over 10 per cent for Ontario, a little over 22 per cent for Quebec. Not that "literacy" in itself is much more than a statistical abstraction!

In the university area, our own day has seen more expansion than any previous period, both in numbers of students and of institutions, but in 1900, the more prominent of our Canadian institutions had already been established for a good many years. None of them, however, was large, none wealthy, none ambitious, none aiming at more than good undergraduate teaching and all very conscious that they were just reflections of that great civilization across the sea from which most of their pro-

fessors had come. The census of 1901 gave the country thirteen universities having 424 professors and 6,860 students. Even Toronto had only about 1,000 students.

In 1835, the population of the provinces consisted largely of youngish people, for it was an immigrant population just getting on the land. More than that, in those days, families were large. By the end of the century trends with which we are familiar in respect to age were clearly visible. The birthrate had decreased, the number of persons in each age group was shifting quite quickly away from the very young, and towards the middle groups, and the expectation of life had considerably lengthened. The number of old persons (over 70) in the population had increased. The next sixty-five years was to see this trend greatly accentuated: in 1881, for example, the percentage of over 70's was 2.52, in 1901, 3.08 and in 1961, 5.00. But it is to be noted that since the Second World War, the birth rate has once more increased, with the result that the age-pyramid is now rather more symmetrical than in, say, 1941. And here the settlement of the west comes in again, for since settlers are on the average young and have large families, a population that after Confederation was rapidly growing older, became rejuvenated by the heavy tide of immigration that set in about 1896.

Many considerations of a high degree of interest to everyone in speculations upon his own life and mortality come out of inspections of the prosaic statistics of birth and death. For the turn of the century, these are well presented. From them one could comment at length on such subjects as birth rate, death rate, life expectation, infant mortality, causes of death, and the correlation of these primary matters with provinces and smaller subdivisions. One learns that in 1901

there were in Canada nearly 17,000 persons of "Unsound Mind", over 6,000 deaf and dumb (of whom 2,002 were in Ontario and 2,488 in Quebec),

3,279 blind (Ontario, 1,063, Quebec, 1,035) and that of the total of 81,201 reported deaths, 21,328 were of infants under one year of age, about

Scottish immigrants on their way to the Grand Trunk Railway ferry at Quebec. The Scots and their descendants have made a major contribution to national life.

one in four. The principal causes of death were not as accurately defined then as now, but the merest glance at the tables shows the much greater prominence of infectious and contagious diseases (nearly 9,000 of the total from tuberculosis, for example).

The general birthrate was given as 27.82 per 1,000, the death rate as 15.12. The birthrate was thus about the same as today, the death rate higher, 15 as compared with about 8. There were extraordinary regional variations. As might be expected the new settlements showed high birth rates. So did every community in which people of French origin predominated. "Old" Ontario had about

Immigrants from Hamburg, Germany. German immigration first started in the 1750's, and today Canadians of German descent form the third largest ethnic group in Canada.

146

the same birth rate as today, a very low one. Thus Middlesex County ran around 19 per 1,000. In Quebec some counties reached what must have been just about an all-time human high in reproduction, the topmost bough on the tree being grasped by Beauce, 47.92 births per 1,000. That is, for every infant born in Middlesex, about 2.5 infants were born in Beauce. But Beauce had a death rate of 18.55, and of its 2,067 children born in the census year, 1901, 369 died. This still left it with a very nice surplus, even if a considerable number of the remainder did die within the first five years of their lives.

Beauce may be taken as a good example of a "natural" population; almost purely rural, where children came and went much like puppies. English Canada had long since passed this stage and was embarking on that penuriousness of life that has marked the western world as a whole and that today is making its inroads even into rural Quebec.

The new immigration, flooding out on to the western plains or into the slums and shack-towns of the growing eastern cities, was radically to change the nature of the Dominion of Canada. In 1871, the first census of the new Dominion, persons of British and French origin numbered 3,192,000 out of a total of 3,486,000, or nearly 92 per cent. Of the remainder, most were descendants of the Dutch and German stocks that went back to the first days of settlement. In 1901, this percentage had gone down to 87, which, however, is still in marked contrast to the 1961 figure of 74.1. In 1900, in other words, we stood just on the edge of that vast population shift, not yet completed, which has so signally altered the economy and the psychology of Canadians.

Closely related to the growth of population in a country such as Canada are the fundamental subjects of race and religion. Few countries keep as close statistical check on these

Ukrainian settlers in Alberta. Ukrainians form one of the largest ethnic groups in Canada at the present time; immigration on a large scale started in 1897 and reached a peak just before the First World War.

matters as we do, and as a result we are able to make comparisons for long stretches of our history. For the earlier period of our review, 1835, our data are not exact, but they justify us in assuming a French-speaking population for all British North America of about half a million, as compared with an English of about 900,000. Our first exact figure is 1871, when "British races" stood to French as 2,110,000 to 1,082,000. In 1901, the two "races", keeping the figures on the same basis, were in numbers, 2,963,000 and 1,649,000. In 1961, the numbers were 7,997,000 and 5,540,000. These sets of figures give the proportions "British" to "French" of 10 to 5.5, 10 to 5.13, 10 to 5.56 and 10 to just under 7. In the period since

1901 persons of French origin have thus considerably improved their comparative position, but of course the situation is complicated today by the large number of persons of non-British racial origin who have adopted English as their mother tongue and have to all intents and purposes become members of the English-speaking group. This is illustrated by the "mother tongue" returns, which we possess since 1931. In 1931, the two language groups stood in the proportions of 10 to 4.6 and in 1961, 10 to 4.8.

For 1901, there is a census table, hard to equate with mother tongue (Vol. IV, table XIII) which nevertheless gives an approximation to the "mother tongue" category. Persons of French racial origin, as above, were 1,649,000 in number, persons over five able to speak French were 1,515,000. For English, the situation was 2,963,000 and 3,700,000. There are various ways of reconciling these discrepancies: for example, 127,000 "English" were put down as able to speak both English and French and 530,000 "French" as able to speak both French and English. A short reference cannot make a satisfactory analysis, but the bilingualism of the period is to be noted, especially on the part of the French. We would need a cross-classification which we do not possess to ascertain the numbers of the people by origin, language and age, so that a comparison could be made with the figures of the preceding paragraph, but in so far as they go, they show that the situation has not changed materially — far more French can speak English than the reverse. And that is, after all a matter of common, every-day observation.

The present writer would judge that the general purport of these figures is to show that the numerical balance of the two great cultural groups of the country has not altered much in the long period examined.

In the important matter of religion,

we go first to the First Census of the Dominion, 1871, where we find 1,532,000 persons putting themselves down as Roman Catholics and the balance split up among many Protestant denominations. The ratio stands as 1,532,000 to 2,157,000 or 7.1 Roman Catholic to 10 "others". In 1901, these figures and proportions were 2,230,000 to 3,141,000 or 7 to 10, and in 1961, 8,342,000 to 9,896,000, or 8.4 to 10. But of course, in 1961, "others" included many non-Protestant groups, so that in the long period under survey, Roman Catholicism has greatly increased its strength relative to Protestantism.

At the turn of the century, while the emphasis on formal schooling (which let us hasten to distinguish from education) was not as strong as today, the emphasis on the traditional religion was much stronger. Roughly speaking, everyone went to church, and a considerable proportion of people went twice a day. For youngsters, such as the writer, a third hour was added in the afternoon Sunday School. All this seemed natural, not onerous. Genuine religious convictions elude statistical analysis, indeed, any analysis, so no one can say that they were less or more common in those days than today, though then expressed with infinitely greater formality and fervour of behaviour. There were, however, many aspects to church in addition to pure religion: the church was a social centre, it provided music and much of the intellectual stimulation of the day. Its clergy, in the major denominations, were educated men, leaders in their communities, highly respected. I cannot remember ever hearing of hostility to the church as such, though sneering remarks about the shortcomings of ardent churchgoers were common enough. The church was strong, quite at home in its community, which was at home with it, and one only has to read biography to see how influential it was in the life of every young Canadian who amounted to anything.

Let me cite Mackenzie King as illustration. Many people find King's religiosity repugnant because of his evident ambitions for personal success and power. I myself find King quite easy to understand. He was brought up in the full flood of 19th century religious fervour and as an earnest youth could hardly have responded otherwise than as he did. But he was human, like the rest of us, and so the more mundane qualities came out, too.

Canada during the last quarter of the 19th century was a religious country in far more than a surface way: in fact, it is to be doubted if there have been many peoples the world over who have taken to heart more seriously and more intelligently the teachings of their religion. Among an executive people religious conviction expressed itself very readily in "good works" — social amelioration of many sorts. It probably reached its peak in Canada somewhere around the turn of the century; thereafter, the intellectual forces of the 19th century abroad began to catch up with it and the great age of faith began to wane.

In our modern census, everyone, with few exceptions, puts himself down as belonging to one denomination or another: there are few people who either wish or have the courage to put themselves down as "No denomination", though it is to be suspected that the denominational affiliation is often more nominal than real. In 1901, if people said they belonged, they probably belonged. An interesting table (Census, IV, 361) gives the number of "Communicants" of the various denominations: this shows them in much their modern order: Roman Catholics, 1,356,000 ("adherents", 2,230,000), Anglicans, 148,000 (681,000), Methodists, 269,000 (916,000), Presbyterians, 226,000 (755,000), with others similar. "Communicants" would not include young children.

No one can possibly overestimate the place of the church in Canadian life as of 1900. Its place was approximately co-ordinate with the social behaviour of the people, though there were dark areas it had not succeeded in getting light into, notably the swinish drunkenness of the frontier (but have we much improved?). There was next to no divorce (in 1901, of the 81,000 deaths, only 6 were of divorced persons) and probably less illegitimacy than today, though that does not in itself mean difference in sexual behaviour, for there is no area of life

leading citizens in Ontario and Quebec are standing their trial for offences against honesty and good morals. Possibly in 1900 these things might have been hushed up: possibly they did not take place. We can form no index number of good morals. But we can quite readily say that the pressure towards good morals was infinitely greater in 1900 than it is today and that, moreover, it had behind it spiritual sanctions whose authority relatively few were ready to challenge.

that can be laid about the individual and consequently they influence him in every fibre of his being. If space permitted, it would thus be possible to trace out the historic gaps between our two great cultural groups and to estimate from dry statistical detail whether they were approximating each other or not. The probable answer, given the uniformity and intensity of the media playing upon everyone for a long period past, would be that they are. But the gaps remain

Threshing grain near Portage La Prairie, Manitoba. The wave of immigration in the early years of the 20th century resulted in rapid development of the Prairie Provinces.

where there is so much deviousness, so much concealment as in sexual behaviour. Certainly there was none of the openness which marks today in these matters, and instead of a complete lack of inhibition, there was too much. Yet since sexual morals could scarcely be looser than they are today, they probably were tighter — for one thing there were no motor cars! As to honesty of conduct, again who is to say? As these words are written, four

Religion and "race" are the two basic conditioning categories of Canadian life, for they determine all the others. They are the dominant factor in education, school attendance, literacy, size of family, economic status, type of housing, occupation, in birth rate, death rate, life-expectancy. That is, these two categories with the inclusion within them of historical and cultural tradition represent the deepest and most permanent influences

wide and difficulties of crossing them great.

Nothing illustrates this more signally than the public events of the last years of the 19th century. In 1896 Wilfrid Laurier became Prime Minister of Canada, the first French-speaking Prime Minister: his acclaim in Quebec was vast. The next year he attended Queen Victoria's Diamond Jubilee. While overseas he made many speeches, some of which were not

149

The Royal Canadian Regiment and the 1st Gordon Highlanders crossing the Modder River in South Africa on Sunday morning, 18th February 1900, before the battle of Paardeberg. About 7,300 Canadians were recruited and sent to South Africa.

well received by his critics in Quebec because they leaned too far in the direction of the British. Yet when he returned to Canada, the St. Lawrence, from Gaspé up, was brilliant with the celebrations of his return. Laurier was equally well received in English Canada. He had, it almost seemed, brought together the two peoples and calmed the passion roused over Manitoba's action in depriving Catholics of their own separate public schools. That memory, however, was to linger.

In 1899 the Boer War broke out. English Canada was in a fever of excitement, French Canada suspicious. For English Canada, the war woke up every ancestral and emotional memory: here were all the sons of Britain, in whatever far-flung land they dwelt, ready and anxious to come to the aid of their beloved parent. Ancestral emotion was reinforced by economic circumstance. Since Confederation Canada had languished: it had been a hard country to become enthusiastic about. But now, at the end of the century, the tide seemed at last to have turned. The West was being

settled, the C.P.R. had begun to pay for its axle-grease, trade was increasing. There was hope abroad. And with hope, went imagination: 4,000 miles from Halifax to Vancouver, forests unlimited, farms for everyone, a vigorous young people in charge of its own domestic destinies. Between 1896 and 1900, a great constricting load seemed to have been lifted from Canadian shoulders, though French Canada, retreating as it did in the bad days to the ancestral rural roof, was not nearly as much affected as English by the slogans of material progress, not as much impressed by the prospects before the country. Were they also prospects for French Canada? The Manitoba episode carried no reassurances.

Nor could French Canada view the Boer War through English eyes. Voices were raised to contend that the little Afrikaner people of South Africa, then being overwhelmed by the world's greatest power, made a striking parallel to the little people which from 1760 on, had had to live as the conquered under the domination of that same world power.

There is hardly a situation since in general Canadian life which has not brought out the same issues. Consequently, bad luck to us, we have to think in terms of two Canadian peoples, who rarely see eye to eye, but, let it be added, whose daily associations over two centuries have so accustomed them to each other that they cannot regard each other as strangers.

English Canada could not have been kept out of the Boer War. Laurier's hand was forced and troops were sent. They proved gallant soldiers, if not altogether the supermen Canadians considered them. "Are the Canadians present?" the British general is pictured as asking. "Yes, sir." "Then let the battle begin." This good conceit of ourselves was to be expected in a young, vigorous people very close to its pioneer days, many of whose men folk were as much at home with a gun as with an axe and far more at home with either than with a pen. While it was naïve, it was important in our national development, for it showed that we had a consciousness of our own identity, were proud of it, and confident that we were going somewhere. The writer remembers those days well. There was both complete identity with Great Britain coupled with a lively sense of separate identity. The country was far more homogeneous than it is today, which meant that thoughts and emotions could be more direct and more uniform than today. Canada today, thanks to the vast population change she has undergone in the interval, is an amorphous mass: blocks here, blocks there, scattered individuals everywhere, many of them on the run from one place or occupation to another. Through such a conductor the electric current makes its way with extreme difficulty. That was not the case in 1899.

The Boer War marked for Canada what it marked for all the other British overseas countries, the experience the youth undergoes in becoming man. After it, the old simplicities could not obtain. Neither we nor the Australians could any longer regard ourselves simply as "daughters in our mother's house", though long since "mistresses in our own". We must face life for ourselves. And three years into the new century, we — both English and French in Canada, this time — got a shock that awakened us to that fact. This was the Alaska Boundary Award, which nearly everyone in Canada felt as a bitter defeat of British by Americans. There was little tendency to blame the Americans, who could only be expected to pursue their own interests as they always had done, but why had Britain let us down? Few Canadians could face the bitter realization that to Britain her own interests far transcended Canada's.

Thus at the turn of the century, this simple rural people was being prepared by the shock of war and the shock of diplomacy for the real world, the rude world, in which it would afterwards have to live. For many, the shocks also provided a vision: they saw the world that was to be. They could not foresee in detail what the future would bring forth but they could feel that their children were destined to take part in the great work of nation-building and would have the opportunity, if they were wise enough, to lend a hand in rearing a new and hopeful civilization based on the old sure formulae of freedom.

May the writer end by saying that his own life has coincided with that two generations of building and that he is proud to have had his lifetime's share of it.

The First Contingent marches up Wellington Street in Ottawa on their return from South Africa in November 1900. Participation in the South African war increased English Canada's sense of nationalism.

St. Roch *stuck in ice off Boothia Peninsula.*

CONQUEST OF THE NORTHWEST PASSAGE BY R.C.M.P. SCHOONER ST. ROCH

by J. LEWIS ROBINSON

The courage and devotion to duty of the Royal Canadian Mounted Police in Northern Canada shows clearly in this account, from the Canadian Geographical Journal, *February 1945. In 1959, Superintendent Larsen was awarded the first Massey Medal of the Royal Canadian Geographical Society for this feat.*

T HE SEARCH for the Northwest Passage forms an intriguing chapter in the history of Canadian exploration. The stories of early navigators who faced the dangers of polar pack-ice in tiny wooden sailing ships, travelling, with doubtful compasses, along uncharted coasts, are accounts of hardship, courage and persever-

ance. The fruitless quest for a route north of the North American mainland to the wealth of the Far East resulted in the exploration and charting of most of the numerous Arctic Islands of Northern Canada.

The Northwest Passage, which brought many ships to destruction in the ice during three long and arduous centuries of polar exploration, remained unconquered by any one vessel until the beginning of the present century. In 1903, Roald Amundsen, Norwegian Arctic Adventurer, entered Lancaster Sound in a small 47-ton vessel, the *Gjoa*, and took a route southward into uncharted Peel Sound, between Somerset and Prince of Wales Islands. He navigated as far as southeastern King William Island, where his party spent two winters at Gjoa Haven (Petersen Bay), studying terrestrial magnetism near the North Magnetic Pole on western Boothia Peninsula. In leaving the Arctic, Amundsen sailed westward through Queen Maud and Coronation Gulfs but was caught in the ice near Herschel Island, where he passed his third winter in 1906. Next summer he and his crew continued westward, becoming the first persons to navigate the Passage suc-

Staff-Sgt. Henry A. Larsen on St. Roch. *Now deceased, he reached the rank of Superintendent before retirement from the R.C.M.P.*

cessfully from east to west in a single ship.

The boat which was to make history in the Northwest Passage, the R.C.M.P. schooner *St. Roch*, was built in 1928 and entered the Western Arctic around the Alaskan coast. In the following years the 80-ton, two-masted vessel travelled along the Western Arctic coasts and islands as a "floating police detachment", carrying supplies and doing routine patrol work without fanfare, through the same difficult ice conditions which had cost so many ships and lives among the early explorers. These hardy adventurers were able to brave only one or two winters in the Arctic, but the sturdy *St. Roch* has spent ten of her sixteen years frozen into the ice of some Arctic harbour. Four successive winters, 1930-34, were spent at Tree River, in Coronation Gulf, and three winters, 1935-37 and 1938-39, were passed frozen in at Cambridge Bay. Aided by modern equipment and radio communication, the R.C.M.P. boat has been performing feats of Arctic ice navigation equal to those history-making voyages of less than a century ago. But to Staff-Sergeant Henry A. Larsen, who has been the unassuming Captain of the schooner during all of these years, this difficult work of navigation and long winter dog-sled patrols are the usual routine in maintaining law and order in the Canadian North.

On June 23, 1940, the *St. Roch* left Vancouver, British Columbia, beginning the voyage which was to make the 80-ton schooner the first ship to complete the elusive Northwest Passage from west to east. She passed through Bering Strait in a dense fog and entered the Arctic Ocean on July 17.

On July 23, the *St. Roch* rounded Point Barrow spit and met the first loose-scattered ice-floes. By evening the blocks had become more numerous, and the *St. Roch* began the familiar task of slowly "working the ice" — twisting and turning from one lead to another opening, edging around large floes and pushing aside small blocks, drifting with the pack and waiting for a lead to appear; Larsen and the *St. Roch* had been

doing this patient work in partnership since 1928. Progress was slow and it became apparent that this was going to be a bad year for ice along the northern Alaskan coast.

For eighteen days the *St. Roch* struggled in pack ice east of Point Barrow and it was not until August 18 that she completed loading supplies and left Herschel Island to carry out her normal routine patrol work of carrying supplies to the various R.C.M.P. detachments in the Western Arctic. Bad weather, fog and strong winds caused several delays in the eastward trip to Coppermine and Cambridge Bay, but on September 16 the schooner returned to Coppermine with her freighting duties finished.

Captain Larsen had originally hoped to proceed through the Northwest Passage via Prince of Wales Strait between Victoria and Banks Islands after completing the freighting work, but the delays caused by ice and bad weather discouraged any such attempt so late in the season. A decision was then made to winter either on Banks Island or at Walker Bay on central west Victoria Island, and to be ready to navigate the Passage early the next summer. The *St. Roch*, therefore, left Coppermine on September 19 and went to Holman Island and thence to DeSalis Bay, Banks Island.

September 25 was spent in examining the enormous harbour and surrounding country at DeSalis Bay, but when Larsen noted high ridges of rock and gravel pushed up along the shore, indicating heavy ice pressure during break-up in the spring, he considered it unwise to winter there. Since no other good harbours were known in the area, the *St. Roch* sailed for Walker Bay, where the explorer, Collinson, had wintered in 1851-52. The vessel had a total of 5,240 miles to show for a season's work when she was anchored in the southeastern part of this bay.

A continous strong east wind blew during most of October and prevented Walker Bay from freezing over until October 30. It was the latest freeze-up known in this area, and, if Larsen had had any way of knowing that it was to be so delayed that year, it is possible that he might have been able to make his way immediately through the Passage to the Eastern Arctic. The vagaries of Arctic weather are unpredictable, however, and what is done in one year may not be possible in another.

The ice in the harbour began to break up in July, but westerly winds kept Walker Bay blocked with floes for some time. On July 31, Larsen decided to try to work his way out, and, after much manoeuvring, finally reached the trading post and mission at Holman Island.

Here duty intervened. An Eskimo boy, who had been accidentally shot, had to be taken to Tuktoyaktuk, for onward movement to hospital at Aklavik. Whereas Amundsen Gulf had been free of ice until very late in the preceding year, during the summer of 1941 floes jammed the northern part of it throughout the whole season. The *St. Roch* did not complete her supply mission and anchor in Cambridge Bay until August 16.

Larsen decided to continue eastward and attempt the Passage around King William Island and through Bellot Strait. On August 19 he left Cambridge Bay, but strong westerly winds, rain and fog were ill omens. The compass was now useless, owing to the proximity of the Magnetic Pole, and navigation through island-studded Queen Maud Gulf was by experience and seaman's 'sixth sense'. The *St. Roch* proceeded cautiously towards Simpson Strait, south of King William Island, taking soundings continually, since no vessel of her draught (13 feet) had ever been in these waters. She reached Gjoa Haven (Petersen Bay) on the afternoon of August 26.

The sea-faring policemen left this trading post on August 30. A north-westerly storm, accompanied by hail

Captain and crew of the St. Roch *at the end of the first historic voyage, 1940-42. Left to right: Const. W. J. Parry, Cook; Const. P. G. Hunt, Deckhand; Const. E. C. Hadley, Wireless Operator; Staff-Sgt. H. A. Larsen, Master; Const. F. S. Farrar, Mate; Const. J. W. Doyle, Deckhand; Cpl. M. F. Foster, Engineer; Const. G. W. Peters, 2nd Engineer.*

and snow, forced the schooner to the coast in the shelter of Mt. Matheson, on the eastern tip of King William Island. There she pitched and rolled for a day before proceeding northward, with one man continuously sounding with the lead and another

at the masthead on the lookout for shoals.

In the narrowest part of James Ross Strait, northeast of Matty Island, the *St. Roch* was stopped by a solid wall of grounded ice extending from shore to shore. Since the vessel

Loading a basket-sled for winter patrol to Eskimo camps.

154

was not built or powered to break such a barrier, she was anchored near-by to wait for the tide to change direction. Early in the evening the ice began pushing southward in a strong current. The only shelter available was in the lee of a small rocky islet only slightly larger than the schooner herself. The morning of September 2 found them still there and undamaged, and when a south wind began pushing the ice northward they moved along with it.

On September 3, improved weather allowed the *St. Roch* to proceed northward between the coast and the ice. During the day the wind changed to the west, gradually moving the ice closer to the coast. It became apparent that there was a definite danger of being caught and crushed. Fortune was with the valiant ship, however, for Pasley Bay, a long inlet, erroneously shown on the charts as a broad bay, appeared ahead, and the *St. Roch* was forced into it. Soon the ship was completely surrounded by heavy ice and could no longer manoeuvre.

On September 11, the ice movement ceased. New ice soon formed rapidly in the open places, and the whole inlet froze over solidly. As it was now impossible to escape, the ice was cut away from the ship, which was anchored farther off-shore so as not to be grounded in the spring. Preparations were then made to spend the winter in Pasley Bay, close to the North Magnetic Pole on Boothia Peninsula, and the news was radioed outside. The schooner had travelled 1,660 miles during the summer. The season was still early by normal standards, and Bellot Strait and the Northwest Passage were only 100 miles away, but the fickle Arctic had again frowned on the *St. Roch*.

The stranded R.C.M. Policemen had an important task to perform during the winter of 1941-42. In the taking of the census of the Canadian arctic areas, their job was to meet as many as possible of the Canadian

Eskimo in this little-visited region. Towards the end of February, Sergeant Larsen and Constable Hunt, having picked up an Eskimo guide, left their winter headquarters on the *St. Roch* for an epic patrol which was to cover 1,140 miles and extend over a period of 71 days.

The winter weather at Pasley Bay was quite different from any other that Sergeant Larsen had known previously in the Arctic. Continued fog and snow-fall, with variable winds, made visibility poor, while sudden changes in temperature from 30 below zero to zero, and back again within a short time, made it difficult to become acclimated. As summer approached it became apparent that the ice was not going to break up early in this region.

The *St. Roch* and police crew spent eleven months at Pasley Bay. On August 4, fresh water draining into the harbour loosened the ice and allowed them to move out of the inlet. On the shore behind they left a new cairn and grave. On February 13, Constable Chartrand had had a sudden heart attack and died almost immediately; his death was the only tragedy of the trip.

Captain Larsen navigated shoreward of the main pack-ice and made 15 miles northward along the coast before being stopped by a solid mass of floes. He then put the vessel into a small lead extending westward to await a break-up. The opening closed, however, and the schooner was caught and held there helpless for twenty days. On several occasions, while they were beset, severe pressure lifted the boat high in the ice and threatened to turn her over. At these times charges of black powder were set off near the vessel to relieve the pressure, while the police crew worked with ice-chisels to keep free the propeller and rudder. An easterly

wind carried the schooner farther and farther away from the coast.

On August 24 a strong northerly gale split the ice and opened a long lead. It took two anxious days for the *St. Roch* to break through the short distance to the lead and then to follow the twisting, grinding opening to the safety of a deep anchorage in the Tasmania Islands. A strong current set back and forth with the regular 5-foot tide, and on August 29 Larsen decided that the leads looked promising. They worked northward and soon found easier going to Bellot Strait.

With the Northwest Passage practically in their grasp, tragedy almost struck the *St. Roch* and crew in Bellot Strait. The western end of the strait was free of ice, but the tide was

Staff-Sgt. H. A. Larsen on the trail — visiting Eskimo camps.

155

changing direction to the eastward as the vessel entered. The ice from Peel Sound was carried in behind them. Half-way through the strait, Larsen suddenly saw that an ice-jam had formed ahead from shore to shore. They could not turn back and were headed for a large, thick, grounded floe. Then, just as they were about to crash and be wrecked, a smaller floe hit the larger one and broke off its southern half. The next moment the *St. Roch's* prow went into the widening crack and she drifted forward between the two floes.

The *St. Roch* left Fort Ross on September 2, surrounded by moving floes, and worked north in Prince Regent Inlet, with young slush ice already forming. The hurrying schooner entered Navy Board Inlet and stopped at the Pond Inlet post on Northern Baffin Island to discharge stores and coal for the police detachment. On September 10 she left this Eastern Arctic post and travelled through numerous bergs and storms southward along the Baffin Island and Labrador coasts.

After stopping at Labrador, Newfoundland and Sydney, Nova Scotia, the *St. Roch* and crew arrived in Halifax on October 11, having travelled 2,840 miles *en route* during their third summer season. The historic news that the *St. Roch* was the first ship to complete the west-to-east voyage through the Northwest Passage in Northern Canada was then released. To Staff-Sergeant Henry A. Larsen this historic feat was an achievement of which to be proud, but nothing about which to become excited. He and his police crew had been travelling around amid the ice-floes of the Western Arctic in good and bad seasons for fourteen years, and had conquered the Passage as a side-activity while successfully carrying on with their other police duties. Larsen discounted his long winter patrols by Eskimo dog-team and sled as something which the R.C.M. Police are doing every winter throughout the

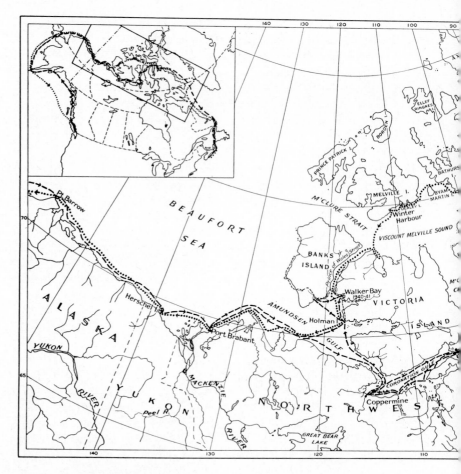

Arctic in keeping contact with our migratory Eskimo population.

During the 1943 navigation season the *St. Roch* had a change of scenery while patrolling the Eastern Arctic detachments. She entered Hudson Strait after most of the ice had gone, and had little trouble in sailing around in this new region with no ice impediment except the huge bergs met off the eastern Baffin Island coast. The Eastern Arctic, however, is not always so friendly.

During the spring of 1944 the *St. Roch* was provided with greater engine-power, one mast was removed, and she was fitted with the luxury of a new gyro-compass. The R.C.M.P. were going to patrol another route through the Arctic Islands as part of Canada's work in maintaining sovereignty over these barren, uninhabited islands, and the partnership of Larsen and the *St. Roch* was scheduled for another history-making voyage.

On July 22, 1944, the *St. Roch* left Halifax, but developed engine trouble which forced her to put in to Sydney. She left there on July 26, but had to moor again at Curling Cove, Newfoundland, to make further engine adjustments. On July 28, she put to sea once more, and thereafter had no further engine difficulties. Cape Chidley, the northern tip of Labrador, was passed on August 2, and the next day the patrol was greeted with the familiar sight of pack-ice off Baffin Island. The ice was broken, but tightly packed, and progress was impossible, so Larsen swung over to the usual open water off the Greenland coast on August 4. On August 6 he turned westward towards Baffin Island, and again met pack-ice and fog slightly south of River Clyde. For several days the gyro-compass had been unreliable, and would suddenly change 10 to 20 degrees; finally it had to be ignored as useless. Larsen's nav-

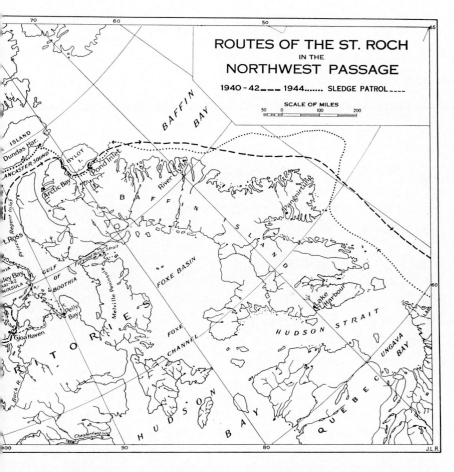

ROUTES OF THE ST. ROCH
IN THE
NORTHWEST PASSAGE

1940-42 ___ 1944 .... SLEDGE PATROL ____

SCALE OF MILES
50 0   100   200

unoccupied buildings in good condition. On the evening of August 19 the first snow fell, heralding the coming winter. Larsen and the *St. Roch* continued westward, but the coastline was usually hidden by frequent heavy snow-squalls. On August 20, they arrived at historic Erebus Bay, Beechey Island.

Wellington Channel was clear of ice as far as could be seen to the northward, but the first floes were met drifting eastward at Cornwallis Island. Larsen followed leads through the tightly-packed floes, staying inside of the line of Griffith, Somerville and Brown Islands, along the Cornwallis Island coast. Since the ice was packed solidly to the south, Larsen turned north along Cornwallis Island as far as Cape Airy, where he found leads pointing westward towards Bathurst Island, the south shore of which was obscured by a heavy snow-storm, Despite being turned and buffetted by the ice, the *St. Roch* maintained a forward course, and Cape Cockburn was reached about noon on August 23. Here solidly-packed floes blocked further progress. The tide set to the east, and the *St. Roch*

igation from then onward was by sight, experience and the wavering magnetic compass.

After a stop at Pond Inlet to un-load detachment supplies, the *St. Roch* arrived at the former R.C.M.P. post at Dundas Harbour, Devon Island, on August 18, and found the

St. Roch ready to leave Pasley Bay, August 1942, after spending eleven months there.

157

Remains of Kellett's cache on Dealey Island, 40 ft. by 14 ft., stocked with supplies to support sixty-six men for seven months.

Cairn built by Capt. Henry Kellett's expedition in H.M.S. Resolute *and* H.M.S. Intrepid *in 1852, to guide mariners to the accompanying cache.*

was carried 20 miles back to Ackland Bay before anchoring close to shore. Larsen's difficulties were further increased by the failure of his magnetic compass, which had pointed fixedly at the bow of the schooner for several days. For the remainder of the voyage he had only his Admiralty charts and amazing sense of direction upon which to depend as navigation aids. Even the sun was hidden by continous snowstorms.

Early in the morning of August 24 the *St. Roch* once more slipped along the coast to Cape Cockburn and anchored. From this high cape it could be seen that Viscount Melville Sound was filled with ice to the horizon. Since he could not proceed westward, Larsen decided to try a route north of Byam Martin Island. After patiently working back and forth from one small opening to another, shoving the floes when possible, or letting them drift by, the *St. Roch* made the north coast of Byam Martin Island on the afternoon of August 25.

August 26 began with clear weather and a fresh westerly wind. After

rounding the northern tip of Byam Island, the expedition found open water to the westward. Melville Island was soon sighted, and the men saw a herd of twelve musk-oxen grazing on the grassy lowland. Except for a long patrol by the late Inspector Ernest Joy of the R.C.M.P. to the island in 1929, no white man had visited Melville Island since Stefansson's party in 1917.

South of Griffith Point, Melville Island, the *St. Roch* was forced to travel slowly, due to shoal water of 4 to 8 fathoms for 2 miles off the coast. At midnight the expedition anchored off Palmer Point, with still no ice in sight. An excellent harbour north of the point was examined the following morning, when thick weather discouraged further sailing. At noon on August 27 the weather cleared, and they approached Dealey Island, where the huge cairn, topped by three barrels on a post, could be seen for miles at sea.

They left Dealey Island on the morning of August 28, and travelled along the low coast to Winter Har-

bour, about 30 miles to the southwest. Larsen and his crew left Winter Harbour on August 30 and had a clear run 30 miles to the south before meeting heavy ice. Due to mist and rain, they moored to a large floe to await visibility and replenished their freshwater tanks from pools on the ice. Early the following morning they began working their way through the heaviest ice yet encountered, as it pushed eastward from the Arctic Ocean through M'Clure Strait.

They drifted throughout September 1, but towards evening of September 2, after they had worked forward again, the fog lifted and a cape loomed ahead. Larsen did not know which coast of Prince of Wales Straits the cape marked, but decided to turn eastward. The cape proved to be Peel Point, and he soon realized that he was in Richard Collinson Inlet. Since there was much ice in the inlet and more pouring in behind the boat, Larsen did not consider it wise to explore the inlet to its head, and so turned around and retraced his course to Peel Point.

The *St. Roch* entered Prince of Wales Strait on September 3 in bright, clear weather. No ice blocked the passage and good time was made to the southward. Holman Island was reached in mid-afternoon of September 4, and the exciting news that the vessel had come through the Northwest Passage was given to the amazed Hudson's Bay manager. Although many explorers had spent years in unsuccessfully trying to work through the eastward-moving ice, it had taken Larsen and the *St. Roch* only eighteen days from the time they entered Lancaster Sound until they were at Holman Island in the Western Arctic.

Larsen received instructions from Ottawa to proceed outside to Vancouver and to complete the coast-to-coast voyage if he could. The *St. Roch* and her determined crew were not to be denied. Towards evening on October 16, she came into Vancouver Harbour with all flags flying and a large white banner proclaiming the successful trip through the Northwest Passage. Three hundred and sixty-eight years after Martin Frobisher first attempted to enter the Arctic, seeking a northern route, the R.C.M.P. schooner *St. Roch* became the first ship to complete the Passage in a single year from east to west, with a total elapsed time of 86 days. As Captain Larsen expressed it: "We were lucky and had the breaks. No one can predict ice or navigation conditions in the Arctic. What we accomplished this year might be repeated the next, or it might be many years. Much would depend upon the type of vessel used, and the ice conditions of that particular year. Our voyage showed that the Northwest Passage can be traversed in a single year, but does not prove that this could be accomplished every year."

Arrival in Vancouver, B.C., after successfully traversing the Northwest Passage — for the first time in a single year. St. Roch *was withdrawn from service in 1954 and after many vicissitudes has now been restored and is resting in the Maritime Museum at Vancouver, B.C.*

"*The scene is magnificent . . .*" (*Air Board file*).

"*Downward air drafts are frequently met, which have been known to force down even so powerful a machine as a DH9A, 3,000 feet at a time.*" (*Air Board file.*) *South of Golden, British Columbia, October 13, 1920.*

Although the weather was better on the 17th of October, cloud still rested on the hills. Coquihalla Pass, British Columbia.

THE FIRST
TRANS-CANADA FLIGHT—1920

by Wing Commander R. V. MANNING, DFC, CD
Director of Air Force History

The pioneers of the air route across Canada, now flown regularly by large modern jet aircraft, deserve a place in our history along with the early explorers. With them should also be remembered the "bush" pilots, who with even fewer facilities by way of weather information and airport services, made our Canadian North readily accessible and so helped to speed its development.

FOR THE THIRD time in as many days, the two weary men pointed the nose of their small, single-engined aircraft to the west and under the lowering cloud in Coquihalla pass. Twice before, the roof of the cavern

formed between the cloud and the forest top had descended until, at last, with a steeply-banked turn, the flight had had to be broken off before the aircraft became trapped in a cul-de-sac of rock, trees, and mist. To-day, the cloud appeared less dark and occasional breaks where the sun shone through gave promise of better things ahead. The base of the clouds still rested low on the hills, however, and it was not until the low-flying aircraft came out over the silvery trail made by the Fraser River in its narrow valley that the two men could let themselves think that their historic flight was nearing its end. The date was Sunday, the 17th of October, 1920, and Canada was on the point

of being spanned by air for the first time.

The Flight is Planned

All that spring and early summer the argument had waged back and forth in the Air Board offices on Sussex Street in Ottawa. Should this small organization, hardly a year old, undertake an unprecedented flight from one coast of Canada to the other? The young veterans of the First World War who staffed the Air Board were eager for an opportunity to show that the aeroplane, developed in war to a high state of utility, could transform transportation in many civilian fields. The more cautious of them, however, were keenly aware of the lack of ground

161

The F3, which had only recently arrived from the United Kingdom, was assembled in the Canadian Vickers plant in Montreal and was to be used as a standby aircraft.

facilities that existed in Canada for any kind of long-distance flight, and feared that a spectacular failure would cause aviation a set-back from which it might take years to recover. The issue had been substantially decided when Wing Commander J. S. Scott[1] on the 12th of August, 1920, sent a memorandum to the Secretary of the Air Board asking that the meeting called for the following week approve a transcontinental flight from Halifax to Vancouver to be

[1]Later Air Commodore J. S. Scott, MC, AFC.

carried out in a few weeks time — "to demonstrate the feasibility of such a flight from the commercial point of view; to prove the possibility of a fast trip from coast to coast without undue strain on the pilots or machines; and to serve as recruiting propaganda for the Canadian Air Force and to stimulate an interest in aviation by commercial firms and the public generally." His estimate of the flying time was 40 hours. The Board accepted the proposal and directed that responsibility for the enterprise

should be shared by the three arms of the Board: the Certificate Branch, the Flying Operations Branch, and the infant Canadian Air Force.

Detailed administrative arrangements were to be made by Wing Commander Scott, whose position as Superintendent of the Certificate Branch was to be designated later as Controller Civil Aviation. Landing areas had to be arranged, gasoline supplies deployed, wireless communication prepared, and civil authorities notified. In a small miracle of organization, ten sites suitable for night flying and ten sites with mooring facilities were ready when the flight began.

When it was reasonably sure that the flight would take place, letters were written to all the provinces offering to carry messages of greetings from the eastern to the western provinces. Similar letters were prepared for the principal cities en route. All correspondence was forwarded to the starting point of the flight, the air station at Dartmouth, Nova Scotia, by 25 September, 1920.

Flying was to be shared by the two

TRANS-CANADA FLIGHT
October 7-17, 1920

HALIFAX-WINNIPEG————— SEAPLANE
WINNIPEG-VANCOUVER —— AEROPLANE

0   Scale of Miles   500

VANCOUVER · MERRIT · REVELSTOKE · CALGARY · MEDICINE HAT · REGINA · WINNIPEG · KENORA · SAULT ST. MARIE · OTTAWA · RIVIÈRE DU LOUP · FREDERICTON · ST. JOHN · HALIFAX

other branches of the Air Board, the Flying Operations Branch, which had been formed the previous December under the superintendency of Wing Commander R. Leckie, DSO, DSC, DFC[2], a peppery go-getter who had returned to Canada as one of the

held commissions in the latter. When they were working in the Operations Branch on government civil operations, such as forestry patrols, they had the status of civil servants and wore civilian clothes on duty; when they served with the CAF at its

Wing Commander Leckie would take-off from the air base at Dartmouth, across the bay from Halifax, on the afternoon of the 27th of September, and would fly non-stop to Winnipeg, where he would arrive on the evening of the 28th. The aircraft

The Fairey Trans-Atlantic Seaplane, which had been redesigned from the Fairey C3, had an endurance of 30 hours and was to fly the leg from Halifax to Winnipeg non-stop.

most highly decorated aviators of the First World War, and the Canadian Air Force, formed a couple of months later on 23 February 1920, and placed under the command of Air Commodore A. K. Tylee[3], OBE, an officer of considerable administrative experience. Serving officers of both the Operations Branch and the CAF

military flying training base at Camp Borden, they wore its dark blue serge uniform. To Wing Commander Leckie and his men of the Operations Branch fell the task of completing the journey from Dartmouth to Winnipeg by "hydroplane." From there the CAF, using DH9A landplanes moved from Camp Borden for the purpose, would carry on across the prairies and over the mountains to Vancouver.

The Flight Gets Underway
Originally it had been planned that

that he would use was to be the Fairey Trans-Atlantic Seaplane[4], which had been made available to the Air Board, and was being erected at the Canadian Vickers plant at Montreal. Its reputed range of 30 hours at 60 mph would permit a non-stop flight to Winnipeg, if all went well. Things were not to go at all well, however.

With only a few days remaining

[2]Later Air Marshal R. Leckie, CB, DSO. DSC, DFC, Chief of the Air Staff, RCAF.

[3]Air Commodore Tylee had retired to civil life from the Royal Air Force after the First World War, having served as commanding officer of the large RAF training establishment in Canada towards the close of the war. He was commissioned in the Canadian Air Force and served as its chief for some eight months, when he again retired to civil life.

[4]The Fairey Trans-Atlantic Seaplane, a modification of the Fairey C3, had been designed for the trans-atlantic race of 1919, but the project was abandoned after the successful flight of Alcock and Brown.

The air station at Dartmouth, Nova Scotia, where the flight began.

The Curtiss HS2L in which Squadron Leader Shearer went to the rescue of Leckie and Hobbs.

until the planned departure date, W/C Leckie accompanied by Squadron Leader Basil Hobbs, DSO, DSC[5] left for Montreal on the 22nd, hoping to pick up their aircraft and to fly through to Dartmouth the following day. Bad weather delayed a departure initially, and then a test flight revealed that the aircraft was unable to become airborne with a full load of fuel. It was still hoped to use this aircraft for the eastern portion of the trans-Canada flight, but the start had to be postponed for ten days, and two refuelling stops added at Ottawa and Sault Ste. Marie. Also, most fortunately as it turned out, an F3 flying boat which had just been assembled at Vickers was hastily pressed into service as a spare aircraft and sent to Rivière du Loup with Flight Lieutenant H. A. Wilson as its pilot.

At Montreal, Leckie and Hobbs at last got airborne in the Fairey seaplane on the 29th of September and set out for Halifax. While they were still 14 miles west of Fredericton, the

[5]Later Group Captain Hobbs, OBE, DSO, DSC.

prevalence of fog persuaded Leckie that it would be prudent to land on the St. John River. This was accomplished successfully, but heavy rain that pelted down on the aircraft caused a complete failure of the aircraft ignition system. The Air Board had to be wired for two mechanics and spare magnetos. By the night of the 3rd of October, repairs to the engine were complete, but the number of logs in this part of the swollen river prevented a take-off. The aircraft had to be towed to Fredericton, developing on the way a leak in the aft compartment of one float. On the morning of the 4th Leckie and Hobbs attempted to take-off again, but the aircraft would not leave the water — "probably owing to water in float." Repairs could only be made after the aircraft was slung under a foot bridge. At last, on the afternoon of the 5th, the aircraft was serviceable once more, and the two men took off for Halifax, arriving without further incident.

Bad weather postponed the take-off of the trans-Canada flight for one

day in the Halifax area, but, on the 7th, the two pilots lifted their aircraft into the air at 8 AM with its precious bag of letters, and set course for the west. A message dropped by Leckie over Saint John at 10.47 AM, reporting "am bucking a 40 mile north-west wind; machine and engine OK", gave reassurance that the first trans-Canada flight was successfully on its way at last.

Halifax to Ottawa

The absence of detailed and up-to-date weather reports en route was to handicap the flight throughout. At the time that Leckie and Hobbs had planned to be well on their way to Rivière du Loup, Flight Lieutenant Wilson, who was standing by at that city with the F3 flying boat, was sending a message to the Air Board: "Very strong north-west wind and heavy sea running", ending on what for him, undoubtedly was not a frivolous note: "Please advance some money." Things meanwhile were not going according to plan with Wing Commander Leckie.

When the seaplane left Halifax that morning, it had been intended that Squadron Leader A. B. Shearer, the officer in charge of the air base at Dartmouth, would accompany the trans-Canada aircraft in a single-engine Curtiss HS2L flying boat as far as Saint John, in case Leckie had trouble. Unfortunately, turbulent air over Halifax harbour made the HS2L so difficult to control that Shearer developed a cramp in a leg that had suffered a war wound, which forced him to return to Dartmouth. Consequently, he was on the ground when word was received that Leckie and Hobbs had crashed west of Saint John. He took off at once and, after contending with rough air for four hours, and a cramp in his leg that forced him to seek the aid of his mechanic on the rudder, he landed near the disabled Fairey Seaplane at Whelpley's Point on the St. John River.

Leckie and Hobbs had been uninjured in a forced landing made necessary by the loss of the engine cowlings, which probably had been weakened by a stormy passage over the Bay of Fundy. One cowling, as it broke away, had damaged an externally mounted pump, which released fuel that blew into the face of Leckie at the controls. At the same time the airstream, no longer directed by the engine cowlings, flowed under the fabric covering of the fuselage, loosening it, and causing it to flap like a banner about the tail surfaces of the aircraft. Only airmanship of a high order on the part of the pilot permitted the aircraft to be landed with no more than moderate damage to the propellor, an undercarriage strut, and a float.

On Shearer's arrival, the stranded pilots lost no time in taking over his aircraft and flying to Fredericton for fuel, landing a few minutes after 6 PM. After the lapse of an hour, they were airborne again, flying a compass course in misty weather for Rivière du Loup, four hours away, where shortly before midnight they landed in the dark under a low ceiling and in a driving rainstorm.

The original plan had called for only a refuelling stop at Rivière du Loup[6], and a night landing at Ottawa. Leckie, a short time before the departure from Halifax, had received a message from the Air Board assuring him: "all deadheads removed from river Rockcliffe with exception one tree on which a red light will be hung."[7] The very bad weather at Rivière du Loup made a night departure inadvisable, so the airmen transferred their gear and bag of letters, to the F3, and waited for dawn[8]. The storm was only slightly abated at 6.20 AM of the 8th when the F3, driving through waves that broke over the top plane of the aircraft, lifted itself from the water and headed up the St. Lawrence bound

[6]The flight was dependent on extensive help from local authorities along the route. At Rivière du Loup, for example, buoys had been put in place by the local authorities but an exceptionally high tide had submerged them and they had had to be put in place a second time. Warm appreciation for the help received from Mayor Viel and other citizens of this city is expressed in the files. Letters of thanks to governmental agencies and private persons take up a substantial part of one file.

[7]A novel arrangement at Ottawa when a night landing was expected was to be the firing of rockets from the Government Printing Bureau at ten-minute intervals 15 minutes after the aircraft was sighted passing Grenville 50 miles down the river from that city.

[8]Foreman mechanic C. W. Heath, who had assembled the F3 at Montreal, joined the crew at Rivière du Loup for the flight to Winnipeg.

165

for Ottawa. For the first part of the journey the cloud base was at 300 feet, but by the time that Montreal was passed at 10.55, the weather had cleared and the aircraft proceeded to Ottawa in brilliant sunshine, landing at Rockcliffe at 12.30.

Departure from Ottawa had to be postponed until the following morning because of an unserviceable engine, giving the crew a well-deserved rest, and permitting Wing Commander Leckie to deliver the letter from the Mayor of Halifax to the

Some of the pilots standing by at Winnipeg on O...ant C. W. Cudamore is in the centre.

The crew who took the F3 through to Winnipeg are, left to right: Flight Lieutenant G. O. Johnson, Squadron Leader B. D. Hobbs, Wing Commander R. Leckie, and Foreman Mechanic C. W. Heath.   W/C R. G. Ford (ret'd)

Mayor of Ottawa, and to arrange for the letters fo the mayors of Fredericton, Quebec and Montreal, which had not been dropped as planned, to be sent to them by rail.

Ottawa to Winnipeg

When the F3[9] departed from Ottawa at 8.45 AM on the 9th, Flight Lieutenant G. O. Johnson had joined Wing Commander Leckie and Squadron Leader Hobbs as navigator for the long, difficult flight to Winnipeg.

The aircraft passed without incident over Pembroke, Mattawa, North Bay, Little Current, Blind River and Thessalon, landing at Sault Ste. Marie at 4.35 PM. Mechanic J. E. Davies, who had been sent ahead as a ground party, serviced the aeroplane, bit a dense fog that had settled in frustrated an attempt to take off that evening. By the following morning, Sunday the 10th, the fog lifted sufficiently for the aircraft to depart

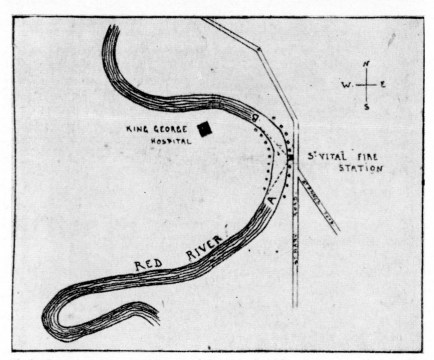

The landing arrangements at Winnipeg included two rows of flares (dots) and two searchlights (dotted lines) between A and B on the river for a night landing. Bad weather forced the F3 to land in the Red River at Selkirk instead.

[9]The F3 had as gallant a crew as could be found anywhere. Wing Commander Leckie had the distinction of being the only Canadian to destroy two Zeppelins in the recent World War, Squadron Leader Hobbs was the only Canadian to destroy both a Zeppelin and a submarine, and Flight Lieutenant Johnson, while serving as a fighter pilot on the Western Front, had acquired the creditable score of 13 enemy aircraft destroyed.

rangements for its share of the flight. Of the four DH9A bombers brought west by rail from Camp Borden, one had been assembled at Morley, Alberta, and was now waiting at Calgary with Flight Lieutenant G. A. Thompson, who would fly the last leg of the flight. Of the three remaining aircraft, which had been assembled at Winnipeg by a party of six airmen from Borden under the charge of Flight Sergeant R. G. Ford[10], one had been sent to Moose

and Air Commodore Tylee, the head of the Canadian Air Force, as passenger.

As soon as the letters had been received from Leckie, the two men took off into the night sky. It was 4.30 on Monday morning, the 11th of October[13]. Dawn was an hour away.

Spotters reported the aircraft over Grenfell at 7.39 AM and Regina at 8.45 AM. A report that the aircraft has passed safely by Regina was premature. Trouble was developing

[10]Later Wing Commander R. G. Ford, RCAF (ret'd). An Air Board memorandum at the time the trans-Canada flight was being planned expressed the hope that: " — the presence of a man of Ford's type in C.A.F. uniform in the west will do much to stimulate recruiting."

[13]One of the shivering spectators of the pre-dawn take-off was an early Canadian pilot who later became a distinguished aviation historian, Mr. Frank Ellis, who has reported his feelings at the time: "We were greatly impressed by the determination of the flyers to keep going. Nothing but the most threatening weather was allowed to delay them." *Canada's Flying Heritage* by Frank H. Ellis.

the western half of the flight. Flight Lieuten-

at 7.30 AM, crossing Lake Superior in 4½ hours, and landing at Kenora at 3.55 PM EST, for a total flight time of 8 hours and 25 minutes.

A leaking engine radiator delayed the departure of the aircraft from Kenora until 8.15 PM CST. The Winnipeg River made a convenient navigational aid and was followed northwestward to Lake Winnipeg. From this point, a course was set for the mouth of the Red River; then the river was followed to the south by the reflection of the sky in the water, until an increasing ground mist made it evident that Winnipeg could not be reached. A night landing was made at Selkirk, and the letters were sent to Winnipeg by train so that the flight could continue by landplane at dawn. The next morning, Leckie brought the F3 to Winnipeg to complete the first half of the transcontinental flight.

Winnipeg to Vancouver

While Leckie had been making his way from Halifax to Winnipeg in the face of varied misfortunes, the Canadian Air Force had completed ar-

Flight Lieutenant Cudamore and Air Commodore Tylee arriving at Calgary on 11 October 1920.

Jaw, with Flight Lieutenant C. W. Cudamore[11] as pilot, to serve as a relay aircraft; one had crashed on a test flight; and the third was standing by at St. Charles's aerodrome, Winnipeg, with Flight Lieutenant J. B. Home-Hay, MC, DFC[12], the pilot,

[11]F/L Cudamore, MC, DFC, was on the reserve and had been called up for training.

[12]Flight Lieutenant Home-Hay, MC, DFC, had had an active career on the Western Front in artillery co-operation. He too had been called up for training with the C.A.F., after which he returned to civilian life.

in the DH9A's Liberty engine, and Home-Hay made an unscheduled landing at the latter place. Cudamore was hastily summoned from Moose Jaw with his standby aircraft and Thompson was instructed to leave Calgary for Medicine Hat. At 11 AM CST, little more than two hours after the trouble developed, Cudamore and Tylee took off for Medicine Hat, arriving there at 1.45 PM MST, and meeting Thompson with the last DH9A. The two aircraft then took off at 3.10 PM, landing at Calgary at 5.10 PM[14].

Flight Lieutenant Thompson had intended to depart with Air Commodore Tylee the following morning, but " — snow, rain, and fog in the mountains" forced a postponement until Wednesday, the 13th, when they got airborne at 11.55 AM. Heavy broken cloud filled Kicking Horse Pass, but they were able to pick their way through, landing at 3.10 PM at the Crowle Ranch, four miles south of Revelstoke, to be greeted by the mayor and a substantial number of townspeople.

Very bad weather now settled into the area and no attempt could be made to pursue the flight until Friday, the 15th, when the weather improved somewhat. At 11.50 AM, the aircraft lumbered into the air and, in the absence of a head wind to contend with, made good a ground speed of 98 mph, until cloud began to close in on the aeroplane as it attempted to proceed through Coquihalla Pass in the Selkirks, and there was no recourse but to land at Merritt.

On the third attempt to get through the pass, made two days later on Sunday the 17th, success was not assured until the bright ribbon of the Fraser could be seen beneath the aircraft. Even yet there were anxious moments as the cloud base lowered and the aircraft had to be flown closer to the floor of the canyon, but at last the two men were out from between the rocks and over the flat delta country. They knew that their goal would be reached. At 11.25 PST, the DH9A was set down on Minoru Park, Vancouver, ten and one half days after the start of the trans-Canada flight[15] and after a total flying time of 49 hours and 7 minutes.

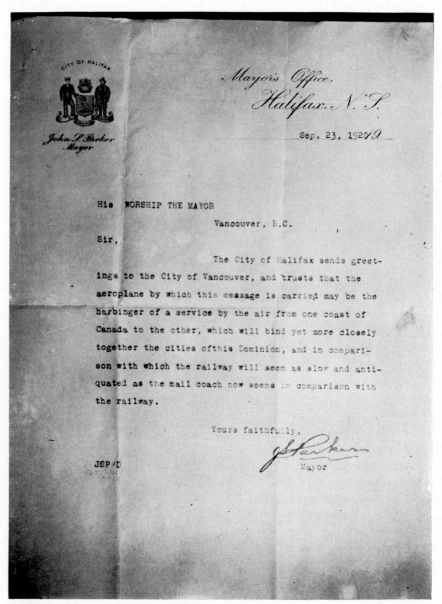

Contents of the letter from the Mayor of Halifax to the Mayor of Vancouver taken on the trans-Canada flight.

The Flight in Retrospect

The first flight in Canada from coast to coast had taken over 49 hours flying time, spread over ten and a half days, instead of a planned 40 hours in two days, but the Air Board could take satisfaction in its accomplishment. A "pioneer effort" had demonstrated that long-distance flight by night and day was quite feasible in Canada. Air fields would have to be built, aicraft given a means of communication with the ground, and "wireless directional apparatus (placed) on the ground to guide the machines as they are flying." Not even the most optimistic member of the Air Board, however, likely foresaw the transformation of long-distance transportation of mail and people that aviation was to bring about in Canada in the short space of four

[14]Flight Lieutenant Thompson, described by a contemporary as " — a man to remember," was a skilled and resourceful pilot who had been chosen for the dangerous mountain leg of the flight for this reason. In later years he had a successful career in civil aviation.

[15]Although the official log of the flight makes no mention of a stop at Agassiz on the last morning of the flight, it would seem from Vancouver newspaper reports of the day examined by Frank Ellis that one was made. There is a reference in the files to the probability that one would be made. No reason is apparent for a stop on one of the shortest legs of the trans-Canada flight (155 miles).

decades, a reduction in transcontinental time, for example, quite as pronounced as that brought about by the building of the first Canadian transcontinental railway.

Epilogue

A return flight across the country that had been planned was discussed but was quietly dropped. Thompson's DH9A was sent back to Calgary by rail and, together with Cudamore's aircraft, handed over to the Air Board base at Morley, Alberta. The other two were dismantled at Winnipeg. The F3 spent the winter in storage on the bank of the Red River. The HS2L, which filled in so capably on the first leg of the flight, went back to Dartmouth. As for the Fairey Transatlantic Seaplane, a signal on the 7th of October ordered its

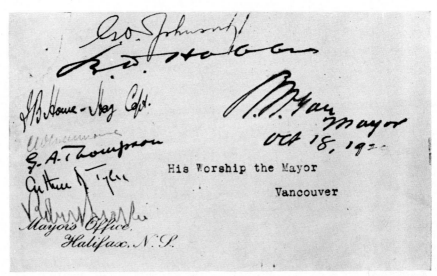

The envelope of the letter opposite, bearing the signatures of the pilots who participated in the actual trans-Canada flight.

dismantling and removal to Dartmouth, the last reference in the records to a little known aircraft that

had had a part to play in binding Canada more closely together "a mari usque ad mare."

Mayor Gale welcomes Air Commodore Tylee and Flight Lieutenant Thompson to Vancouver.

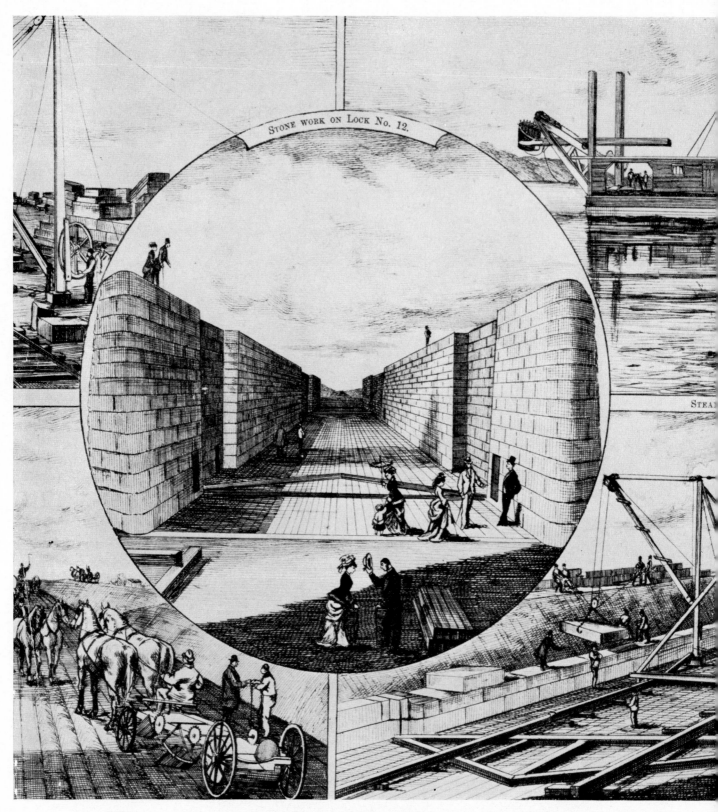

STONE WORK ON LOCK No. 12.

Scenes at the construction of the third Welland Canal, which took fourteen years to build. From sketches by C. J. Dyers in Canadian Illustrated News, January 1876.

THE WELLAND CANAL

by LYN HARRINGTON

The Niagara River was the chief barrier to construction of the St. Lawrence Seaway, and the Welland Canal was the first section in Canada to be built to Seaway standards. This account appeared in the Canadian Geographical Journal *in May, 1947, when completion of the Seaway was an active topic of inter-governmental discussions.*

WHERE NIAGARA's jade-green waters hurl themselves over their precipice to surge down through the gorge, Nature presents one of her greatest challenges to the builders of a nation. In its 28-mile length from Lake Erie to Lake Ontario, the Niagara River drops 326 feet, half of its plunge at the spectacular Niagara Falls.

That mighty cascade wreathed in spray held back navigation for many a year after the first explorers gazed on it in awe mixed with exasperation. The turbulent stream cutting its way deep through the canyon was a tide which no canoe could stem.

In the days of the fur brigades, portages could be made around lesser rapids without too much difficulty, or canoes could be "lined up" from the shore. Niagara Falls, over which the freshwater seas and rivers innumerable poured their drainage, presented a vastly greater impediment.

Portage trails on either side of the Falls carried freight and birchbark canoes. A road from Queenston to Chippawa was opened in 1791, but was expensive in manpower and in toll charges. Moreover, it was risky due to the activities of bandits.

Sailing vessels did manage to get around the Falls, but only by man's sweat and strain. In 1810, a vessel of 100 tons was placed on skids and in winter was hauled over the Portage Road down the mountain at Queenston and launched in the Niagara River there. On at least two other occasions during the War of 1812, transport boats of considerable size were taken up the escarpment and launched at Chippawa for service on Lake Erie — no mean undertaking.

Immediately after the war, the Americans commenced the barge canal connecting Lake Erie with the port of New York, by way of the Mohawk Valley. This would mean that goods coming from the upper lakes would be trans-shipped at Buffalo, and the traffic drained through American canals to American ports. This project was viewed with alarm by Canadians, and patriotic feeling ran high. The future development of Canada was bound up with the Lake Ontario-St. Lawrence highway to the Atlantic.

Enthusiasm for the construction of a canal on Canadian territory was whipped up. It was to be placed well back from the frontier which American troops had overrun a few short years before. Those in authority had misgivings, some even to the extent of hampering the venture. But a few men of the Niagara Peninsula, notably William Hamilton Merritt, pushed on the project. A private company was formed, stock sold, and the first sod was turned in November of 1824.

The Barrier is Conquered

The first Welland Canal began at Twelve Mile Creek, back from the frontier. The builders utilized natural water-courses as much as possible to save expense and labour. The route led up the Twelve Mile Creek from Port Dalhousie on Lake Ontario, following its wavering course to the escarpment. Here a "deep cut" had to be made across the height of land to the waters of the Chippawa Creek (sometimes known as the Welland River). Another long channel led from the Grand River 27 miles away, to serve as a feeder.

Five years later, two small schooners made the first water passage between the lakes. Slowly they passed up the little canal with its forty wooden locks, its shallow draft of eight feet, and its narrow 22-foot prisms. From the "deep cut" they turned into Chippawa Creek, and thus down into the Niagara River.

This route was followed for the next four years. Usually sailing vessels had to be towed up the Niagara against its strong current and unfavourable winds. A "horned breeze" as the sailors called it, was provided by eight to fourteen yoke of oxen hauling from the tow-path. Ice jams in early spring also held up navigation. An extension of the canal was therefore necessary. It was made directly south of Port Robinson on the Chippawa Creek, to Lake Erie, a tremendous undertaking. Miles of rock had to be pierced with the simple tools of those days. The low waters of the creek were led below the canal by an aqueduct. To hinder matters further, an epidemic of cholera broke out, killing many of the labourers.

The new water highway was widely touted in order to bring settlers and trade development to the Niagara Peninsula. In short order, grist and

171

saw mills, potteries and tanneries, cement plants and soap factories sprang up along its banks, using the water power and taking advantage of the transportation provided.

Almost as soon as the first canal was completed, the need was seen for a larger one. In 1842, the provincial government of Upper Canada bought all the shares, and immediately set to work enlarging and straightening out

the canal. Today, only a few remnants of the first locks may be seen, the great squared oak timbers still showing the marks of the adze.

In three years the work was completed, enabling sailing vessels of 750 tons cargo capacity to pass from lake to lake. It was the heyday of the sailing vessels. Schooners predominated, with a following of barques, brigs, sloops and scows. There were some

steamers with their exposed side paddle wheels, and the number of screw propellers increased steadily.

The canal had a 9-foot draft. Twenty-seven locks built of fieldstone, with wooden gates, replaced the numerous locks of the first canal. Scores of horses and mules were employed in towing boats and barges through the canal, a tedious passage. Paper mills sprang up, along with other industries. The new canal gave considerable impetus to industry, and caused some shifts in population.

When the third canal was built, part of this second canal was abandoned. Converted into hydraulic raceways, its waters are now used by numerous paper mills and other industries along its banks. Birds nest in the decaying timbers of the old wooden lock gates, and muskrats tunnel their dens in its reaches.

Confederation of the provinces in 1867 placed inland waterways under federal jurisdiction. The third canal was therefore a much more ambitious project. It was begun in 1873 and was fourteen years a-growing. The number of locks was slightly reduced, the canal was widened to 45 feet, almost twice its previous width, and the draft was deepened to 14 feet. The canals on the St. Lawrence were deepened and widened correspondingly, thus providing a gateway to the upper lakes for ocean vessels of that day.

The course of the third canal utilized much of the previous channel, but swung to the east of Thorold, in a flight of locks designed to carry vessels over the escarpment. Steamdriven freighters of 2,700 tons cargo capacity, and requiring a depth of 14 feet, shuttled back and forth through the canal. The volume of shipping grew steadily year by year. By 1928, seven and a half million tons of water-borne freight were passing through the Welland Canal yearly.

As the shipments of wheat and ore from the head of the lakes increased, larger ships were needed to carry this

THE FOUR WELLAND CANALS
DIAGRAMMATIC COMPARISONS

FIRST WELLAND CANAL
STARTED 1824 —— COMPLETED 1829

TYPICAL VESSEL
LENGTH 100 FT – CARGO CAPACITY 165 TONS

TYPICAL LOCK

LENGTH BETWEEN GATES ....110 FT.
WIDTH OF LOCK .... 22 FT.
DEPTH OF WATER OVER SILLS......8 FT.
SINGLE LIFTS ....6 FT. TO 11 FT.
NUMBER OF LOCKS................39

SECOND WELLAND CANAL
STARTED 1842 —— COMPLETED 1845

TYPICAL VESSEL
LENGTH 140 FT – CARGO CAPACITY 750 TONS

TYPICAL LOCK

LENGTH BETWEEN GATES........ 150 FT.
WIDTH OF LOCK ....26 FT. 6 IN.
DEPTH OF WATER OVER SILLS...... 9 FT.
SINGLE LIFTS....9 FT. 6 IN. TO 14 FT. 3 IN.
NUMBER OF LOCKS................27

THIRD WELLAND CANAL
STARTED 1875 —— COMPLETED 1887

TYPICAL VESSEL
LENGTH 255 FT – CARGO CAPACITY 2700 TONS

TYPICAL LOCK

LENGTH BETWEEN GATES......270 FT.
WIDTH OF LOCK...........45 FT.
DEPTH OF WATER OVER SILLS.....14 FT.
SINGLE LIFTS..........12 FT. TO 16 FT.
NUMBER OF LOCKS..............26

WELLAND SHIP CANAL
STARTED 1913 —— COMPLETED 1932-33

LENGTH BETWEEN INNER GATES___859 FT.
WIDTH OF LOCK_____80 FT.
DEPTH OF WATER OVER SILLS____30 FT. (REACHES 25 FT.)

SINGLE LIFTS_____46 FT. 6 IN.
NUMBER OF LOCKS__ INCLUDING 3 TWIN_____8
TOTAL LOCKAGE_____325 FT. 6 IN.

THE GUARD LOCK AT HUMBERSTONE IS 1380 FT LONG BETWEEN INNER GATES

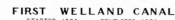

TYPICAL LOCK

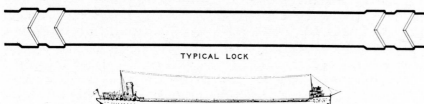

TYPICAL VESSEL
MAXIMUM LENGTH 620 FT. & CARGO CAPACITY 25000 TONS AT 24 FT. DRAFT.

The opening of the first Welland Canal in 1829. The Ann and Jane of Upper Canada was the first vessel through.

freight economically. Trans-shipment to smaller boats at the Welland Canal was costly. The canal had become a bottle-neck to navigation. To remedy this situation the fourth, or Welland Ship Canal, was planned. During the years of its construction, the third canal was maintained in operation. Part of its course was retained, much of it abandoned. Some of it has been filled in; part serves as supply weir and pondage for the fourth canal. Near Thorold, east of the ship canal, may be seen the old flight of locks. The masonry walls are chinked with grasses and moss, and a quiet atmosphere of forgetfulness lies over the picturesque ruins.

These remnants of the first lock still show the marks of the adze on the oak timbers.

Bound for Lake Erie, these ships must pass over the syphon culvert by which the waters of Chippawa Creek are carried beneath the canal.

The twin flight locks at Thorold.

Waiting its turn to be unloaded outside Thorold, a pulp freighter from the north shore of the St. Lawrence ties up at the dock.

The Welland Ship Canal

Work on the new Welland Canal was on heroic proportions. The canal must be built to look after more than existing vessels, large enough for the needs of several generations. The Dominion of Canada therefore in 1913, took steps to construct such a channel. Work began that year, and carried on until halted by World War I.

Unsettled conditions and high prices held up construction for a time. Engineering problems demanded the utmost care and consideration, but all were met and solved. In 1932, the Governor-General of Canada, the Earl of Bessborough, officially opened the Welland Ship Canal. "I hereby declare the Welland Ship Canal open to the commerce of the world," he said gravely as he turned the lever.

The course was radically changed at the Lake Ontario end of the canal, so that it runs practically in a straight line across the Peninsula, a distance of nearly 28 miles. An expenditure of $130 million has been justified in the increased tonnage, which in 1945 was almost twice that of the best years of the previous canal. Especially during the war years was the canal a vital artery to Canada and the United States.

The ship canal starts at Ten Mile Creek, three miles east of its former entrance. An artificial harbour was built and excavated to a depth of 25 feet, which may be deepened by dredging. Embankments a mile and a half long reach out into Lake Ontario to protect the entrance to the canal. Temporary railway tracks were laid down during construction to bring rock and earth from the excavations farther up the canal. The ends and inner sides of the embankments are reinforced with concrete.

The new canal has a width of 80 feet in the locks, and is much wider in the canal reaches, 310 feet being the narrowest. The depth of water over the sills in the locks is 30 feet. Seven locks, and one guard lock, have replaced the forty tiny locks of the first canal. The locks have a usable length of 820 feet, and lift the ships 46½ feet at each lock.

Safety devices are used throughout the canal. Radiophones, telephones, special construction of the massive gates, and steel fender-booms reduce the danger of accidents in the canal. Moreover all controlling machinery operating the valves, gates, fenders and signals is so electrically interlocked as to protect the equipment of the locks and prevent disasters.

Twenty highway or railway bridges span the Welland Canal. Eleven are of the vertical-lift type, whereby the bridge rises horizontally into the air, between tall towers, giving a clearance of 120 feet from the surface of the water. They move surprisingly quickly with heavy weights and chains counterbalancing the weight of the bridge. Power to operate the bridge costs only four and a half cents each time the bridge is raised. Gasoline motors are also maintained in case of failure of electricity.

Other bridges are of the bascule or rocking-chair movement type. Great concrete bases counterbalance the weight of the moving span as the bridge cants upward to an 80-degree angle. A ship hustles by, and the bridge locks down in place once more. Only two swing bridges of the turntable type are used on the canal for the railroads, since they limit the width of the shipping lane.

Through the Canal

Past the harbour light, past the lighthouse, steams a freighter; entering the canal at Port Weller, it glides between the long piers guarding the approach to the first lock. The first seven miles of the canal south from Lake Ontario lead through the intensively cultivated fields and orchards of the Niagara Peninsula. Three locks lift the ship a total of nearly 140 feet, bringing it to the foot of the escarpment.

Most impressive is the flight of twin locks at Thorold, similar to those at Gatun on the Panama Canal, but of greater height. These locks are built in double flight, so that ships

may mount to Lake Erie on one side, while other ships are locking through downbound on the opposite flight. At the foot of the flight locks is the power house with its surge tank, which supplies electricity throughout the canal for lighting and operating all locks and bridges. Not far off are the remnants of the third canal, which store additional water for the operation of the flight locks.

The flight locks comprise Locks 4, 5 and 6, a triple set which together elevate the ship another 140 feet in less than half a mile. Lock 7, very slightly farther along, raises the ship another 46½ feet, bringing it to the level of Lake Erie. A guard gate above this lock is maintained in case of any disaster on the canal below.

Beyond are highway and railway bridges, and the canal stretches across lush farming country. The wayfarer is amazed to see ships apparently sailing across the fields, through windbreaks of grey-green Russian olive trees, and other trees of rapid growth.

At the city of Welland, the ship

steams over a most interesting feat of engineering. Where the canal crosses the sluggish Chippawa Creek, a siphon culvert carries the waters down and across underneath the canal. Each of the six huge tubes is large enough to accommodate the

The gates are gone from the flight locks of the third canal, where they mounted the escarpment east of Thorold, but the rivers are picturesque.

biggest locomotive. Great difficulties attended this piece of construction.

Just a mile from Port Colborne, at Humberstone is the longest lock in the world, a guard lock. It brings the vessels to the fluctuating level of Lake Erie, the lift being determined from day to day by the lake itself. The lake is given to rapid variations caused by the wind direction, and the difference in level may be as great as eleven feet. From that last lock, through the Port Colborne channel, out into the harbour with its breakwaters and lighthouses, the ship steams into Lake Erie.

Canal Shipping

She has passed many other vessels in the course of her seven- to nine-hour journey through the Welland Ship Canal. The traffic is of international character, much of it originating in American ports. Tramp steamers from the seven seas ply up and down the lakes, picking up cargoes here, unloading there. The cargo might be a load of bulbs from Holland, poppy seed or enamelling clay, odd items of manufacture from the Scandinavian countries, or vintage wines of France.

Tankers carrying gasoline, kerosene or fuel oil, with the warning red flags flying amidships, move smartly through the canal. Tugs and barges pass in orderly fashion through the locks and canal prisms. "Upper lakers" steam ponderously across the countryside carried by water. "Canalers" shuttle back and forth with cargoes of grain from the government elevator at Port Colborne, with iron ore for Hamilton, with package freight or coal. Huge pulp piles rise at the mills as the freighters bring in loads of logs from the north shore of the St. Lawrence or of Lake Superior. Sulphite, limestone, agricultural products traverse the canal, since water shipping is still much less costly than any other means of transportation.

Pig-boats towed by powerful ships, gleaming yachts making passage through for regatta or cruise, whale-backs — that novelty of the lakes — and the occasional passenger liner making a cruise to the Thousand Islands of the St. Lawrence, all contribute colour and interest to the shipping scene.

With no thought of catering to tourists, the Welland Canal has nevertheless proved of great interest to visitors. Extensive afforestation has been done along the banks of the canal, and many of the trees have now reached a considerable height. The roots bind the soil of the banks, halting erosion and, more important, serve as windbreaks, protecting the ships in the canal. The park-like areas along the canal are not only useful, but transform a gaunt concrete commercial waterway into a zone of scenic beauty. Many varieties of

birds add song and vivid life, outstanding being the flashing activities of the black-capped tern.

The founders of the first Welland Canal would see their dream realized in the vigorous industrial life that flourishes along the waterway. With cheap electrical power and an adequate labour supply, with transportation by rail, highway and water available to bring in raw materials, the area has had everything to make it develop and prosper beyond their imaginings.

The Welland Ship Canal has meant incalculable advantage to the whole country in the development of both internal and export trade; so much so that a distinguished observer* declared: "It is the lung of Canada, carrying commerce into our arteries and remote veins, expelling our goods, our wheat, our minerals."

With the enlargement of the St. Lawrence canals, the Welland Ship Canal will increase in strategic importance and value. Our inland harbours will become ocean ports, and on a scale greater than ever before, "open to the commerce of the world."

*Bruce Hutchison, *The Unknown Country.*

Rapids in a by-pass channel at Merritton, now used only for power purposes. Remains of now-unused portions of the first, second and third canals and associated works may still be seen.

177

C.W.A.C. officer cadets on an afternoon route march at Ste. Anne de Bellevue, Quebec.

The first airwomen of the R.C.A.F. at the Manning Depot in Toronto in October 1941.

Probationary Wrens on parade at the basic training establishment at Galt, Ontario.

CANADIAN WOMEN ON
ACTIVE SERVICE

World War II brought demands on Canadian manpower for the armed services, for industry and for the farms which could not have been met without the great effort put forward by Canadian women in all three sectors. This article, which appeared in the December 1943 issue of the Canadian Geographical Journal *explains their part in the armed services. Their contribution to industry and to agriculture was at least as great.*

WOMEN in the Forces were an innovation which Canadians were hesitant to accept at first, just two years ago. It was "unwomanly". If woman's place was not still exclusively in the home, it at least wasn't in the uniform of her country. There was gossip for a while. Even Commanding Officers did not want women cluttering up their establishments. That was at first.

The first trained detachments which went out to the camps and air stations changed that. It was only a matter of days before hard-bitten critics had to admit that those girls could do the jobs they had assumed just as well as any man, sometimes better. They quickly recognized, too, a change in the demeanour of the men: the men became a little more careful of their appearance — and their language.

Those first detachments have been followed by an ever-growing flow of Canadian young women into the Services. At present there are more

than 32,000 in the Women's Royal Canadian Naval Service, Canadian Women's Army Corps and Royal Canadian Air Force. From all walks of life, they have taken over jobs which were formerly done by men, thus releasing them to join their fighting comrades, the job for which they enlisted.

Starting with the taking over of such familiar duties as office work and the preparation and service of food, the women of the Services have proved their adaptability to a steadily lengthening list of Service trades, many never before done by women, many done much better by women.

The only practical limits now on the scope of women's employment in the Services are their numbers and their physical inability to do the heavier types of work.

The Services sift out potential recruits carefully within the general qualifications: that they are between the ages of 18 and 45, in good health, have at least Grade VIII schooling and are single, or married without dependent children.

On acceptance, new recruits are given four to five weeks of basic training, the Navy at Galt, Ontario, the Army at Kitchener, Ontario, and Vermilion, Alberta, and the Air Force at Rockcliffe, Ontario, just outside Ottawa. There they are documented, inoculated, fitted with uniforms and completely equipped. The courses give considerable physical training and drill, instruct them in general Service regulations, etiquette and procedure. This is essentially a period of transition from civil to Service life.

With the completion of basic training the girls go to various trade schools where they are given specialists' courses in diverse trades for which they have been selected on a basis of experience and aptitude. These courses vary from two weeks to three or four months, and, in some cases, six months.

When the new recruit finally takes up her regular duties, she usually finds herself living in barracks. Her posting may be anywhere and will likely be changed within a year. The girls are encouraged to make their quarters as home-like as possible.

Their general welfare is a major consideration of their officers. Meals are the best and scientifically pre-pared. Health is closely watched, as is their social welfare. While the girls work hard and often long, they also have time for fun. They have their own recreation rooms, where they may entertain friends several evenings a week. Week-end passes are granted when routine permits.

As the tempo of the war rises women are bound to play an increasingly vital role in Canada's Armed Forces. While the pool of available manpower is lower than ever, more and more men will be required to do the actual fighting, to man the ships, the planes, the tanks, the guns. That means more and more Canadian women will be required to take over non-combatant duties in the Services, just as the women of Britain, Russia, China and the United States have done in their hundreds of thousands.

ROYAL CANADIAN AIR FORCE (W.D.)
By Wing Officer WILLA WALKER, Senior Staff Officer, Women's Division

THE Women's Division is part of Canada's blueprint for victory; a print in Royal Canadian Air Force blue. It is a monument to the foresight of those who, in war days of 1940, looked to a time when all-out aerial warfare would impose such requirements of manpower on the Dominion that womanpower would be needed in the second line.

For this there was precedent. The Royal Air Force, even before that time, had begun to rely on the Women's Auxiliary Air Force — the "WAAF" — for much of the ground staff duty that helps keep aircraft flying. During the Battle of Britain they proved more than worthy of the responsibilities that were theirs, accepting the rigours of active service life like veterans, and sticking to their jobs in the face of great danger.

Accordingly, the Canadian Women's Auxiliary Air Force came into being by Order-in-Council dated July 2nd, 1941. Shortly after its first recruits went on active service the name was changed to the Woman's

trucks and carried their kitbags around an ice-covered parade square to their barracks. Then they lined up in the drill hall to be interviewed and assigned to their duties.

That was the beginning. After-

wards, squadrons of airwomen went to new schools of the Air Training Plan week by week till every Service Flying Training and Bombing and Gunnery School of the R.C.A.F. had its staff of airwomen. The service grew, and so did its roster of duties: airwomen in the control towers, timing the flying hours of student pilots; airwomen in the hangars as aircraft helpers, testing spark plugs, cleaning aircraft, doing light maintenance work; airwomen plotting student bombers' scores.

By June of 1942, the first group of operations' room clerks were completing training, preparing for duty in the secret "ops rooms" of Canada's coastal defence, where aircraft, shipping and submarine movements are charted. In July of that year, airwomen sailed for Newfoundland; the first to be posted for duty outside Canada. Less than a month later, a draft of airwomen, trained for Air Force clerical duties, left for Britain, the first draft of any of Canada's women's services to sail overseas.

The brass band of the R.C.A.F. (*Women's Division*) leads a graduation parade at Rock-cliffe.

Christening ceremony at HMCS Conestoga, Wren basic training establishment at Galt, Ontario.

Division, recognizing the fact that it is not and never has been, an auxiliary, but an integral part of the Royal Canadian Air Force.

They enlisted, as men did, "for the duration". Their officers were granted the King's Commission after first entering the ranks. The first group reported for duty at the Service Flying Training School at Uplands, near Ottawa, on January 3rd, 1942. In the six months of its existence the Women's Division had enlisted and trained its first officers, enlisted its first squadrons of airwomen, and trained them, too, in the life of the Air Force.

At seven-thirty of a freezing morning, after an all-night journey in day coaches, they climbed out of big blue

Out on the tarmac at a service flying training school. Airwomen in dungarees and "station" caps help service training aircraft. Many of the components in the aircraft will also have been given routine maintenance by airwomen specialists in various fields.

Soon, airwomen entered the trade of photographer, taking an eleven weeks' course that qualifies them for more than mere shutter-snapping. They learn to load aerial cameras, to process films, to operate enlargers, to patch the pictorial mosaics that mark a "Target for To-night". Others studied the Morse code, then learned to read that same code by Aldis lamp flashes; to interpret messages in semaphore, and to do minor repairs to radio equipment. This involves a six months' course, the same as that taken by airmen.

Airwomen also entered the trade of meteorological observer, and now, on many stations, maintain 24-hours-a-day weather maps for the guidance of men who fly. They became tele-printers, too, and — completing their assumption of communications' work — went into the trade of code and cypher.

Thus, more men were released for flying duty or heavy mechanical work

essential to flying. But woman's work was not forgotten. Shortly after airwomen began cooking for the service, came the innovation of qualified dietitians, enlisted as messing officers. Under their guidance, improved nutrition, more variety to menus, less waste, and more kitchen efficiency are attained.

Women doctors have had a place in the Division since the start. Qualified medical officers are on duty at training centres of the W.D., at headquarters, and big Air Force hospitals in both Canada and Newfoundland.

Airwomen are now on duty in Canada from coast to coast, in Newfoundland, the United States and Great Britain. The call is for more and still more.

Airwomen do essential work in both training and operational fields of the R.C.A.F. The importance of

The thrill of the photographic course — a "flip" with an aerial camera.

their part is best shown by the many duties they perform when a bomber crew goes "on ops". It is equipment airwomen who issue the crew's flying suits and parachutes. Fabric workers

and parachute packers have checked and folded the silk "umbrellas" that are a lifebelt of the air. Cooks and messwomen prepare the sandwiches that will be eaten miles away from the station and thousands of feet above it. Deft-fingered armament workers have tucked each machine gun bullet in its belt.

The crew must bail out? Probably a girl in blue will receive their distress signal at her wireless post. Another has packed the rubber dinghy that will save their lives. Yet another will be at the wheel of the transport that brings them back to the station, and if any are hospitalized because of exposure, airwomen will help the nurses and doctors bring them back to health. The telephone operators

wings, or clean and check the aircraft for its next journey.

In two years, the strength of the Women's Division has expanded to a hundred times its original size. Its trades have grown from nine to more than forty. Men who have worked with the sister service have only one complaint. They say there are not enough of them for the jobs that must be done.

CANADIAN WOMEN'S ARMY CORPS
By Lt.-Col. MARGARET EATON, Assistant Adjutant-General (C.W.A.C.)

MORE than 13,000 women in Canada wear the insignia of Athene, Greek goddess of war and

demonstrated daily in the camps, offices, store-rooms, laboratories, and other branches of the Army. They do a score of jobs — in many cases with more speed and natural ability than men. They drive the heaviest of Army trucks, use highly-specialized technical equipment. Just as her civilian sister can now operate lathes and welding torches in munitions' plants, the C.W.A.C. can repair an automobile or adjust a gun-sight.

Those who have had an opportunity to study first hand the contribution of this Army say that its members have a new keenness, a new outlook on Canadian life, and a new determination to contribute more fully to the national development.

The story of the Canadian Women's Army Corps goes back to early 1940 when the need to enlist women in the Canadian Forces became sharply apparent. All types of office workers with experience were urgently needed to handle the paper work of a rapidly-expanding Army. The need to staff the Corps of Military Staff Clerks, the Royal Canadian Army Service Corps, Royal Canadian Ordnance Corps, and administrative branches was a severe drain on the ranks of fighting men.

The women themselves were anxious to do their part. Many organizations were appealing to the Government for official recognition of their war role.

The final decision to form a corps of women whose chief task would be to replace soldiers in non-combatant duties was made during the summer of 1941. The Canadian Women's Army Corps was authorized by an Order-in-Council on August 13, 1941.

First recruits for the new Corps were attested in September, 1941, when companies were set up in the eleven Military Districts of Canada. As the new Army took form, personnel were quartered in barracks wherever possible, going out daily to their places of Army employment. The Corps established its head-

Routine inspection of all parachutes, as well as parachute packing, is a responsibility of the Women's Division.

are Women's Division; so are the stenographers, the bookkeepers who log each minute of every aircraft's flying time, the teleprinters whose flying fingers send important coded messages. Others do instrument repair, mend the fabric of bullet-torn

wisdom. They are members of the Canadian Women's Army Corps, an integral part of Canada's Armed Forces, now in its third year of active service.

The results of their well-organized role in the nation's war effort are

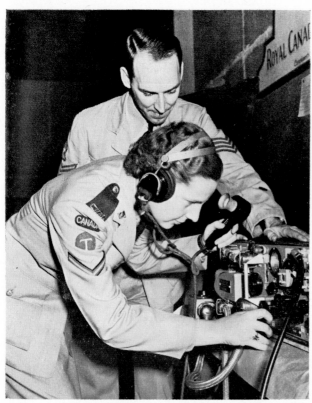

A C.W.A.C. radio mechanic learning her trade.

Automobile brakes are relined by C.W.A.C. mechanic.

quarters in Ottawa, the nation's capital. Lieut.-Col. (then Major) Joan B. Kennedy, of Victoria, British Columbia, was appointed Officer Administering. Thus did a new kind of force begin life.

Recruits are required to take a four weeks' training course at basic training centres. Here a special syllabus is given, and, upon completion of the course, the recruit is despatched to a Military District, there assigned to the job she will fill best.

Training is carried out on almost exactly the same lines as in the camps of the regular Army. While the C.W.A.C. does not receive arms drill, its members are instructed in the art of self-defence and in protection against enemy aircraft and gas.

Promotions in the Corps are made on a basis of merit. Officers come up from the ranks, and candidates are required to take Officers' Promotional Courses at an Officers' training centre. First commissioned rank in the C.W.A.C. is that of a second-lieutenant. In a similar fashion, promotion is made to non-commissioned and warrant officer ranks.

Early in 1942, the first training centre was opened at Macdonald College, Ste. Anne de Bellevue, Quebec. In June, the first cadet course was started, and since that time graduation exercises have been held periodically. In July of the same year, Western Basic Training Centre was opened at Vermilion, Alberta. 1942 also saw the establishment of an Eastern Basic Training Centre at Kitchener, Ontario, with facilities for training 1,000 C.W.A.C. personnel a month. Highlight of 1942 was the arrival overseas in November of the first group of Canadian Women's Army Corps personnel.

Many trades' training establishments have been formed this year, which open new and varied trades to the personnel of the Corps. In February, National Defence Headquar-

ters announced the establishment of a C.W.A.C. driving and maintenance wing at Kitchener, Ontario. Here selected members of the Corps are trained as drivers of motor transport vehicles following completion of their basic training.

On April 26th, twenty-one selected members of the C.W.A.C. commenced a mechanics' course at the Central Technical School, Toronto. On completion of the course certain of the successful candidates were posted immediately to Royal Canadian Ordnance Corps Workshops Sections. The remainder were given further instruction on predictors.

With the formation of a pipe band from a nucleus formed in Vancouver, British Columbia, the Corps now has two bands, brass and pipe.

Women will be taking their place with men behind anti-aircraft artillery. They will be trained as plotter-telephonists. Women in England

A C.W.A.C. Armourer in an Army Ordnance shop.

have been used on similar duty for some months.

With the arrival of a fourth draft in Britain, C.W.A.C. overseas strength has been brought up to the six hundred mark. The demand for relatively small drafts continues steadily and will be met as required.

That members of the C.W.A.C. will continue their service to Canada after demobilization is indicated by the fact that this year's agenda includes the study of post-war rehabilitation plans through which they learn what further contributions they may make to Canada's future development. Thus, determined to be well equipped in Peace as in War, the girls of the Canadian Women's Army Corps resolutely fit themselves to keep pace with their brothers in khaki.

A battery of tabulating machines at National Defence Headquarters operated by C.W.A.C. personnel. Machine operation is a specialty within the general category of clerical trades at which women have proved to be exceptionally efficient.

WOMEN'S ROYAL CANADIAN NAVAL SERVICE
By Commander
ADELAIDE SINCLAIR
Director, W.R.C.N.S.

SIXTY-SEVEN girls in plain navy blue smocks stood at attention before Commodore H. E. Reid, Vice-Chief of Naval Staff, R.C.N., at Ottawa. They had lived in those smocks for four weeks — their basic training period as the first class of Wrens in Canada — and now they were undergoing their official inspection and a formal march-past in the sole item of uniform yet issued to them by the Navy.

As he launched the first members of the Women's Royal Canadian Naval Service into their career with the Royal Canadian Navy, Commodore Reid told them: "You are badly needed by the Navy to replace men for active duty, and I know you will be welcomed by them".

That was September 26, 1942. The originals had come from every part of Canada to be the first women in the Royal Canadian Navy. From that group, the W.R.C.N.S. has grown to more than 3,500 members. Recruiting officers estimate that the Wrens will number 5,500 by March, 1944, filling jobs at ports, shore establishments and naval reserve divisions across Canada as cooks and secretaries, stewards and sail makers, typists and transport drivers, and all the dozens of categories which women can fill to release men who want to go to sea. Wrens are now in Washington, D.C., Newfoundland, and the United Kingdom, on active service.

From the beginning, the new service relied on guidance from the Women's Royal Naval Service in Great Britain. Captain Eustace A. Brock, who had been serving overseas with the British Admiralty as Canadian liaison officer, was named as Director and returned in mid-April, 1942, to set the new organization in motion.

On May 12, 1942, three British Wren Officers arrived to assist him: Superintendent Joan Carpenter, Chief Officer Dorothy Isherwood, and Second Officer E. M. Sturdee, who, immediately upon consultation with

Canadian officials, began a tour of Canada, picking out possible recruiting depots, examining prospective quarters and interviewing hundreds of applicants from coast to coast. By May 18, there had been 800 applications from Canadian girls who wanted to join the Navy.

Of the first class of 67, 22 Wrens were recommended for commissions, and many of the others were promoted to higher ranks as the months went by. Once trained, they were detailed to posts as recruiting officers, or to Galt, Ontario, where accommodation had been secured for a training establishment. Here, in five modern brick buildings, preparations were made for the incoming drafts of recruits, the first of which arrived in October. Somewhat bewildered and uncertain about their new life, they left 27 days later — enthusiastic Wrens.

Recruiting went on apace during the autumn months of 1942, as applicants were called up for training at Galt and then posted to duties at ports, inland establishments and Naval Service Headquarters at Ottawa. New drafts arrived each week,

Navy and Air Force co-operate in staffing joint services' operations rooms on east and west coasts. Women act as wireless and telephone operators helping to feed information into the centre, and also as recorders and plotters.

Wrens relax in quarters after a full day of duty. "Double-decker" beds in large barrack-rooms do not make for much privacy, but do ensure companionship.

and have done so every week since October, 1942, with about 400 Wrens-in-training at Galt most of the time.

By February, 1943, six months after organization had begun, the Women's Royal Canadian Naval Service had more than 400 Wrens on active service, and this number had doubled by March. In February, the first Officers' Training Course was held in Ottawa, and the Service acquired the former Preston Springs Hotel to accommodate Wrens being trained at Galt. By the end of April there were 1,000 Wrens on active service, with about 230 at Naval Service Headquarters.

In March, Director Dorothy Isherwood succeeded Captain Brock who returned to England, as did Superintendent Carpenter.

April brought the first taste of foreign service for the Wrens, when eight were sent to Washington to serve on the staff of Rear-Admiral V. G. Brodeur, then Naval member of the Canadian Joint Staff. In May, the Honourable Mr. Macdonald paid an official visit to Galt, now commissioned as a ship of the Royal Canadian Navy, H.M.C.S. *Conestoga*.

Wrens in the Fleet Mail Office at Halifax.

as Staff Officer for the Canadian Service. Two Canadian officers were appointed in their places — Commander Adelaide Sinclair as Director and Lt.-Commander Evelyn Mills as Staff Officer.

With increasingly important jobs opening to them, and the rapid growth of Canada's Navy demanding more and more ships and more men to fight them, the Wrens have a bright outlook for their second year. Heaviest responsibility is the supplying of Wrens in domestic categories, for cooks, stewards and laundry assistants are badly needed to replace men in these trades. They are needed, also, to staff ever-increasing numbers of shore establishments, where thousands of sailors are being trained for their jobs at sea.

Canadian Wrens know that the foundation laid by the Wren officers from Great Britain is adequate for any conceivable expansion, and, under the direction of an All-Canadian ship's company, the enthusiasm and capacity for hard work, which has been so well demonstrated, augurs well for the future.

Biggest news of the year to most Wrens was the announcement in August that the first group of W.R.C.N.S. members would proceed overseas shortly for service with the R.C.N. Application for overseas duty may now be made by any Wren to her Unit Officer for consideration at headquarters. Twelve Wren ratings and two officers arrived in the United Kingdom on the first of September and took over jobs formerly done by English Wrens in the office of the Senior Canadian Naval Officer in London.

On August 15, another significant announcement was made, affecting Canadian Wrens. Captain Dorothy Isherwood had been recalled to her duties in the United Kingdom, together with Lieutenant-Commander Lorna Kellett who had been acting

A Wren messenger delivers a document at ship-side.

PATTERNS OF CHANGE

When the conversion from a wartime to a peacetime economy had been completed following World War II, Canada found herself emerging as an industrial nation, with factories which looked beyond local markets and were actively competing in the markets of the world in many products. Industry itself was changing as the development of machines, and especially automatic processes, gave special advantages to large factories which could exploit their use.

As successive areas of Canada had been settled, local industries had been established — a grist and flour mill, a tannery, a cheese factory, a saw mill. This pattern was repeated across the country and supplemented by shoe factories, foundries, furniture factories, etc., which served wider areas but with few exceptions did not sell their products across even the whole of Canada. Many of these factories closed during the war, as new, larger and more efficient units were built to meet war needs. Following the war this process was continued and hastened; a wide variety of new products was introduced; and the grouping of factories with ever-larger industrial areas was accelerated, because these areas offered advantages in transportation costs and in providing pools of skilled labour.

Similar changes were taking place all around the world, varying in degree and in particular goods produced, depending on the natural resources of the various areas and their stages of industrial and social development. World demand for metal rose on an ever-increasing scale. Canada responded to that demand, increasing her output of metals of all kinds.

This rise of production of metals and of manufactured goods brought ever-increasing demands for power. At the same time, the development of efficient, long-distance transmission of electric power allowed distant sites suitable for production of hydro-electric power to be put to use. To the familiar names of Niagara, Beauharnois, and Shawinigan were added Kemano, Bersimis, Peace and Manicouagan, plus a host of lesser sites. The Nelson River in Manitoba, the Hamilton (Churchill) River in Labrador and the Yukon River are the last great potential sources of hydro-electric power in Canada. When these have been developed, nuclear power should be fully competitive in price to meet the ever-increasing need.

A few of the major developments of this time of expansion and change are covered in the articles of this section. Also included are articles on the present state of development of our natural resources. The pattern of industry, with its many ramifications, would demand a book in itself to show in clear perspective how it has developed to meet Canada's needs and how its various segments are meeting the challenges of the markets of the world.

Change is brought about by people who are themselves reaching for fresh horizons. The skills demanded by technological growth must be taught to an ever-increasing proportion of our people at all levels from the elementary school to the university. Specialization is essential at ever-earlier stages because the amount of new knowledge is growing faster than ever before. Fortunately for Canada, this concern with factual knowledge is being accompanied by a growing interest in the arts, literature, music and drama, which bodes well for the years ahead when a principal concern may be the right use of leisure created by technological change.

City Hall, Toronto. 2, A DC 9 of Air Canada in flight. 3, A Gulf Islands ferry, British Columbia. 4, Planting celery, south of ontreal. 5, A blast furnace at night, Hamilton. 6, Victoria-Vancouver ferries meet in Active Pass. 7, The main dam at Bersimis II as it neared completion. 8, The St. Lambert Lock on the St. Lawrence Seaway.

KITIMAT – A SAGA OF CANADA

by PAUL CLARK

The imagination, technical competence, and ingenuity which characterized this project has been shown again and again at major hydro-electric power developments in other remote parts of Canada. This account, which appeared in the October, 1954, issue of the Canadian Geographical Journal *may speak for all of them.*

HIGH IN THE MOUNTAINS of central British Columbia, 400 miles north of Vancouver and 100 miles south of Alaska, are long, narrow lakes whose beds were gouged from granite during the ice age. Fed by glaciers and snowtopped mountains, the waters of the lakes have for ages flowed eastward, then turned south

to join the Fraser River and meet the ocean at Vancouver.

"A terrible silence, broken only now and again by the dreadful crash of some falling avalanche, reigned over this scene of desolation." Thus wrote Charles Horetzky, surveyor for the railroads in 1874. Searching for a pass through the mountains where a

aroused since Tahtsa Lake, the most westerly water in the intricate and connected chain, was only ten miles away from, and one-half mile above, the Kemano River and sea water. However, high-in-the-clouds Tahtsa Lake and sea-level Kemano River were held apart by a great mountain. This barrier of nature presented many problems. How could man pierce the mountain and allow the waters to drop to sea level? Could the eastward flow be reversed and turned to the west? And who would use the power if it could be made? A quarter of a century ago there were no answers to these questions, so the surveys and the reports were laid aside awaiting a day when the answers would be found.

This, then, was the situation for many years. British Columbia officials often wondered what could be done to use the lakes and their potential power. After fruitless inquiry at many places, the officials invited the Aluminum Company of Canada to send engineers to inspect the site and determine whether the wasting waters could be put to service. Early in 1951 Alcan accepted nature's challenge, and started work on the vast Kitimat Project, the largest job ever undertaken by private enterprise.

Power, the Key to Aluminum

Power is an essential key to low-cost aluminum production. Canada's abundant water power has helped to make her the world's second largest aluminum producer — the United States is first — even though Canada has no bauxite, the reddish-brown ore from which the metal is extracted.

The second essential key to the production of Canadian aluminum is transportation — because bauxite, the ore from which aluminum is made, is found principally in tropical countries. Canada obtains its ore in British Guiana and Jamaica. There

in the hot jungles on the land area banding the equator, bauxite is plentiful. Just as Canada is favoured with water power so is she blessed with a long seacoast and deep harbours to receive ocean vessels carrying the raw material.

The Kitimat Project

The Kitimat Project is really five separate engineering feats. First a dam was constructed to impound the waters of the chain of lakes. Second, a ten-mile tunnel was driven through the mountain barricade to give passage to the falling waters. Third, a powerhouse was carved inside a mountain to convert the energy of the rushing waters into electrical power. Fourth, was the erection of a transmission line to carry the power to the smelter. And finally came the building of the aluminum smelter at the end of a barren fiord. Each of these tasks was a major operation in itself. Their total had never before been attempted.

Kenney Dam

The Kenney Dam, the largest but not the highest rock-fill dam in the

railway could be built, he had led a party of three white men and four Indians to the top of a pass on the mountainous north shore of British Columbia. As he stood there awed by the silence, looking at the "lake of a brilliant light blue colour" (Tahtsa Lake), Horetzky could not foresee that 80 years later the scene would be the centre of an aluminum industry — a metal he probably had never seen.

These lakes were surveyed in 1928 by provincial engineers of British Columbia. The interest of government hydro-electric engineers was

191

The construction camp on ice-covered Tahtsa Lake housed the hard rock miners who were driving a river through a mountain. The ski tracks of the planes which served them and their families may be clearly seen.

time this diversion tunnel was ready. In August, 1951, the River was blocked with rock and earth just at the point where the diversion tunnel started. The water swirled into the tunnel and the main channel was dry.

There are many types of dams. Some are made of concrete, some are called rock-fill dams. To block the Nechako River, the designers decided upon a rock-fill type of dam. This means that rock was built up as a heap on top of the stripped River bed. Then impervious clay was placed on the upstream face of the Dam and covered with gravel. It took 1,000 men six months to fill the Dam with rock and clay. They took a nearby mountain apart, hauled the rock to the Canyon and there put the mountain together again. Every 45 seconds, one of the fleet of trucks dumped its load of rock on the Dam, its driver directed by radio from a central dispatch tower.

Work continued on the Dam during the long summer days of 1952. In November, 1952, the task was nearly finished. The 114-ton gates of the di-

world, finished in December of 1952, is the starting point of the Kitimat Project.

Engineers spent months exploring and sounding several tentative sites for the dam before settling on a location in the Grand Canyon of the Nechako River. Here the engineers could plug the eastern outlet of a 5,500-square-mile drainage area and create a 358-square-mile reservoir out of a dozen large lakes.

Armed with modern construction equipment and with over 1,000 men to operate it, the engineers began the attack on the River. Through one high bank, they bored a great tunnel in a sweeping arc. The thirty-two-foot-diameter tunnel commenced upstream above the Dam site and ran 1,539 feet parallel to the River, but inside the bank, and came out below the site of the Dam. In two months'

Ten-foot-thick concrete slab spread on the bed of the Nechako River to serve as a base for Kenney Dam.

version tunnel were slowly lowered and the storage of water began. Named after E. T. Kenney, former Minister of Lands and Forests in the British Columbia Government, Kenney Dam rises 317 feet above the old bed of the Nechako River and measures 1,550 feet from one side of the Canyon to the other. With a crest width of 40 feet, and containing over 6½ million tons of rock and clay, its life will be measured in geological, not historical, time.

The waters rose against Kenney Dam until 1957, when the 358-square-mile reservoir became full. Discharge of surplus or flood waters is effected at a location part way up the reservoir and remote from Kenney Dam. At a place called Skins Lake a gated spillway has been constructed to discharge waters over Elevation 2,800 through the Cheslatta Lake Basin to re-enter the Nechako River five miles below Kenney Dam.

The Power Tunnel

On December 2, 1953, two begrimed hard rock miners grinned at each other through a jagged opening blasted from solid rock deep inside Mount DuBose. A power tunnel had been cut out through the barrier. For twenty months, hundreds of Canadian miners had worked the clock round. Their machines and skill had carved a 25-foot-diameter, 10-mile-long "river" through a mountain. When it was done, the tunnel looked easy but it was a spectacular accomplishment. Three times world records were broken, the last time in February, 1953, when 282 feet of tunnel were torn out in a single week.

The boring of the tunnel started on October 22, 1951, on the western shores of sky-blue Tahtsa Lake, followed soon on November 4, 1951, by crews headed eastward from sea-level Kemano River. Meanwhile, two other crews prepared to start tun-

nelling eastward and westward at a mid-point adit driven into the side of Mount DuBose at Horetzky Creek. Thus the tunnel job was attacked at four faces simultaneously: two crews working from the middle outward and two other crews working from the east and west portals.

The job took twenty months and when the ten-mile tunnel was finished,

the locked lakes had a new channel to sea-level. The waters could be put to service generating power.

Kemano Generating Station

Kemano is an Indian word meaning "Men of the Rocks". It is well named, for the glacial waters of the Kemano River flow in a deep narrow valley shrouded by mile-high granite

After twenty months of labour, east and west construction crews met on dead centre, deep inside the mountain.

193

peaks. No one ever lived in the Kemano Valley but the small bands of nomad Indians who roamed the area and occasionally broke the silences while hunting bear and mountain sheep. These "men of the rocks" gave their name to the River.

Now the granite mountain shelters some of the world's most powerful electrical generators, with capacity of 112 megawatts each, to power Alcan's smelter at Kitimat.

While it is unusual to build a powerhouse underground, it is by no means unique. Kemano went underground for many reasons, including lack of suitable space in the constricted Kemano Valley; more economic foundations for massive machinery; freedom from landslides, and saving in steel and concrete.

The first generator was on power at Kemano on July 15, 1954, followed quickly by two more. Since then, to the end of 1959, four more 112 megawatt generators were installed bringing capacity at Kemano

to 784 megawatts. However, the great cavern, 82 feet wide by 135 feet high by 700 feet in length has room for still one more generator. To bring Kemano to its ultimate 1,800 megawatt capacity — which is not scheduled at this writing — another 10-mile tunnel will be required; the powerhouse will have to be lengthened some 400 feet and, of course, additional generating equipment will need to be installed.

The Kildala Pass

From Kemano to Kitimat is tough country. The distance is only 50 miles but the land rises from sea-level at Kemano to mile-high Kildala Pass and back to sea-level at Kitimat. A mile up and a mile down. And glaciers, crevasses and sharp rocky clefts and cliffs are all in between. The question was not so much how to build the transmission line; the real doubt was whether a line could be built at all.

Today, the transmission line spanning Kildala Pass is a monument to

Canadian engineering courage and skill, persistence and science. It was the most difficult and unique phase of the entire project.

Surveys and investigations of the route began in 1949. On the summit, 2,000 feet above the timber line, a test span was erected between two 26-foot-high aluminum towers. Automatic measuring instruments festooned the line as though it were a Christmas tree and made their record of gales from the Pacific Ocean and ice formed from snow and rime. To supplement the machines, men were stationed in cabins along the transmission route and spent lonely days where snow lay 20 feet or more deep. In time, the calculations showed that the transmission line must withstand winds of 80 miles per hour and ice loads five inches thick, weighing 40 pounds per foot.

Back in the laboratories, scientists collated the data and made their calculation. Then they put together a test length of the largest overhead transmission cable ever made. Thick as a man's wrist, 2.295 inches in diameter and made of 108 strands of aluminum over 37 strands of steel; weighing only 4.77 pounds per foot, yet having an ultimate strength of 135,700 pounds, this cable proved it could do the job.

While the cable problem was solved, the men seeking a path for the transmission line were falling behind. Mired in muskeg and hindered by snow fields, progress was slow. Helicopters had done yeoman service for the military forces. Maybe the whirly-bird could "chart" Kemano Valley.

One of Canada's most renowned airmen, Carl Agar, was summoned to Kemano to pioneer high altitude landings and take-offs, — about which the instruction book said nothing. In the thin air and treacherous down drafts, Agar's pilots found

Excavating over half a million tons of rock for the man-made cave to house the generators at Kemano.

new hazards and learned new flying techniques to overcome them. In a few weeks, surveys were completed aloft that would have required months, maybe years, by men on the ground. The route of the transmission line was mapped.

Accurate surveys are one thing, but towers and cable are not moved over a paper road on a blueprint. After six snow-blown months, a road had been edged part way up the valley. Only six miles away was the top of Kildala Pass — but what a six-mile stretch! Rising rapidly, about a thousand feet to the mile, the road would have grades up to 25%. Miles of "switchbacks" must be blasted, despite snowslides and avalanches. These six miles would take a long time unless heavy equipment could be miraculously dropped on the summit. Then the road could be pushed from the bottom and from the roof.

Albert Charron and his helper Bill Henry volunteered to pilot an International TD-24 crawler tractor up a steep snowfield, — 150 feet deep at the base. Stopping only to eat and sleep, Charron and Henry covered about a mile a day. In seven days they reached the top, their tractor a black

Aerial view of towering Mt. DuBose.

dot on the blinding snow to the anxious group watching from below. Though much remained to be done, Kildala had been conquered. The entire access route was ready by December, 1952, and the construction of the transmission line commenced.

Again helicopters played a major role in saving time. Supplies and equipment were bundled on the ground, helicopters hovered over the load while sling hooks were attached and then sailed away to the erection crews the 'copters had spotted along the right-of-way. On four-hour shifts, the 'copters never touched the ground. On favourable days, 75 round-trips

A helicopter approaches on a specially-constructed platform.

195

The workmen of Kemano lived well in their city in the valley. They came from every part of Canada and some from lands overseas. The "meal call" was the most popular call of the day. To a thousand men at a sitting, the chefs served pie for breakfast and steak for lunch.

were circled with the precision of a drilled racing team. The transmission towers began to dot the wild terrain.

On July 15, 1954, a switch was closed. Power surged to Kitimat. Three and one-half years of labour by tens of thousands of men employing $275 million of capital were the prelude to this day.

Kitimat — A Dream in the Wilderness

Why did Alcan choose Kitimat? To the casual observer, 80-mile-long Douglas Channel ends on mud flats

without promise. However, the Kitimat Valley proved to be the only large open area between Powell River and Prince Rupert which would invite a town of the size envisaged. Kemano River Valley was too small, while five-mile-wide Kitimat Valley reaches 40 miles to the flourishing community of Terrace. Then too, aluminum loves tidewater!

The summer of 1951 saw Kitimat's smelter and townsite under way. Maybe because there was no river to divert nor a mountain to tunnel or a

cliff to climb, 3½ years of toil went almost unnoticed in the building of Kitimat harbour and smelter. However, it was a spectacular venture.

The preparation of the smelter site was the "time-taker". The 70-acre area, on the west side of the Kitimat area was a low delta of mud and fallen trees. To gain a firm foundation for the massive buildings to be erected there, the soggy soil was removed, then replaced with clean strong fill.

Some of the gravel required came from the bottom of the harbour

Powerhouse construction men smile as the Duke of Edinburgh pauses for a friendly chat.

A guard of honour of Wolf Cubs stands on Kitimat wharf as the Duke of Edinburgh comes ashore.

where dredging was necessary for the ship channel. The Kitimat Constructors' dredge pumped 12,000 cubic yards of fill a day — equal to the size of 30 bungalows — until at the end 2¼ million cubic yards had flowed through the 24-inch pipeline.

Additional fill was needed and fortunately a mountain of gravel was found about four miles away. Just as at Kenney Dam, the mountain was moved truck by truck. Over 200,000 truck loads of fill moved from the gravel mountain to the smelter site four miles away!

Meanwhile tugs were making the four-day run from Vancouver, towing barges loaded with aluminum siding, steel girders, cement and the host of materials for the smelter itself. Slowly and surely the smelter area took shape.

On August 3, 1954, Kitimat was ready. The first phase of the smelter involved 12 acres of industrial buildings. Dominating the scene were the two potlines, where the raw material from Jamaica is reduced to aluminum. At 3:00 p.m. on August 3, 1954, the first metal was poured in the presence of a notable gathering. H.R.H. The Duke of Edinburgh "tapped" the first 50-pound ingot. Smiling at his side was the then President R. E. Powell of Alcan watching his dream come true.

The Kitimat Project is a saga of Canada. Won from the wilderness, Kitimat will grow with Canada. Its power from Kemano will surely, in time, make more aluminum and draw other industries. The forests, long ravaged by winter storms, are the nucleus for more and more services to each one of us. All who built Kitimat — the manufacturers, the engineers, the workmen and Alcan — did so with the high purpose of a better way of life for today and all the tomorrows awaiting North Americans.

The rotor of a 112-megawatt generator being lowered into position in the Kemano powerhouse. Seven such generators are now installed.

The Trans-Canada Highway approaching Banff from the west.

THE TRANS-CANADA HIGHWAY

by EDWARD J. MARTEN

This assessment of the impact of the Trans-Canada Highway on Canadian development was written one year after the official opening of the highway and appeared in the Canadian Geographical Journal *in September 1963. Since then the growth of trucking services within Canada and the building of facilities for travellers has continued apace and shows no sign of slowing down.*

IN MANY AREAS, along the Trans-Canada Highway, the roar of the bulldozer has now been replaced by the ring of the carpenter's hammer. New motels and hotels are springing up; restaurants and service centres are a-building; camp sites and picnic areas are being carved out of the wilderness; preparations are being speeded up to accommodate an ever-increasing influx of visitors to Canada.

The big attraction and main cause of all this activity, Canada's newly opened national highway, is having an exhilarating economic impact on hundreds of communities both big and small along its route. Already, according to travel officials, it has surpassed even Niagara Falls in tourist interest and the Canadian Government Travel Bureau uses such adjectives as "fantastic" and "amazing" when describing the world-wide interest generated by it.

And this interest is still growing. One of the most significant facts is that many of the enquiries this year were from "repeaters" — visitors who travelled on a portion of the highway last year and enjoyed it so much that they planned to come back again to see some more of our country by travelling over a new section of the "longest national highway in the world".

The motor coach industry expects to see a continued upsurge in bus travel. "Packages tours," advertised in the United States and in Europe, are causing a great deal of interest, and senior officials of the industry are confident that the highway will prove to be a great stimulus. The all-Canada route is already being vigorously promoted.

Another segment of Canadian industry which has kept a watchful eye on the highway with a view to assessing its ultimate benefits, is the trucking industry. With long-established truck routes through the United States, Canadian trucking firms have from the outset adopted a wait-and-see attitude. Slowly, however, they have become convinced of the advantages of the all-Canadian route.

Although the highway was officially opened to traffic last year, construction is still going on in a number of sections. However, the 4,860 miles from St. John's, Newfoundland, to Victoria on Vancouver Island, are virtually all paved with the exception of Newfoundland, where a large portion of the provincial mileage still has a gravel surface. In other parts of Canada, the unpaved portions are in short sections where the highway has been re-routed from existing roads, or where bypasses around communities are being constructed. In all such cases, good alternate routes are available.

The official opening ceremony took place in the late summer of 1962 in Glacier National Park, at the summit of Rogers Pass. The Pass has been described as a "defile of boundless beauty", as it twists and turns its way through the range of mighty mountains that separates the Canadian

Prairies from the western seaboard.

It was fitting, too, that this site was only a few miles from Craigellachie, where, in 1885, the last spike was driven to signify the completion of another great transportation artery, the nation's first trans-continental railway. Many of those present at Rogers Pass on September 3, 1962, felt that they were witnessing an equally historical event. The romance surrounding the construction of the highway, especially the section through Rogers Pass, had caught the imagination and aroused both national and international interest and consequently a crowd of more than 3,000 people assembled alongside the highway for the event. Representatives from each of the ten provinces were on hand to take part.

Developments which paved the way for this event began many years ago. Following the First World War, an unprecedented expansion in motor vehicle registration caused a sudden need for more and better roads. Initially, the demand was not for long distance travel, but for local and inter-regional roads within the provinces. As time went on, and as automobile traffic increased, some of these roads became the basis for a system of trunk highways in each province. Throughout this period of road development, there were various proposals for a national highway from coast to coast, but when the emergency of the Second World War intervened, nothing was done about them.

Immediately following the war, the great increase in motor vehicle registration and an expanding freight trucking industry made the need for a trans-Canada highway even more apparent. A Dominion - Provincial

The covered bridge at Hartland, New Brunswick, 1,282 feet in length and the longest covered bridge in the world, can be seen from the Trans-Canada Highway.

Conference was called in 1948 to discuss the possibility of co-operating in its construction. The Trans-Canada Highway Act was passed unanimously by the Federal Parliament in 1949 and given Royal Assent on December 10th of that year.

The Provinces of Manitoba, Saskatchewan, Alberta, Ontario, British Columbia and Prince Edward Island, in April, 1950, signed agreements with the Federal Government. New Brunswick signed in May, 1950; Newfoundland in June of the same year; Nova Scotia in May, 1952; and the Province of Quebec in October, 1960.

Under the original Act, the federal government agreed to pay 50 per cent of the cost of construction. Later, by an amendment to the Act, the federal government agreed to pay an addi-tional 40 per cent of the cost for 10 per cent of the mileage in each province. In essence, this meant that the Canadian Government paid 90 per cent of the cost of the most difficult 10 per cent of each provincial route. While the provinces undertook to build the road, both the design and construction procedures were subject to the review and approval of federal authorities. Federal engineers of the Department of Public Works inspected the work as it progressed.

Strict specifications for the high-way were required under the Trans-Canada Highway Act. It called for a minimum right-of-way of 100 feet and a minimum pavement width of 22 feet. Curves were not to exceed 6°, except in isolated instances where the terrain would not permit this with reasonable economy. Wherever possible, curvature was to be maintained at 3°. Grades were not to exceed 6 per cent except in very mountainous country where gradients of 7 or 8 per cent would be acceptable for short distances. Wherever possible, minimum horizontal and vertical sight distances were to be kept to 600 feet. This meant that a driver of a passenger car travelling on the highway should see an object 6 inches high on the pavement in front of him at a distance of 600 feet.

The federal government pays the full cost of construction within the boundaries of the national parks. This has proved to be a major task, since in Newfoundland, British Columbia and Alberta, these sections were right in the middle of the most difficult areas. Terra Nova National Park in Newfoundland is astride the highway route, while, in British Columbia, the road cuts through the magnificent Glacier, Yoho, Banff, and Revelstoke Parks — magnificent from a scenic point of view, but a tough job from the viewpoint of the highway engineer.

In Newfoundland, much of the 540-mile route was through virgin country where no road of any kind existed. In Northern Ontario, around the north shore of Lake Superior, there were two roadless gaps over extremely forbidding territory and in British Columbia, the route through Rogers Pass was to be cut out of the very heart of the Rocky Mountains.

Today, in Newfoundland, while the highway is far from finished, it is possible to drive the 540 miles from Port aux Basques to St. John's with-out too much difficulty. Certain sections — about 200 miles in all — have now been completed, including the stretch through beautiful Terra Nova National Park. The location of the highway through this national park was so inaccessible that construction materials for parts of it had to be brought in by boat and barge from the sea. In order to meet Trans-Canada Highway standards here, it

The Canso Causeway linking Cape Breton Island and the Nova Scotia mainland, is part of the Trans-Canada Highway.

was necessary in some cases to excavate the muskeg to a depth of twenty-five feet. On the average, each mile of highway through this park required the handling of almost 175,000 cubic yards of earth, rock or granular material and cost about $490,000.

When the highway is completed in Newfoundland, it will have tremendous tourist potential. The scenery is breathtaking — countless lakes and streams beckon the camper and the angler. At the moment, tourist facilities are still being developed in some areas, but the provincial government

Newfoundland's salmon streams attract anglers from all over North America.

is making great strides in providing camp and picnic grounds adjacent to the highway. This is being done under a program in effect in all provinces with federal assistance for the development of camp grounds and

highway. This year alone, according to a conservative estimate by Newfoundland officials, at least a dozen new motels are going up, as well as several times that number of restaurants of various types.

of the ferry from the mainland. It is not all due to the Trans-Canada Highway, of course, but the volume of tourist traffic in Prince Edward Island increased by over nine per cent last year. This compares with a seven per cent increase in the previous year. This steady increase in tourism has caused a similar increase in the provision of tourist facilities. Since 1961, the provincial government has established five new camp sites and picnic grounds, with three more scheduled for future development.

The "Promenade des Gouverneurs", foreground, leads to Dufferin Terrace which overlooks lower-town and the St. Lawrence River at Quebec.

picnic areas along the Trans-Canada Highway.

Not only the government is preparing for increasing tourist trade in Newfoundland — individuals and private funds are adding every year to existing service facilities along the

The highway through Prince Edward Island was one of the first provincial sections completed and the "Garden Province" has been reaping the benefits. Witness to this is the long line of cars that, during the tourist season, await each departure

In Nova Scotia and New Brunswick, where almost all the route is paved, it is regarded as a contributing factor in increased tourist business. Tourist traffic in Nova Scotia is up by some fifteen per cent, while the tourist bureau in New Brunswick reports that during the past five years, it has increased by twenty-one per cent. This has prompted a flurry of building activity such as new motels, restaurants and service stations.

The five camp grounds and picnic areas begun four years ago by the Province of Nova Scotia were completed last year and planning is already well advanced for two more camp sites. New Brunswick's three new camp sites were completed last year and plans for two more are currently on the drawing boards.

Quebec was the last province to enter into a Trans-Canada Highway Agreement. The province is, however, making up time and a very active construction program is in progress. For the most part, the 398-mile route is on existing highways that do not need a great deal of work to bring them up to specifications. Bypasses around the towns and cities, and an extensive grade separation program, are major features of construction.

Quebec has long had an effective tourist promotion program. This has lately been stepped up and its "Hospitalité spoken here" slogan is becoming increasingly familiar throughout the whole of the North American

continent. Tourist officials are quick to promote and take advantage of provincial attractions ranging from the quaint rural life of the Gaspé Peninsula to Quebec City with its old world charm and to the bustling modern and cosmopolitan city of Montreal. By 1967, Canada's Centennial year, all roads will lead to Montreal for the Canadian edition of the World's Fair.

The Trans-Canada Highway traverses 1,453 miles of Ontario, more than twice the distance of any other province, and it is virtually completed. Construction operations will be encountered in some areas but

Motorists pause at one of the numerous rock-cuts which are a feature of the Trans-Canada Highway along the north shore of Lake Superior.

203

Ontario is generally considered to have a fine highway stretching from the Quebec border to the Manitoba boundary.

At the beginning of the work in Ontario, there were two gaps where no highway existed previously. The bridging of the first gap in 1959, a comparatively short link through a section of the Muskoka district south of Parry Sound, opened up a portion of this lovely summer resort area which previously had been accessible

The second gap, and by far the more formidable, was along the north shore of Lake Superior between the Agawa River and Marathon, a distance of 165 miles. Geologists tell us that, millions of years ago, this area was the centre of a chain of mountains loftier even than the Himalayas. Erosion and glacial action lowered the great peaks and ridges to the level we know today and left behind a wildly rugged terrain of great outcroppings of rock,

one 590-foot span over the Big Pic River, east of Marathon.

The gap was closed in the early fall of 1960, and traffic has been rolling over this section of the highway in a steady stream ever since. With traffic, came an economic development which is still expanding.

Another development in Northern Ontario that can be at least indirectly linked with the construction of the Trans-Canada Highway is the opening this year of three new provincial parks. Neys Provincial Park, just south of the highway, fifteen miles west of Marathon, will contain some ninety camp sites in its 8,000 acre area. At Obatanga Provincial Park, on the Highway twenty-three miles east of White River, there will be 1,000 camp sites with all conveniences, while Killarney Park, a huge new camping ground on the north shore of Georgian Bay, can also be reached from the Trans-Canada Highway. In addition to the provincial parks, the tourists can also take advantage of a large number of municipal parks, private camping grounds and public and private picnic grounds. The Ontario Government is steadily increasing the number of information centres it maintains along the entire route.

Construction of the highway through Canada's vast central plain created relatively few problems for the road builders. Near Winnipeg, the thick sticky gumbo of the Red River Valley provided a challenge to both men and machinery, and unique construction methods had to be applied in one instance, to span the Assiniboine River. In this case, a bridge was built on dry land and the river re-channelled and re-routed later to pass underneath it.

Across the rest of Manitoba, through Saskatchewan, and as far west as the Alberta foothills, there were no major obstacles, with the result that this portion, 1,000 miles in length, was completed and in full operation long before most other

The marina at Falcon Lake in the Whiteshell Forest Reserve, Manitoba.

only by boat, train or air. There was, of course, an immediate up-surge in traffic not only on this new link, but on highways leading from the larger centres, such as Toronto and Hamilton, into the resort area. This in turn sparked a rash of construction which led to the opening of a larger number of motels, commercial tent and trailer parks, restaurants, snack-bars, and grocery stores, all catering to the tourist trade.

deep gorges and dense forests. This area was all but inaccessible; to clear the right-of-way, men and equipment had to be brought in by boat from Lake Superior, and aircraft were used extensively to carry supplies to the field camps. Before this section could be completed, it was necessary to construct twenty-five bridges over fast-running northern rivers. These were major bridge projects, many of them over 200 feet long, and included

A view of the Trans-Canada Highway through the golden wheatlands near Indian Head, Saskatchewan. The wise traveller soon finds that the western provinces have much to offer in addition to their flat prairies.

sections. Certainly the Prairie Provinces have benefited from it. It has provided for the first time a fine all-Canadian truck route linking the Prairies to the markets east and west of the area. Thousands of motorists who previously travelled over the better highways in the northern United States are now travelling the Canadian route to see Canada instead. The increase in truck traffic, combined with the influx of tourists, has necessitated the construction of all kinds of service centres.

Saskatchewan reports that traffic last year increased by almost seven per cent over the previous year. While no comparable figures are readily

available for the Province of Manitoba, they report that there is definite proof, based on accommodation and service figures, that there has been a decided increase both in tourist and commercial traffic.

There has been an indirect benefit too. With the federal government bearing a big share of the cost of the great east-west Canadian artery, these provinces have been able to spend more on improving their north-south access roads. The result has been an improved transportation system, not only throughout the individual provinces, but throughout Western Canada as a whole.

At least a part of this interest and

increased tourist traffic can be traced to a rather unique promotional venture. In order to promote Western Canada as a whole, the western provinces, in addition to their own individual programs, pooled resources to sponsor a joint advertising program featuring the Trans-Canada Highway. While it is difficult to estimate just how much interest this campaign generated, the provinces feel that results have been encouraging.

To build the Trans-Canada Highway in sections of British Columbia, it was necessary literally to move mountains or at least parts of them. This was true particularly of the

205

route through Rogers Pass, the short cut through the Selkirk Range which cuts 100 miles off the tortuous Big Bend Road. The Big Bend, a 190-mile route that follows the Columbia River between the towns of Golden and Revelstoke, was impassable in winter and difficult even in summer.

When it was announced that the highway would be built through Rogers Pass, and that it would be an all-season road, there were more than a few skeptics. This, they pointed out, was avalanche country, an area where the average winter snowfall measured over thirty feet in depth. How could it be kept open under these conditions? Well, the road has been built and has successfully undergone a "baptism of fire", for the winter of 1962-63 was one of the worst in memory. Snowfall reached a record height — one storm alone dropped over 100 inches — and there were many avalanches. But Greyhound Coachlines lost only one scheduled run through Rogers Pass all winter long!

This remarkable record was achieved only as the result of the most thorough pre-construction planning and study by federal and pro-

vincial engineers. Federal authorities, responsible for the section of the pass through Glacier National Park, set up an Avalanche Research Group and, for several winters, carried out a comprehensive survey of all avalanche zones. Similar studies were carried out in the area under provincial jurisdiction. As a result, when construction of the road commenced,

Protection against avalanches is given by these snow sheds near Revelstoke, British Columbia.

The three-dimensional abstract effect is heightened by the lighting in the China Bar tunnel in the Fraser Canyon, British Columbia.

avalanche routes had been plotted and effective defences designed. The construction of these defences was, in the main, completed when the route through Rogers Pass was opened for traffic in the summer of 1962.

It was first thought that very extensive use would have to be made of snow sheds throughout the Rogers Pass section. These are, of course, the most effective, but also by far the most expensive, form of defence against snow slides. By devising other types of protection, the engineers more than halved the original estimate of the number of snow sheds required, saved several millions of dollars, and in no way reduced the safety factor of the highway.

This was accomplished by a novel "defence in depth" method where potential danger existed. Instead of snow sheds, a series of earth mounds and dams were built into the mountain sides to break up avalanches and divert them from the highway. Only where the road was particularly vulnerable was it found necessary to build snow sheds. From last winter's experience it is apparent that the studies into snow conditions paid off in big dividends.

Avalanches were of course only one of the many great problems facing the road builders in the Rocky Mountains, and, more particularly, in the area of Rogers Pass. This indeed, from a construction standpoint, was one of the most difficult mountain areas on the continent. Including avalanche defences, the cost of the Rogers Pass route through Glacier averaged almost one million dollars a mile, much the highest of any section of the highway. It is regarded as money well spent however, for not only does it provide a fast, safe, all-Canadian, all-weather route through the mountains but also some of the grandest scenery to be found anywhere in the world.

Motor car ferries make the link from the mainland to Vancouver Island where the Trans-Canada Highway ends at Victoria.

The opening of this "road through the Rockies" has had a startling economic effect on the mountain towns that lie astride the highway. In the Revelstoke area it has been described as "instant prosperity."

It is here in the West that the benefits of the Trans-Canada Highway are especially noticeable. Traffic counts show that in the two months following the opening of Rogers Pass, the volume of traffic increased by as much as 294 per cent in some sections. Much of this was due to commercial traffic.

It is probably difficult for the average person to appreciate the magnitude of the job that has been done in building the Trans-Canada Highway. It may help to say that from the time work started in 1949 up to March of 1963, it is calculated that more than 12,000,000 man-days of employment (at eight hours per day) were provided. In addition to this, the off-site employment, that is the employment involved in producing materials for the highway, servicing equipment and so on, is estimated at more than 20,000,000 man-days. Some 1,500,000 feet of culverts and more than 12,000,000 tons of paving materials were used in the work. It has involved the construction of more than 640 highway bridges. The earth and rock used in building the road bed would weigh about 800,000,000 tons, which, if put into standard 60-ton freight cars, would require enough of them placed end to end to encircle the earth five times at the equator.

Canadians have every right to be proud of this billion dollar investment and they can expect to enjoy the dividends that are currently being declared along the entire length of the highway. High-flown phrases about "national unity" and "national purpose" are fine when kept in perspective. There is no doubt that it has increased our national unity and will further increase it in the years ahead. But the tangible return on our investment is another good way to determine whether or not it has been successful. Measured in this light, the Trans-Canada Highway has so far proven itself to be eminently successful and even greater dividends are expected of it in the years to come.

The effect of large-scale mining activity on the landscape is shown in this 1957 view of Gagnon Mines near Knob Lake. A hillside of iron ore has been removed to feed the blast furnaces of modern industry.

KNOB LAKE ON CANADA'S NEW FRONTIER

by W. GILLIES ROSS

The setting of this article from the June, 1957, issue of the Canadian Geographical Journal *is Northern Québec, but it could be almost any other province in Canada. The physical surroundings and the mineral sought might be different in another location, but the story of the winning of the wealth of our natural resources would be the same.*

KNOB LAKE lies near the Quebec-Labrador boundary in the heart of the immense peninsula of Labrador-Ungava. For centuries a neglected area of barren, windswept desolation, it is today one of Canada's most valuable assets; its rich deposits of iron ore are now being relinquished to modern industry. Where twenty years ago human activity was confined to a few Montagnais Indians tending winter trap lines, there is now on the shores of Knob Lake a community of over 2,000 people, served by air and rail. Its name is Schefferville, after Monseigneur Lionel Scheffer, O.M.I., Bishop of Labrador, whose spiritual missions in his vicariate of 350,000 square miles have become legend.

Schefferville was built by the Iron Ore Company of Canada. This group of American and Canadian mining companies decided in 1950 that the iron ore deposits of the Knob Lake area could no longer be ignored. The steel demands at the time of the Korean War, and the foreseeable depletion of the iron ore of the Mesabi Range of the United States, were both factors in this decision to open up the centre of Labrador-Ungava. Briefly, the company's project consisted of the construction of dock facilities and a townsite with adequate power supply at the port of Seven Islands, the building of a railway from Seven Islands to the ore deposits at Knob Lake, the construction of a town at Knob Lake, supplied with power from a dam at Menihek, thirty miles to the south, and the development of the mines themselves.

The beginning of this project in 1950 was a historic event. The interior of Labrador-Ungava, an immensity of some half-million square miles, had long been one of the world's least-known areas. Even today, despite the exploration and development in certain regions by mining interests, the construction of early warning sites on two defence lines across the peninsula, and the research projects carried out by students of the natural sciences, the area has been hardly touched.

Continually bypassed by explorers, traders, and settlers, this land was an uninviting wilderness north of the convenient waterway of the St. Lawrence through most of the last four centuries. La Salle reached the Gulf of Mexico in 1682, and Mackenzie crossed to the Pacific in 1793, but it was not until 1826 that Hendry travelled from Hudson Bay overland to Ungava Bay to mark the beginning of exploration of Labrador-Ungava.

In the years which followed, voyages by Erlandson, McLean, Babel, Low and others brought the first knowledge of the interior to the civilized world. Low's marvellous canoe voyages were undertaken less than seventy years ago; the first mineral concession in the interior was granted only twenty years ago, and the first ore was shipped out of Knob Lake only in 1954.

Consequently, knowledge of the area and its inhabitants before the entrance of white man is patchy. Sometime in the past, Indians of Algonkian stock moved eastward into

The Roman Catholic church at Schefferville was built largely by the volunteer labour of the congregation.

A street in Schefferville. The houses, built by the Iron Ore Company of Canada, are rented by employees and may be purchased by them eventually.

the peninsula in successive waves, and with pressure from Iroquois and Micmac tribes in the sixteenth and seventeeth centuries respectively they became more and more isolated from other Algonkian tribes. They became known as Montagnais along the north shore of the St. Lawrence and in the southern forests, and as Naskapi in the northern forest-tundra region. The establishment of fur-trading posts, first along the coasts, and in the interior during the nineteenth century, converted many Indians from subsistence hunting to trapping. When the mysterious decline of the caribou population was noticed by Low nearly seventy years ago, the Indians were turning to economic ties with the white man in sheer desperation. Unfortunately, the

notorious fluctuations in fur prices, and depletion of animals, made the trapping life insecure and generally unrewarding. It is significant, therefore, that the recent mining development in the Knob Lake area has offered important new opportunities to the Indians and has attracted large numbers from both Montagnais and Naskapi bands.

In the industrial penetration of Labrador-Ungava, the event which "broke the ice" was the construction of the Quebec North Shore and Labrador Railway from the port of Seven Islands northwards to the iron ore deposits of the Knob Lake area — 360 miles over exceedingly difficult terrain. The first equipment was unloaded at Seven Islands in the autumn of 1950; a base was established, docks were constructed, and crews began building a road-bed up through the steep-walled valleys of the incised rivers cutting through the rim of the Laurentian Plateau. Slowly work progressed as the route twisted up the Moisie, Nipissis and Wacouno Rivers, crossing seventeen bridges and going through two tunnels. Frequent landslides, and a mean winter snowfall in excess of 150 inches were only two of the many difficulties which beset the construction crews. At Mile 150 and altitude 2,055 feet above sea-level the climb was finished. Construction was somewhat less spectacular across the lake plateau country, although the notoriously bad drainage of this glaciated Canadian Shield topography was a serious problem. High winter winds and low temperatures made severe conditions for working and living. In February, 1954, four years after the project was begun at Seven Islands, the last spike was driven at Schefferville.

A singular feature of the railway's construction was its supply by air.

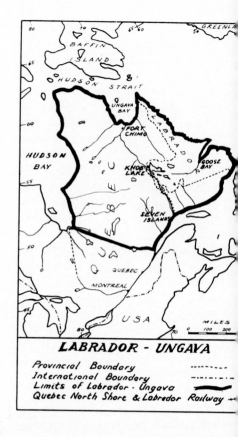

LABRADOR - UNGAVA

Provincial Boundary   ----------
International Boundary   ---·---·---
Limits of Labrador - Ungava   ▬▬▬
Quebec North Shore & Labrador Railway ~

The fifteen planes of Hollinger-Ungava Transport, a subsidiary of the Iron Ore Company, leap-frogged up the line along a series of fourteen landing strips, carrying men, food, fuel, material and equipment. Trucks, tracked vehicles, and two helicopters transported cargo from the strips to the construction sites. At the peak of activity almost 7,000 men were employed, involving complicated problems of messing and accommodation. The railway has been described as "one of the longest stretches of railroad construction on the continent in this century and the only one in history built by air". Under the difficult conditions imposed by climate and topography it was an enormous undertaking, and a great achievement for Canadian engineers.

As the railway pushed northward, there was much activity in the vicinity of Knob Lake, so that by the time it was in operation there was a mining community, supplied with hydro-electric power from the Menihek

These cascades of water, dropping down a long steep rock face, are one of the many picturesque features of the railway's route from Seven Islands to Knob Lake.

Lakes, and already producing iron ore. During the summer of 1954 over two million tons of ore were transported by rail to Seven Islands, and shipped to markets.

The problem of location of the Schefferville townsite was mainly to find a well-drained area reasonably close to the ore bodies and to a good airfield site. Burnt Creek was originally chosen; but when a chance drilling revealed that directly underneath the proposed site there were more than ten million tons of high grade ore, the location was changed to its present one on the neck of fluvio-glacial sands and gravels separating Knob and Pearce Lakes. The town of Schefferville is served by the air-strip on the east and the railway on the west. The Ruth, French, Gagnon and Gill mines are only a few miles to the north-west.

Today at Knob Lake the orderly streets of the modern town of Schefferville run in arcs between symmetrical rows of brightly painted houses. Construction is everywhere in progress; homes, a school, a church, a cinema, a bank, are triumphant, even arrogant, manifestations of man's conquest of nature. It is a transplanted civilization cast up boldly among the silent spruce. From this hub of settlement man's conquest spreads radially outward in power-driven tentacles, pushing the lichen woodlands back with shovels and trucks, men and toil. In the vast, gaping, dusty pits huge machines scrape incessantly at the lifeless ore, the food of man's industry.

The appearance of Schefferville nowhere suggests that it was planned with a special consideration of the climate. It looks like any well-laid-out mining town of lower latitudes, yet it seems adequate. The single, double, and four-family dwellings, although possibly an uneconomical answer to the demands of northern housing, have the advantage of giving the inhabitants a sense of privacy and eventual ownership that is more ap-

Twelve miles north of Seven Islands, an ore train crosses one of the seventeen bridges along the 360-mile route of the Quebec North Shore and Labrador Railway from Knob Lake. Several trains make the trip every day during summer, each with more than 100 cars.

pealing than any system of large centralized apartment buildings. The town plan is characterized by a division of functional units which contributes to convenience and efficiency, as well as to comfort and appearance. Its elements are a central core, which contains a school and a church, with provision for other religious and educational units; the living area of family dwellings on a modified circular plan surrounding the core; the commercial area of shops, public utilities, a bank, a cinema, a service station and a hotel; and the peripheral area containing the offices, warehouses, garages and bunk-houses of the various firms, and the railway station and airport.

The Knob Lake development has attracted a number of Indians who, as it was pointed out earlier, were basically discontented with the trapping existence. In June 1956 there were about 130 Montagnais, formerly from Seven Islands, living at Knob Lake; by mid-August 1956 the number had increased to almost 300, after the Indian Affairs Branch urged the 170 remaining Naskapi Indians to vacate the Chimo area in preference for Knob Lake. Almost all the firms in the area hired some Indians, despite the fact that they tended to fade away silently into the woods if caribou were reported or if the fishing was particularly good. In August more than seventy were employed, about one man per family. They now live on the shores of John Lake, two miles east of Schefferville, in a collection of wooden cabins and tents. This relocation of a significant number of Montagnais and Naskapi Indians constitutes one of the major secondary effects of the mineral development in the Labrador Trough. These people will enjoy a greater measure of opportunity and security than they have ever had before, through the advantages of education, medical supervision and employment. This is especially true of the Naskapi, who were poor, primitive folk, untouched by education until now.

The population in the summer of 1956 reached a peak of 2,830 people, almost one-half being employees of the Iron Ore Company of Canada, and another one-quarter their families. The third largest group consisted of the employees of the firms working on construction in and around Schef-

At the Iron Ore Company of Canada's dock at Seven Islands a cargo vessel loads iron ore, while tugs stand by to assist her departure against an on-shore wind.

ferville, civilian air crews and
R.C.A.F. personnel engaged in air
supply of the Mid-Canada Defence
Line sites stretching across the peninsula between the Labrador coast and
Hudson Bay. The Indian population
constituted ten per cent of the total.
However, several fluctuations in this
population should be mentioned in
order to demonstrate that the figure
of 2,830 was valid only for the time
of the survey. First, there is the seasonal variation in the personnel of
the Iron Ore Company of Canada;
low winter temperatures prohibit the
transport of ore to Seven Islands, and
the labour force must be reduced.
Second, there is uncertainty as to
the permanence of the Indian settlement, and its size. Third, there has
been the gradual withdrawal of men
working on the Mid-Canada Defence
Line as it has approached completion. There is also a withdrawal of
construction firms as the housing
project in Schefferville tapers off.

Although dusty streets, gaping excavations, and the gaunt frames of
unfinished buildings were hardly con-
ducive to an appreciation of its aesthetic qualities in the summer of 1956,
there was evidence that Schefferville
would one day be a very attractive
town. While primary construction
still assumed priority in the building
program, it was heartening to observe
the erection of traffic signs and the
laying of sidewalks, and to know that
landscaping would eventually do
much to beautify the town.

Inevitably, one attempts to visual-
ize the future. Knob Lake is a mining
area, and present estimates of ore
reserves indicate a potential annual
production of about twenty million
tons for several generations. When,
however, one considers the possibility
of other large deposits in the area,

and the probable exploitation of
lower grade ores, it seems apparent
that the life of Knob Lake will be
very much longer. It also seems likely
that it will have a strategic importance
for civil and military aviation as
well; its location on the Mid-Canada
Defence Line makes it a suitable
centre for air defence of north-eastern
Canada, and its climatic advantages
have already suggested to some the
possibility of its supplementing, or
even conceivably replacing, Goose
Bay as a stop-over on trans-Atlantic
air routes.

The pioneer venture at Knob Lake
has broken through the wall of climatic severity and inaccessibility to
open up the long-ignored interior of
the peninsula. This has encouraged
other industrial companies to come
in. The British Newfoundland Company is building a road into Grand
Falls, one of the largest potential
sources of hydro-electric power in the
world. Canadian Industries Limited

are building a plant at Seven Islands.
Canadian Javelin are working at
Wabush Lake to extract low grade
iron ore. The Cyrus Eaton associates
are busy along the west coast of Ungava Bay, where a short ice-free season and some of the world's highest
tides will be only two of the problems
in the removal of iron ore. Interest is
high in the nickel-rich Chukotat
River belt of northern Ungava. Along
the north shore of the St. Lawrence
the lure of mineral resources is supplemented by the wealth of large
forests, access to ocean shipping
routes, and the advantages of abundant, inexpensive power. These are
big attractions for industries such as
pulp and paper, aluminum and chem-
icals. Today settlement is filling in
behind an advancing frontier of industrial development, a twentieth
century method of colonizing vacant
lands. It can honestly be said that the
"ice" of Labrador-Ungava has been
broken.

Aerial photograph of the construction area of the South Saskatchewan River Project looking south, taken in September 1959, when construction was just well begun.

THEY ARE CHANGING THE FACE
OF SASKATCHEWAN

by PHYLLIS MacNEILL

The right use of our water resources is a matter which challenges every Canadian. This project, whose story appeared in the May, 1960, issue of the Canadian Geographical Journal, *combines the elements of power generation, irrigation, flood control, and recreation.*

THE INDIANS called the river Kis-is-ska-tche-wan, the swift flowing, and so the province became Saskatchewan, land of the rapid river. It is well named. In the early days of the west this river was a highway into the hinterland for fur traders and voyageurs. Today, as in the past, the destiny of the province is closely linked to the future of this mighty water-way.

Since the first influx of farmers, Saskatchewan has periodically watched agriculture, its largest industry, suffer the ravages of drought while through the centre of the arid region the river rolled northward to waste its precious water in the vast

214

In May 1966, the dam is nearing completion and the water is rising in the reservoir which will stretch 140 miles above it. The detail may be compared with the artist's concept of the completed work, below.

expanse of Hudson Bay. This extravagance is soon to cease. Mighty machines are now at work night and day moving tons of earth into the valley to build one of the world's largest earthen dams. Within a few years the flood waters of the swift river will remain on the prairies to provide a new water resource for a thirsty province.

This is a project that will surely change the face of Saskatchewan. The main dam, north of the elbow on the South Saskatchewan River, will rise 210 feet above the river floor and stretch three miles across the valley. The secondary dam at the summit between the South Saskatchewan and Qu'Appelle River basins will be 90 feet in height and about two miles long. Eight million acre-feet of water will be impounded in a new lake

Stabilization of Saskatchewan's livestock industry through increased fodder production will be one of the most immediate benefits of irrigation from the South Saskatchewan Project. This is the feedlot at the federal government's Pre-Development Farm at Outlook.

stretching 140 miles south and west almost to the Alberta border. Along its 475 miles of shoreline parks will flourish providing new playgrounds for vacationers. New and more abundant crops grown on the 500,000 acres to be irrigated will stabilize the agricultural industry over a wide area of the province. New industries will appear utilizing water from the reservoir and power from new hydroelectric installations. Towns and cities will expand to serve the growing population of the area. Urban centres in southern Saskatchewan will have virtually unlimited water supplies for the first time in history. Downstream from the new dam floods will be controlled, river flow maintained, and power sites improved. Throughout the province the waters of the river will give new impetus to economic and industrial development.

A Joint Federal-Provincial Project

The project is to be built under a federal-provincial agreement which provides that the federal government will acquire the necessary lands and will design and construct the reservoir, including the two dams and related works. The relocation of highways and other public works in the area to be flooded will be carried out by the province under a supplementary agreement yet to be negotiated. The cost of reservoir construction will be apportioned, 75 per cent to the federal government and 25 per cent, up to a maximum of $25 million, to the provincial government.

The province is solely responsible for the planning and development of the benefit phases of the project including irrigation, power, recreation, water supply and flood control. No time limit has been placed on this development except that 50,000 acres must be ready for irrigation when the reservoir is completed. The federal contribution to the benefit phases is limited to 25 per cent of the cost of penstocks required for a generating capacity of 200,000 h.p.

The cost of the main reservoir, and the power and irrigation facilities is estimated to be between $164 million and $192 million.

When the reservoir is completed title to the lands and works will be transferred to the province which will assume immediate responsibility for operation. The federal government will remain responsible for reservoir maintenance for a period of ten years, sharing maintenance costs equally with the province during the last four years.

Canada's Largest Rolled Earth Dam

The site for the South Saskatchewan dam, 18 miles up-stream from Outlook, was selected on the basis of topography and location of materials. Foundation conditions dictate that the dam be of rolled earth construction. A structure as high as a seventeen-storey building and nearly three miles long, it will be the largest dam of its kind in Canada and one of the largest in the world. Forty-five million cubic yards of earth will be used to build the embankment; the cement needed would fill 3,000 freight cars. Trains could pass with ease through

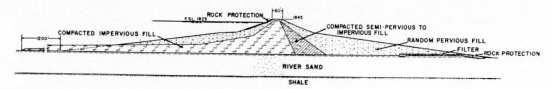

Cross sectional plan of the South Saskatchewan River dam.

any of the five diversion tunnels. During the eight-year construction period a labour force exceeding 1,500 men will be employed.

The dam will be 3,800 feet wide at the base. In cross-section the main embankment will be triangular, 2,600 feet across at the base and 60 feet in width at the top with slopes on both sides varying from 7 degrees at the bottom to 26 degrees at the top. An earth blanket varying in thickness from 10 to about 34 feet will extend beneath the reservoir 1,200 feet upstream from the heel of the embankment to prevent water leaking under the structure. The upper 40 feet of the up-stream face of the dam will be covered with riprap for protection against wave action.

While the main fill is under construction, water from the river will be diverted through five reinforced concrete tunnels, each 20 feet in diameter and stretching about 4,050 feet through the west embankment of the dam. When the dam is completed three of the tunnels will be used to deliver water to turbines in the power station at the down-stream toe of the dam.

A reinforced concrete spillway to be built about one mile south-west of the main fill will utilize a natural depression created by the Coteau Creek, a small tributary which flows into the river just below the dam. The spillway will be 17,000 feet long and will have a discharge capacity of 265,000 cubic feet per second.

The Qu'Appelle dam, a rolled earth structure 90 feet high, 9,000 feet long and 700 feet wide at the base, will be built at the divide between the South Saskatchewan and the Qu'Appelle drainage basins at the head of Aiktow Creek. It will prevent the waters of the reservoir from escaping down the Qu'Appelle Valley, and will permit controlled diversion into the Qu'Appelle system for municipal water supply, recreation and other purposes.

When the reservoir is full, 109,600 acres will be flooded. Most of this area is immediately adjacent to the river and of little agricultural value except for grazing; only 5.2 per cent is now under cultivation.

A Multi-Purpose Project

By 1966, a great new water resource will have been created in an area that has long suffered from recurring drought. The economic and social benefits of the project, direct, indirect and intangible, will develop gradually over a period of several decades. The ultimate impact of the project on the province is a matter of speculation at present. But one thing is certain, through irrigation, power,

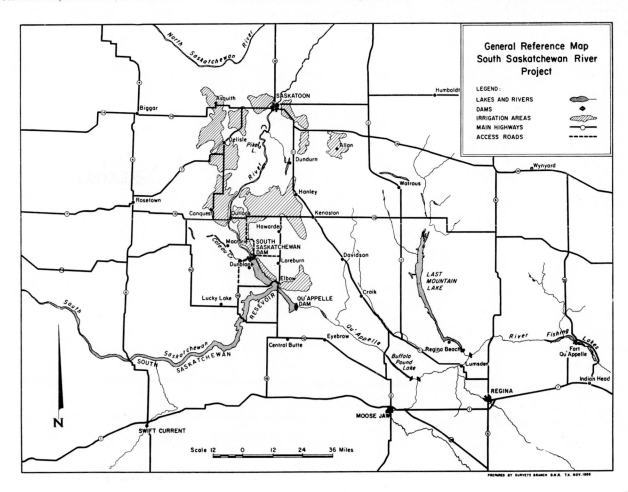

A crop of oats sown on the University of Saskatchewan's irrigation project at Saskatoon which has received only natural moisture.

The other half of the same field shown in the during th

water supply, recreation and flood control, the South Saskatchewan Project will give this province the greatest economic boost experienced in its short history.

The Change in Agriculture

Since it will take at least a generation to develop the full irrigable potential of the South Saskatchewan River Project, the final impact on farming in the area is necessarily somewhat speculative. The transition from dry-land to irrigation farming will be gradual, with most farmers bringing additional acreage under the ditch each year until the complete change is made. The first real effect may not be felt for fifteen years and full development may take as long as twenty-five years. However, if one could look twenty-five years into the future, these are the changes he would probably find.

There will be more farms and they will be smaller. When all of the acreage has been brought under the ditch, more than 1,000 dry-land farms will have become about 2,000 irrigated farms. However, these farms will be larger than most irrigated farms in other projects of today and yesterday. A few years ago a farm of 160 acres with 100 to 140 acres irrigable was considered the maximum size for a family unit. The advances in irrigation technology over the past few years should make it possible to increase the size of farms on this project to about a half section with 200 to 250 acres irrigable.

The irrigation farmer will enjoy a higher income than does the dry-land farmer and this income will be assured. Production per acre is expected to double or triple. Although more intensive agriculture will also mean higher costs per acre, with full development of the irrigation system the costs of operation should be more than offset by increased income.

The large irrigation farmer in Saskatchewan will probably continue to grow wheat, oats, barley and flax and will also diversify to produce forage crops, beef cattle and dairy products.

A typical rotation during the initial stages of irrigation may have one-third to one-half of the land in grain and the remainder in hay or pasture crops. One acre of irrigated pasture will support one or two cattle and should produce about 600 pounds of beef per season; or one acre should yield two or three tons of hay, enough to carry one animal through the winter. Farmers will probably finish their cattle on course grains and fodder produced on their own land.

As the project matures, specialty crops may be introduced but this development is uncertain. Specialty crops will depend on the growth of markets in Saskatchewan's major cities and the availability of capital for processing plants and specialized farm equipment.

Smaller farms and more intensive agricultural methods will mean an increase in the population of the irrigated area, and this increase will be augmented by groups providing business, commercial and other services.

Direct benefits will be felt not only

An irrigated potato crop on the Pre-Development Farm. Note baled alfalfa in the background. Varied crops and various methods of irrigation were studied.

ure. This half of the crop was irrigated twice

in the irrigable area itself but also over a wide area of central Saskatchewan. An immediate result of irrigation will be stabilization of the province's livestock industry through guaranteed supplies of fodder. Winter feed for livestock has always been a major problem in Saskatchewan and supplies of fodder are frequently imported from other provinces at great cost to the provincial treasury and to the industry. Fodder grown on lands irrigated from the new reservoir should be sufficient to supply the agricultural industry throughout a large part of the province, permitting farmers to diversify and stabilize their operations.

Hydro-electric Power

The importance of power to Saskatchewan's rapid economic and industrial expansion is reflected in the fact that the province's requirements for electrical energy are doubling every four years. At present, this power is generated exclusively in thermal stations. The construction of

The federal government's Pre-Development Farm at Outlook. Since 1950 the farm has been conducting irrigation experiments and demonstrating irrigation techniques to farmers.

new hydro stations and their integration with the existing system of the Saskatchewan Power Corporation will permit great flexibility of operation and the generation of base and peak power from the most economical plants.

The initial capacity of the power installation at the South Saskatchewan dam will be approximately 225,000 kilowatts. Three of the five diversion tunnels will be lined with steel penstocks to convey water from the reservoir to three giant turbines in the power house. Construction of the power works is expected to begin shortly after river diversion in the fall of 1963, and to be completed when the reservoir reaches minimum operating level. The facilities will generate in excess of 500 million kilowatt-hours annually, depending on river flows.

Though the hydro development at the dam is important, perhaps a more significant benefit of the project is its effect on the potential of power sites down-stream, particularly at Squaw Rapids, Nipawin, and Fort-a-la-Corne. Together they have six times the energy potential of the South Saskatchewan dam. However, very little storage is available at Nipawin and la Corne, and the development of these sites depends on river control and regulation through storage provided by the South Saskatchewan Project.

Recreation

The development of the reservoir for recreation will directly affect more people than either irrigation or power. The immense lake to be created by the dam will have a shoreline of 475 miles and will stretch from the centre of Saskatchewan almost to Alberta. Since recreation sites in this area are few and badly overcrowded, the new lake is certain to become one of Saskatchewan's largest playgrounds. Careful planning and controlled development should make it a major beauty spot in western Canada.

It is apparent that if the reservoir is to be attractive for recreation extensive afforestation will be necessary. With this in mind the Department of Natural Resources is establishing a new nursery near Prince Albert, which, within three years, will be producing over two million seedlings annually. Seedlings for afforestation will also be obtained from the other nurseries in the province.

Early reports indicate that the lake will support an abundance of both commercial and game fish. For the hunter, both waterfowl and upland game birds will be found in large numbers. Indeed, thousands of waterfowl are expected to nest in the area, and the main migration routes which are presently west of the river will probably shift so that ducks and geese can take advantage of the new expanse of water. Experiences elsewhere indicate that irrigation will bring about an increase in the population of pheasant, a popular game bird in Saskatchewan.

The South Saskatchewan Project will also substantially improve several existing playgrounds in southern Saskatchewan. Diversion from the reservoir into the Qu'Appelle Valley will maintain water levels in Last Mountain Lake and the six lakes in the Qu'Appelle chain. Periodically the level of these lakes falls and various types of algae flourish, making the water unsuitable for swimming.

Urban Water Supply

To urban residents of southern Saskatchewan an adequate water supply will be one of the greatest benefits to be derived from the Saskatchewan Project. Southern cities and towns have been searching for an adequate water supply constantly since they were established. For the first time in history they will be assured of virtually unlimited water for domestic and industrial use.

Regina and Moose Jaw now obtain part of their water from Buffalo Pound Lake, the lake level being maintained by pumping from the South Saskatchewan River into a high-level canal which carries the water over the summit into the Qu'Appelle River. When the reservoir is completed it will be possible to maintain the lake level by gravity flow from outlet works in the Qu'Appelle dam. Alternatively, water for southern cities could be piped directly from the reservoir.

Throughout the southern and central area of the province small urban centres can also look forward to the convenience of modern water and sewer systems. The provincial government may offer some assistance in a municipal water and sewer programme, perhaps in the form of grants, loans or technical assistance.

Industrial Development

Industrial development came late to Saskatchewan. Before and during the Second World War agricultural products accounted for most of the province's output. But within the last fifteen years a resource and industrial boom has raised the proportion of non-agricultural production from less than one-third to about two-thirds of provincial production. The power, water supply and irrigation phases of the project will all contribute directly or indirectly to an acceleration of this industrial growth.

The province's current industrial expansion is based on resource development and a central position in the western market. The South Saskatchewan Project will add new power and water resources to these basic factors. Because industrial development is a cumulative type of growth, the ultimate effects of the project on industrial expansion are difficult to estimate. The direct effects of irrigation will probably take the form of expansion in the feed and meat-packing industries. When the irrigation phase of the project matures and specialty crops are grown on a large scale, processing and canning factories may be established.

Flood Control

A serious flood hazard exists at several points along the south and main branches of the Saskatchewan River. Floods may occur once, twice or several times a year and have three main sources: snowmelt on the plains in April, snowmelt in the mountains sometimes accompanied by heavy rains in June, and prolonged intensive rainfall anywhere in the drainage basin. The regulation permitted by the huge capacity of the reservoir will virtually eliminate flooding on the south branch down-stream from the dam, particularly in the Pike Lake area south of Saskatoon.

Floods on the main branch below the forks also will be greatly reduced. This is of special significance to the agriculturally rich Carrot River Valley and Saskatchewan delta region. The Saskatchewan delta is a gently sloping plain about 30 miles wide and 120 miles long. Most of the sediment carried by both branches of the river has been deposited here for ten thousand years as the course of the river changed frequently, spreading the rich deposits of soil over a wide area. Settlement of the fertile delta land has not been possible because of periodic flooding and poor drainage. The reclamation of even part of this region could mean the development of a new farming area which would be of particular importance in the future as northern resources are developed and northern populations rise.

A Province Looks to the Future

The South Saskatchewan Project is the largest and most expensive enterprise ever undertaken by this province, and it is being undertaken at a time of high and rising costs. Estimates of $118 million to be spent by the provincial government for the dam, irrigation works and initial power facilities represent only a part of the investment made necessary or generated by the project. The actual private and public investment in irrigation development, recreation facilities, water supply, flood control, and power installations at the site and down-stream may well amount to hundreds of millions of dollars over a period of years.

Saskatchewan expects its tremendous investment to be repaid many times over in agricultural stability, industrial expansion, and in a more attractive life for its people. Premier T. C. Douglas made this point when he spoke at the official start of construction in 1959. "The future of Saskatchewan", he said, "depends on our ability to diversify and stabilize our economy . . . The building of the South Saskatchewan River dam can be a turning point in Saskatchewan economic history. With its realization I feel confident that this province will move forward to the high destiny which we all believe lies ahead."

A potential park area in southwestern Saskatchewan. When the reservoir is filled, this part of the valley will become a part of the lake. Extensive afforestation has begun on many such sites.

About 22,000 acres are devoted to grapes in Ontario; most of this acreage is in the three Niagara counties of Lincoln, Welland and Wentworth.

LAND UTILIZATION IN CANADA

by TREVOR LLOYD

CANADA IS IN THE unusual position of having more land than it knows what to do with. This, of course, was one of the driving forces behind the waves that populated North America during the great days of agricultural migration in the latter part of the nineteenth century and the early part of the twentieth. Land was always the great attraction, whether to the Scots crofters who made the Selkirk settlement in the Red River Valley possible, or to the East European peasants who saw no future in cultivating the land of others for a pittance, when broad acres were going begging in Canada.

For decades governments, the railway companies, the Church and the pull of relatives and friends kept a steady stream of agricultural settlers flowing westward across the Atlantic. That there might have been more effective ways of using the new lands to produce foodstuffs, and a less heart-breaking manner of occupying it, is now recognized, but at the time there were no soil surveys, no climatic data, and only the barest of outline maps.

In this hit-and-miss fashion the land was occupied and the best of it has remained so to this day. Some potentially useful acres were doubtless passed by and a good deal of marginal land was unwisely occupied. In any event, the result has been to transform the map of Canada in less than a century and to imprint on it a pattern which will probably always remain. It seems doubtful now that the area of occupied land can be increased appreciably, granted continuation of present day economic conditions and relatively unchanging world political forces. As we shall see, there has already been some retreat from the old periphery and a certain amount of decay at the centre, at least in terms of rural land use. Urban sprawl, still largely unplanned, eats away some of the best and more accessible land, and elementary economics makes it unprofitable to continue to struggle to extend the old frontier.

Such changes in the map of land use are not the only, and perhaps not the most important, current trends. The manner in which the land is being employed to carry out traditional objectives is also changing, in keeping with a quiet but persistent revolution in Canadian society itself. The quite proper insistence on social security, uniform education and welfare standards, and a degree of personal comfort difficult to achieve in remoter areas, are pulling the population toward the modern urban complexes. Fifty years ago, an unusually discerning World War I songwriter enquired "How Can You Keep 'em Down on the Farm After They've Seen Paree?" and the answer has not yet been found. The consequences of "seeing Paree" are world-wide today

and are appearing on the map which records the changing pattern of Canadian land use.

The Changing Land Use Pattern

A map of the occupied land of Canada demonstrates what is not widely appreciated — how remarkably little of the country is in fact in regular use for agriculture. About 7½% of the total land area is so used and the overwhelming part of it is in the south, within about 200 miles of the United States border. The settling of this belt of farmland is in a real sense the history of Canada, and while there has been a retreat from agriculture as the dominant occupation of the country, it remains of very great importance both as a way of life and a source of national wealth.

After almost three centuries of European penetration, the map shows a curiously scattered pattern of occupation. Politicians have long recognized that there are two agricultural Canadas — the east and the west split, which has its origins in both physical and social causes. The prime factor is, of course, in the existence

of a mass of Pre-Cambrian Shield lying to the north of Lake Superior, which effectively separates the farms of Manitoba from those of Western Ontario.

Within the two large east and west areas there are, of course, significant sub-divisions. The scattered pockets of farmland in Newfoundland have little in common with the almost uniform agricultural land use of Prince Edward Island, and of the St. Lawrence Lowland, a relatively small but remarkably diversified farming area. These, too, contrast dramatically with the Shield immediately to the north of the St. Lawrence — an agricultural no-man's-land — and the rolling Appalachian country to the south, where farming as a way of life is retreating and once-cleared land is returning to wilderness.

Even within the forbidding Shield, there are extensive areas which are productive. They are usually lake basins or river valleys and, while in total area they are significant, the conditions restrict much of the land use to "hay and dairy" activities. In Quebec and Ontario together there

A field of sorghum, a new crop of several uses, grown near Pembina in south-central Manitoba. This field is being cut to supplement summer pasture for dairy cows.

Pure-bred Ayrshire cattle on excellent pasture in the county of Deux-Montagnes, not far from Montreal in the province of Quebec.

Canada and in the east, there is an abrupt falling off in the utilization of the land surface. Statistically speaking, the amount of agricultural land in Northwest Territories and Yukon is negligible, perhaps 1,000 acres, mainly in low-lying areas near streams and lakes. The significance of northern farming can be greater than this miniscule acreage would suggest, particularly since intensive use of the land near settlements can provide a valuable local source of fresh vegetables and dairy products.

In summary, while the number of farm units in eastern and western Canada is approximately the same (250,500 and 230,400 respectively) the area of land in use is very different. Thus the acreage under crops in the east is 14,400,000, while in the west it is 48,000,000, a ratio of farmland in the two areas of about 2 to 7.

Following three-quarters of a century of intensive agricultural settlement of the country, it should now be possible to compare the extent of present agricultural land with what may be expected in future. The key fact is that the tide has already turned; there has been a falling off in the area of land so employed. This reflects some of the economic and social factors already mentioned, but also the unwise expansion of farming into areas which would have been better under their original forest cover. From a peak of 174,000,000 acres of agricultural land reported in the 1951 census, there was a decline to 172.5 million acres in 1961, and since then probably a continuing proportionate loss.

The impact of this decline has been felt most in the east (45.5 million acres to 38.3 million acres over the 10-year period), and it has been going on longer. The double effect of farm abandonment and the spread of urban construction has been responsible. Another change in the east has come from an increase in the proportion of intensively cultivated land, so that the abandonment of marginal occu-

are more than two million acres of such land in use. It has been suggested that the Shield could still provide another ten million acres of useful land and that almost half as much unused land still remains in the Atlantic Provinces.

While the land-use map of Eastern Canada necessarily has a spotty and confused pattern, there is a broad simplicity about that of the Prairies. The rolling and flat lands have fairly uniform characteristics over a large area, and what was formerly a region covered largely by grass, or grass with patches of trees, was readily

adaptable to grain farming. Shortage of moisture in the southwest led eventually to use of dry-farming techniques, while in the wooded land that framed the former grasslands, the more podsolized soils, the higher precipitation and shorter season led to mixed farming.

The situation in the western mountain areas of British Columbia is unique. Cultivated land is limited to more level areas accessible to markets for truck farming and fruit growing, with the addition of grazing land on the higher interior plateaus.

Farther north, both in western

pation has gone on side by side with emphasis on more remunerative use of the land still employed. In the west, despite some farm abandonment, there has been a small but steady increase in total acreage, although this is locally less noticeable than re-arrangement of the pattern of farm occupation. Consolidation of farms in the prairies has gone on apace — with a resulting fall in the number of occupied farms — though not in the acreage cultivated. This is but another indication of the drift toward higher capitalization of farms and reduction in the ratio of labour to land — both a manifestation of increased rationalization and mechanization.

Nevertheless, in contrast to some other parts of the world where large-scale agriculture predominates, Canada is still a land of farmers rather than farm managers. "Canada is typically a country of family farms, with the farmer in the role of owner, operator and manager."[1] Thus 77% of farms are operated by owners and less than 1% by managers. In Quebec, where family ties with the land have been long established, 95% of the farms are occupied by their owners. The quite fundamental change in the part played by labour on the farms is perhaps the most striking contrast between the period following World War I and today. Harvest gangs of seasonally hired labour long ago vanished, and "the hired man" himself is becoming rare on many farms. Even since the end of World War II the farm labour force has almost halved (1,186,000 in 1946 in contrast to 674,000 in 1961), so that as a way of life farming today occupies barely 10% of the Canadian population. These changes are demonstrated clearly by the following figures:[2] "The amount of land under cultivation per farm worker increased by 67% between 1941 and 1961, the livestock population by 93% (despite mechanization) and the amount of power and machinery owned by 21.3%". Naturally, the capital value of individual farms has changed with the other factors. So large is the investment today that it is difficult for a young man aspiring to be an owner-farmer to get a start. The direction in which agriculture is moving in Canada appears to be clear. Farms are becoming larger, and more highly mechanized, and labour requirements are falling. Greater specialization is coming about and with it more expert techniques are demanded of the farmer. In many areas truck farming and livestock production are becoming typical. A greatly enlarged local urban market has become available, as have widespread overseas markets, particularly for grain.

Farming today is caught in a period of revolutionary change. The demand for foodstuffs and agricultural raw materials of uniformly high quality, at competitive prices, is compelling rationalization. Just as the way of life of the individual craftsmen or guilds was swept away with industrialization, so it seems may be the small

[1]Weeks, Camu and Sametz, *Economic Geography of Canada with an Introduction to a 68 Region System*, p. 166.
[2]Weeks et al, *op cit*, p. 167.

An apple orchard in full bloom.

farm today. The essential purpose of farming is to produce food and raw materials. Doing this in the world of the late twentieth century may well require new methods and these will be reflected in a changed pattern of land use.

Forest Land Use

It is of the nature of forest-based enterprises that they are usually carried on remote from urban centres and beyond the ken of most of the population. Unlike agricultural land use, at least in Canada, they are not operated by family units with a continuing stake in a specific piece of land. On the contrary, they are often heavily capitalized and centrally controlled, usually at a distance from the scene of operations. In a very real sense they are directly tributary to the nation's industrial complex, whereas farming has until now rarely been so.

In spite of these large-industry-oriented arrangements, most of the country's forest lands are in fact publicly owned. That is, title to them is held by government, essentially the Provincial authorities, to which control of all natural resources has been allocated. The use of forests as a source of industrial raw materials is today a highly technical matter and an internationally competitive one. For this reason alone research is essential, not only to maintain the best possible supply of trees but also to utilize them economically and to devise improved uses from the wood so provided. Here again, the stress is on size, central organization and, of course, cost.

While the industry itself is involved in such research, the main weight of it has always fallen on the Federal Government. Yet despite the centralized control of much of the industry, and the major contribution provided by the taxpayer through research facilities, utilization of the forests of Canada appears to be less efficient than it could be, and this particular

Miles and miles of golden wheat fields greet the fall traveller crossing the western prairies on the Trans-Canada highway.

land use harvests at present far less than it might each year. Some of the reasons for this will be commented on later.

Of the two to three million dollars of production per annum, almost 90% originates in Quebec, British Columbia and Ontario, with the first somewhat in the lead of the other two. Such a distribution is not apparent from examining a map showing the area of activity, if only because B.C. has very intensive and productive lumbering operations in a relatively restricted region. The distribution of mills producing pulp and paper or sawn products shows them to be for the most part marginal to agriculture areas, with the limitation

that pulp and paper centres are often also found close to urban areas: e.g. along the St. Lawrence and Ottawa rivers.

Canada's forests extend from coast to coast in a belt of varying width but at its greatest about 1,300 miles from south to north. Of the 1,700,000 square miles, roughly 1,000,000 are potentially productive. Not all of this huge area can at present be worked economically; transporation routes are in some cases not available to get workers in and the products out. Soft woods are found across the whole of the forest belt while most of the hardwoods are now cut in southern Ontario. Both varieties are available in the Maritimes and in the St.

Lawrence valley. The industry based on these forests is essentially directed towards exports, but practically all of the exports have, in one way or another, received some processing within the country. As a primarily export industry, and one owned to an appreciable extent in the United States, it is sensitive to variations in the prosperity of other lands.

The migration of the forest industry during the past two centuries illustrates its changing relationship to the economy as a whole. Initially a by-product of the Napoleonic wars, it provided cash income from the sale of timber and at the same time improved the value of the newly-settled lands by the mere fact of being removed. Such a close relationship between farming and forestry has continued to be characteristic of parts of Quebec, New Brunswick and Nova Scotia. The St. Lawrence valley and the Ottawa valley were also early centres for large-scale lumbering and in this case rafting of the logs was possible, so that they could in effect be sawn and shipped at sea-level. It was this early utilization of forest accessible to sea-going ships that made lumber the principal Canadian export until the beginning of the present century.

As lumbering cleared the accessible land suited to farming it extended farther into the Shield country and there assumed an independent character, becoming an industry of its own. The speed with which the better forests of Ontario were cleared was remarkable, and also regrettable. The destruction of the forests of the north-eastern United States only added to the demand for Canadian timber.

During the first decade of this century, British Columbia began to develop a timber industry which was always distinct from that of the east. The forests were made up of more massive species, the terrain and cli-

mate were very different and influenced forest practices in their own way, and the sea was close at hand. By 1920, the West Coast was producing more wood than Ontario and six years later was cutting more than half of all the wood produced in Canada.

Viewed as an aspect of land use, the forest industry has complicated political and social relationships. Traditionally, in eastern Canada it has been related to farming, and the decline of the small farm has raised the hope among many that wood-cutting might salvage the dying countryside. It seems clear that this cannot be if the methods of wood gathering are to be efficient and competitive. Central organization and large-scale operations would seem to be imperative. On the other hand, most wood-cutting is being done on Crown lands so that there is a basic public interest in ensuring that it shall be done with a minimum of waste and a maximum of continuity. This naturally leads to close govern-

ment supervision of the allocation of forest lands to the industry. The time may come when careful restrictions will be necessary to ensure that the long-term yield of the forest, about 12 billion cubic feet a year, is not exceeded in a desire to sell as much as possible. At present the amount used up each year is rising steadily but not yet so as to endanger the natural supply.

Contemporary Assessment of Canada's Land Use and Potential

Resource management and the planned development of the rural landscape are comparatively new ideas in Canada. In this, the country has lagged far behind the United States. While the coincidence during the 1930's of an economic depression, which was world-wide, and a local series of dry years in the agricultural heart of the Middle West, shocked the United States government into action which has had dramatic consequences, Canada recognized no such national calamity and produced

On a large ranch in the Cariboo district of British Columbia the cattle are rounded up from the woods and gullies in preparation for calf-branding.

Logs piled up against a picturesque 1885 covered bridge over the Coulonge River, not far from where it flows into the Ottawa.

no corresponding nation-wide response. In fact it was not until 1961, when this particular emergency was past, that an over-all examination of the situation became possible. Then, a broadly representative national "Resources for Tomorrow Conference" was held, which in effect announced that the old carefree "laissez-faire" days were ending. As far as land resources were concerned, there was, parallel with the Conference, development of a strictly governmental agency with responsibility for a national overview of the situation.

Under the Agricultural Rehabilita-

tion and Development Act (ARDA) of 1961, new policies began to take shape and might have moved ahead faster but for the need to work in harmony with ten provincial administrations. This, for Canada, revolutionary change in direction was the political result of profound social changes in the countryside. There were more and more cases of failure to make an adequate living from the land; "rural slums" were spreading through formerly prosperous agricultural communities; there was an obvious and growing contrast in living standards between urban dwellers and those directly dependent on

the farms and forests. One consequence of public concern over this was the setting up of a Senate of Canada Special Committee on Land Use, in part because of the personal awareness of the then Prime Minister (Rt. Hon. Louis St. Laurent), that the old prosperity of the Eastern Townships, where he spent his earlier years, had disappeared, leaving behind abandoned land and marginal living conditions.

Very properly, one of the initial acts of the new ARDA administration was to assess the whole rural situation. Never before had there been a reasonably accurate "Domesday Book" of the land of Canada. The Canada Land Inventory, initiated in 1964, sought to assemble information on how the settled parts of the country are used and, often a very different matter, how they are capable of being used. For the present, this stock-taking is limited to the parts of the country which are, or have been, used for agriculture and to the nearby areas which have a significant effect on employment in this region. In round figures, the area to be covered is about 1,100,000 square miles, or about 32% of the land area of the country.

This is an enormous task and could only be contemplated through use of the most modern techniques. The basic source of data is the aerial photograph, from which information is extracted according to a carefully tested classification. This information is transferred to existing map sheets on a scale of 1:50,000. From the manuscript maps so produced, data can be in turn extracted for use in the computer. Eastern Canada should have been covered by 1968 and the western part of the country about two years later. The basic classification follows:

PRESENT LAND-USE CLASSIFICATION FOR CANADA LAND INVENTORY

Urban
Land used for urban and associated non-agricultural purposes.

(a) *Built-in area*

Land occupied by the built-up portions of cities, towns, and villages, as well as isolated units away from settlements such as manufacturing plants, rail yards, and military camps.

(b) *Mines, quarries, sand and gravel pits*

Land used now, or in the past, for the extraction of earth materials.

(c) *Outdoor recreation*

Land used for private or public outdoor recreational purposes. The sub-category includes the land occupied by summer cottages and associated beach areas, parks, golf courses.

Horticulture
Land used for the intensive production of vegetables and small fruits. Market gardens, nurseries, flower-growing areas and sod farms are included in this category. Farm holdings are usually small and intensively cultivated.

Orchards and vineyards
Land used for the production of tree fruits and grapes.

Baling Christmas trees near Goshen in Guysborough County, Nova Scotia. While many Christmas trees still come from farm woodlots, increasingly they are being treated as a special crop grown on land unsuitable for other purposes.

Cropland

Land used primarily for cash crops, usually in rotation. Cash grains, oil-seeds, sugar beets, potatoes, field beans and peas, and any associated fallow land are included in this category. Feed grains grown for use on the farm are also included in this category.

Improved Pasture and Forage Crops

Land used primarily for the production of improved pasture and hay.

Unimproved Pasture and Range Land

Grasslands such as natural range, rough pasture and scrub grassland.

Woodland

Land covered with tree or scrub growth.

(a) *Productive woodland*

Land bearing forest of a commercial character. Artificially restocked areas, or plantations, are included in this sub-category, regardless of age.

(b) *Non-productive woodland*

Land covered with scrub growth. The sub-category includes recent cut-over and burnt-over areas.

Swamp, marsh or bog

Open wetlands of all types.

Unproductive Land

Land that is biologically unproductive in its present state.

(a) *Sand flats, dunes and beaches*

Land on which an exposed sand surface predominates.

(b) *Rock and other unvegetated surfaces*

Rock barrens, badlands, eroded river banks, etc.

Such an "inventory" is really a supplement to the continous gathering of data by the regular Census of Agriculture. The one provides a reasonably accurate distribution pattern of the various land uses, the other a statistical summary of the changing activity in agriculture based on predetermined census districts. Of course, maps compiled from Census Data cannot locate accurately the position of the various categories of land use.[3]

This is in part because a county unit (the basis for displaying data) may include diverse soils or topographic features with contrasted land use, something which data for the country as a whole cannot reveal.

It would be misleading to imply that the whole of the responsibility for assembling the Canada Land Inventory falls on one agency of the Federal Government. In fact, the project is a remarkable example not only of inter-government co-operation at all levels, but also of collaboration between government, universities, private corporations and individuals. Out of the project there should emerge not only a set of maps which will probably be published in colour at a scale of 1:250,000, but also an analysis of the capability of the land for use within categories having practical application — for example, soil capability from an agricultural point of view. This latter should eventually provide, on a uniform basis, the facts needed to appraise the economic potential of the land, which in turn will make planned use of it for specific crops far more reliable.

Similarly, the soil will be assessed for its suitability for forestry. Any utilization of land for forests must recognize that a decision once made cannot readily be modified because the "crop" is a long time in coming. Again, new maps will be prepared for use by those making decisions on land use for forestry, on a scale of 1:50,000 for planning purposes, and probably 1:250,000 for public use.

New thinking about the better employment of the land of Canada is taking account of needs which were barely discerned a generation ago — among them the setting aside of areas suited to recreation and for the benefit of wildlife. The former is an outgrowth of the intense urbanization not only of Canada but even more so of nearby parts of the United States, the source of many of our tourists.

[3] J. B. McClennan, *Geographical Bulletin, Vol. 7, No. 2*, pp. 74-75.

The demand, particularly by city dwellers, for open-air recreation is growing enormously and, if not met with forethought and intelligence, it will undoubtedly lead to widespread devastation of the more accessible countryside.

The immediate need is to learn where such recreational lands are, how extensive they are and what they are individually suitable for. Priority in this will need to be given to study of areas near the larger cities, but modern transportation enables urban dwellers to move a long way in a short time, so the survey cannot end there. Such an inventory has long been needed in Canada, and there is urgency in perfecting the techniques for providing it. The beginnings of such a system exist in the National Parks Administration but to make a nation-wide survey will call for far more elaborate facilities than it alone can provide.

Wildlife management — and the assessment of land suitable for it — is another neglected field. It is a complex matter because it must take account not only of the terrain itself — which can be mapped — but also the requirements of the various wildlife species and the interests that the population may have in them, whether for hunting and fishing, for scientific study or for conservation and protection.

Conclusion

As for the future, the trend seems to be clear. First, must come an inventory of how the land is used, then an assessment of how it could best be used in terms of productiveness, recreation and conservation. Then a slow but steady re-arrangement of the former to conform to the latter. The days of carefree, open-handed resource disposal are ending. Wise use of the land of Canada is an essential prelude to providing the population, within the country and abroad, with the maximum benefits of which this greatest of all natural resources is capable.

Three generations of one family have cut red spruce, white pine and hemlock from this stand of timber.

In this refinery tankhouse, there are 684 nickel plating tanks, each containing 29 anodes and 28 cathodes. A unit man checks the quality of a nickel cathode halfway through its ten-day growth in a plating tank.

THE THOMPSON

PROJECT

by SYLVIA SEELEY

The commemorative medallion specially struck for the dedication ceremonies at Thompson. It was designed by the Toronto sculptor Dora DePedery-Hunt, and depicts an engineer's dividers pushing back the northern forest to make way for the Thompson project.

Typical of the problems to be solved as mines are developed further north were those of the Thompson nickel project. This article appeared in the November 1961 issue of the Canadian Geographical Journal, shortly after the official opening of the mine and smelter.

ALONG THE PATH that leads to Canada's centenary of 1967 are many outstanding milestones which fully justify the faith of those far-seeing leaders who planned Confederation. In their wake has arisen in every walk of life a series of leaders to pilot Canada into projects of enterprise and energy that command the attention of the business world. After a long line of successes in industry where hand labour was the chief factor, the nation progressed into such specialized achievements as the Kitimat Project, (1954), Knob Lake, (1955), the St. Lawrence Seaway, (1959), and now the most recent of these advances in Canada's industrial life is to be found in the Thompson Project, where land that was an unprofitable wilderness in northern Manitoba as late as 1957 has rapidly been transformed into a community with the second largest nickel producing centre in the free world 75,000,000 pounds a year.

On the cessation of the Second World War, industry became free to renew the search for fresh fields. As a result of developments during the war, airborne methods of ore detection beneath the surface were rapidly coming into use, which speeded up the discoveries of new orebodies. As early as 1946 attention had been focussed on the Canadian shield in northern Manitoba and The International Nickel Company of Canada resumed its prospecting with the aid of airborne devices by which ores can now be detected in the absence of

geological outcrops where the metal lies sleeping far below the surface, unused and defying the earlier conventional methods of prospecting.

In order to perfect these procedures, new airborne equipment was designed. Even so, the discovery of the ore in sufficient quantity was by no means plain sailing. The terrain was difficult and the surface teams who followed up the aerial findings had to be transported by helicopters, tractor trains, snowmobiles, muskeg tractors, and even canoes. The least accessible points could only be reached on foot. Patience, faith, and a great deal of money had to be stretched out over a period of ten years. Some fifty thousand linear air miles of aerial survey had been flown, and there had been headaches and heartaches enough over test drillings that proved abortive, but in 1956 faith and perseverance won out and

a big new orebody was discovered twenty-two miles southwest of Moak Lake, four hundred air miles north of Winnipeg.

It was on the fifth of December 1956 that the (then) Premier of Manitoba and Henry S. Wingate, (then) President of the International Nickel Company jointly announced the inception of a project for the development of the newly discovered orebodies and the project was to be named in honour of Dr. John F. Thompson who had just completed fifty years service with the company. Immediately following this announcement the company set to work with a will on the herculean tasks of felling trees, clearing land, building roads, and laying pipe-lines. Every particle of equipment from hammer and nails to bulldozers, from bread to blankets, had to be transported to the site over rough ground.

Inserting nickel starting sheets in the electrolytic tank at the refinery. The pure nickel is deposited electrolytically on these thin sheets.

By dint of running "the snowball express" twenty-four hours a day, seven days a week, the tractor trains moved thirty thousand tons of material during the winter of 1956-1957. The seventy-mile round trip over snow-covered muskeg and frozen lakes took fourteen hours. It was a desperate race against time to bring in the power shovels, cranes, fuel oil tanks, building material and hardware of every description before the oncoming spring weather would render transport impossible.

Work also proceeded apace on the thirty-one mile branch railway line which links the Thompson works with the Hudson Bay line of the Canadian National Railways line at Sipiwesk. This at once meant the arrival of more workers, more equipment and more materials, and in the period following, hoists were installed, shafts were sunk with narrow gauge transportation lines to connect them underground. There was heavy mechanized equipment to be moved into place; temporary housing and feeding facilities for 3,000 contractors' employees had to be erected on ground which offered peculiar difficulties. It was covered with super-saturated clay which had to be cleared away, for it was frozen rock-hard in winter, and became a quagmire as soon as the spring thaw had set in, making the transport of heavy material impossible.

In the course of road construction this far north, one of the obstacles to be overcome is the permafrost. In this district the road builders found it easier to work while the snow was on the ground as it gave the machines better traction, and a heavy shovel, together with a ripper when necessary, had little difficulty in cutting through the permafrost to excavate for water and sewer mains. Wherever permafrost was encountered it was usually removed from the trenches and the space was backfilled with granular material. Sometimes, where the permafrost was exceptionally deep the trenches were undercut several feet beyond the normal grade and then backfilled. This was an accepted risk which proved to be about fifty per cent successful. In the building of roads it is necessary to guard against the possible results of subsidence or consolidation; also the builders must return to areas where permafrost has existed and add yet more granular material after the frost is out.

At present there are twenty-four miles of provincial highway south of Thompson, six miles of road to the north connecting Thompson with the airport, and ten miles of road laid to the lakes, to the railway and to give access to the river. Within the town area of Thompson itself there are fifteen miles of roadway, which adds considerably to the amenities of the town for permanent residents. There is also passenger service six days a week by rail from Winnipeg. Three of these trains proceed on to Churchill while the other three return directly to Winnipeg. Air service between Thompson and Winnipeg on a six flights a week basis is also available.

It is obvious that newcomers to this district require some period of adjustment on arrival, specially if

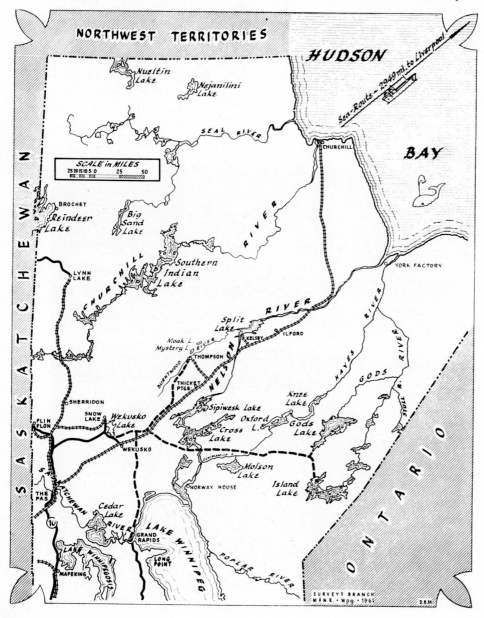

A section of Thompson from the air. A portion of the business district is in the upper centre, and includes the municipal administration building, a hotel, the Manitoba Telephone System building, a theatre, and the Hudson's Bay Company store.

There is a spacious look about the layout of houses at Thompson, but otherwise this might be any new suburb.

The concentrator, which contains the largest ore grinding mills in Canada, has a capacity of 6,000 tons per day. The grinding circuit is controlled from the panel on the left. Behind the panel is one of the three huge concrete fine ore bins, 56 feet in diameter and 63 feet high.

they come from the big cities where most household needs can be obtained at the touch of a button. But it seems axiomatic that a well-adjusted family unit remains well-adjusted irrespective of location, and at Thompson reasonable assistance is always forthcoming to aid a new family start life afresh in strange surroundings. The children appear to enjoy outdoor sports both winter and summer. The winters, though severe, are enjoyable on account of their dryness. As yet, no indoor recreation space is available with the exception of a two-sheet curling rink. No one

appears to suffer unduly from the conditions of life, as the health records are favourable.

Business enterprise is just as free in this new mining town as it is anywhere else in Canada. Neither the International Nickel Company nor the municipality have any part in it nor sponsor it in any way. Each enterprise stands on the merits of the individual or firm who owns and operates it. Twenty-four business sites have been developed to accommodate fifty different types of business outlets, and in order that suitable homes should be provided for the ever in-

creasing number of workers, application was made to the Metropolitan Commission of Winnipeg to draw up plans for the town of Thompson on a site within easy access of the works. This new mining settlement was to be no sprawling frontier outpost but a well-arranged town with residential and business areas designed for orderly growth and development. Plans for all communal facilities were set in order before the first house was built in 1958. Power for the new town and the mine was made available by the new Kelsey plant developed by the Manitoba Hydro-Electric Board at

Grand Rapid on the Nelson River, fifty-three miles northeast of Thompson. The skyline of northern Manitoba is changing fast.

In order to effect the greatest economy of production all mining processes are mechanized by the newest methods. The production shaft was sunk to a depth of 2,100 feet; the development shaft was sunk to a depth of 1,057 feet. Between the two there are four connections at different levels and the work is chiefly by cut-and-fill mining. The broken ore is drawn to the stopes by the ore cars, and after crushing it is stored at first in an underground bin and then hoisted to the surface storage bins. Minor quantities of cobalt, platinum metals, gold and silver are present in the ores but unlike those of Sudbury they contain very little copper.

The valuable minerals in the ore are separated from the rock constituents by a flotation process. The nickel concentrate is then pumped to the Thompson smelter where it is thickened and then filtered and charged into one of three fluid bed roasters. Thence it is carried with the gas stream from the roasters into refractory-lined cyclones where the solid particles are settled out and dropped to the furnace feeding mechanism below. The roasted concentrates are smelted in three 18,000 kilovolt-ampere furnaces. The furnace matte is transferred in ladles by sixty-ton overhead cranes into one of four converters where iron is oxydized and removed as slag. The molten nickel sulphide or Bessemer matte is cast directly into refinery anodes. After cooling the anodes are dissolved electrolytically in plating tanks producing pure cathode nickel.

This direct method is a recent development and has been used successfully at the Company's nickel refinery at Port Colborne in Ontario. The electrolytic solutions are treated for the removal of impurities and for the recovery of cobalt which is shipped as an oxide. Spent anodes together with an adhering high sulphur residue are crushed and washed. A filter cake obtained from the washings is melted and the sulphur is removed, leaving a precious metals residue which is shipped to the Copper Cliff refinery for further processing. The cathode nickel is sheared in the refinery and shipped to markets in Canada, the United States, the United Kingdom and other industrial areas of the free world to be used for making stainless steel, for the electroplating industry and in making over three thousand alloys that are strong, tough and resistant to heat and corrosion.

All these satisfactory achievements are the end product of much planning and administrative work, which calls for the construction of suitably equipped buildings that must also have room for research laboratories, and engineering, metallurgy and geology personnel. There must be warehouses and workshops, generators and high pressure turbo-compressors and a power room for the power distribution system. In addition there must be changing houses to accommodate both miners and surface workers. All these facilities are provided on the most modern lines.

Situated just two miles from the plant and covering an area of 3,000 acres is the new town of Thompson where 2,200 men, women, and children have permanent homes. The initial plans provide comfortable living facilities for an anticipated population of 8,000, and there are temporary

Mining operations at Thompson. The man on the left is drilling holes for rock-bolting to support the roof.

Handicrafts of all kinds flourish. Here is a leathercraft class for adults.

Shopping at the meat counter in a fully stocked and equipped supermarket.

construction camps housing an additional 2,600 workers. The town is under the administration of the new local government district of Mystery Lake whose chief is appointed by the Provincial Government of Manitoba. As the International Nickel Company defrayed the cost of land clearance, town planning, the installation of all basic necessities such as drainage, sewerage, pure water supply, roads, sidewalks, fire station, fully equipped hospital and schools, the town has the unusual advantage of starting its municipal life free from debt, which means that taxation can be kept to a minimum for the present.

The first elementary school was formally opened on the tenth of September 1959 with 144 pupils. A second elementary school was opened in April of this year and the total student population now stands at 600, taught by a staff of twenty-five teachers. The first high school will be completed by November 1, 1961. The hospital, like everything else in Thompson, is designed for expansion and the same may be said of the churches, shops and recreation cen-

tres. The surrounding wilderness affords unlimited opportunities for hunting and fishing, and it is to the interest of the project that its workers should be contented and willing to put down roots in the new area.

With so much expense in outlay and development it is important for the company to assess correctly, as far as it is possible, the probable quantity of ore that will become available for working and then to adapt the rate of procedures on lines carefully planned to avoid unduly rapid depletion of the orebody. Examples are not lacking which prove the disasters that can be induced by want of such preliminary foresight. Ancient ghost towns give dismal proof of wasted effort in the heedless days of mining rushes when little regard was paid to the possible life of a newly discovered ore bed. Today, a well calculated rate of production is economically measured against the probable life of the mine to avoid premature exhaustion of the ore. This procedure also underlines the fact that the search for new locations of ore-rich terrain must be carried on

all the time so that there will be some new enterprise ready to hand, as each ore deposit is finally worked out to the limit of its economic usefulness.

Another major factor in the success of any project lies in the question of demand and supply. The markets must be carefully watched, because new inventions and discoveries in other fields of labour may enhance or diminish the demand for any given product and mining production must be graduated accordingly, to meet any variations in demand. Without due regard to the supply on hand, and the variability of industrial needs, no mine can be efficiently run, and there must be a ready flexibility of policy and willingness to meet any industrial changes that may affect the demand for the metal or mineral in question.

The new output at Thompson has set the free world's nickel production capacity at an all-time high. Exclusive of Cuban production capacity which has ceased for the present to be available to the western world, it is estimated that the free world production will exceed 600,000,000 pounds by the end of 1961, of which Canada's contribution amounts to seventy-five per cent. Sudbury and Thompson together have an annual production capacity of 385,000,000 pounds. Scientific research is necessary to develop new nickel-containing products and new markets must constantly be sought with the aid of good merchandising, good advertising and all the modern accessories of sales promotion.

The very wide range of uses to which nickel alloys can be put was made clear in an address to shareholders, given by Mr. Henry S. Wingate, Chairman of the International Nickel Company, shortly following the formal opening of the new project at Thompson. In the course of his speech he said, "On March 7, an experimental United States Government airplane — the X-15 — crossed the skies at the greatest speed ever attained by a manned vehicle, 2,905 miles per hour. The metal skin of the airplane reached a temperature of 700 degrees Fahrenheit during flight, yet retained its strength. This metal skin is made of 'Inconel X' alloy, one of a series of high strength, high temperature alloys developed by our research staff and produced in our rolling mills. As a commentary on the versatility of nickel, another nickel alloy we have developed is for use in storing liquefied gases at temperatures as low as 320 degrees below zero, Fahrenheit. This is a nine per cent nickel steel which we successfully demonstrated in 1960."

Further research has resulted in the production of an alloy containing eighteen per cent nickel as well as lesser amounts of cobalt and other elements designed to withstand exceptionally high pressure and stress. These new allows help to create their own markets as they serve to make possible enterprises which could not have been attempted before their invention.

Hockey leagues for all ages flourish, organized and run by the Thompson Athletic Association.

The next expansion of the nickel industry brought about by the Thompson project has the added value of providing employment opportunites for Canadians and immigrants alike and in Mr. Wingate's words, "It is also providing the basis for providing a still greater inflow of foreign exchange to assist in alleviating Canada's imbalance in international payments . . . It also encourages continued confidence in Canada's producers by demonstrating anew to nickel consumers that Canada is the world's most dependable source of nickel supply." This same point was also stressed by the Premier of Manitoba, Mr. Roblin, on the occasion of the opening of the new Thompson mine. In the course of his speech he said, "With the need to create new international markets to sustain our economic growth, the export of a finished product — electrolytic nickel — has important ramifications." He also recalled the fact that it was for the purpose of exploiting the fur trade in this very region that King Charles II had granted a charter to the Governor and company of adventurers of England trading into Hudson Bay in the year 1670. He pointed out that now, nearly three hundred years later, a lump of ore has replaced the fur pelt as a symbol of the richness and the potential of

this great region, and he added, "We pay tribute to a Company of Mining Adventurers — men who without a government charter or special privileges from the Crown have paved the way for the permanent development of this frontier land." He also drew attention to the fact that because of this new development in Canada's nickel deposits, world attention had been rivetted on the northland, the province had experienced an accelerated programme of exploration. Because Manitoba desired to open this great new frontier economically, a new road building project has been planned to speed the work in this great wealth-producing area of the province.

Although Canada is the world's leading producer of nickel, she is a very small consumer and uses only about one-fortieth of her own nickel producing capacity. The chairman of the company therefore emphasises the fact that all the new output from Manitoba must be marketed outside Canada. The work of building up new markets in the United States, Europe and elsewhere is a vital companion enterprise to the mining itself, and will help to determine Canada's own international status in the industrial world, and her potential to meet the requirements of the age of space exploration.

TEEMING WATERS

Spanish pair trawlers at dockside in the harbour of St. John's, Nfld. These and other ships of the international fleet fishing the Grand Banks often seek shelter or take on supplies at St. John's.

The Story of Canada's Fisheries
by MARK RONAYNE

This account is taken from an article which appeared in the Canadian Geographical Journal *in September 1960. At a time when the world's supply of food is of great international concern this Canadian resource is of special interest. On both the East and West coasts the "harvest" has been reaped by fishermen of other nations, as well as by Canadians, for many years, to our mutual benefit.*

WHEN, IN 1957, huge trawlers lowered their nets into the Atlantic off Canada's east coast to bring up copious catches of redfish from hitherto unfished waters, history had once again come full cycle in repeating itself. For, as early as 1497, the year of Canada's discovery, it was being said of the waters of this new world:

"The sea is full of fish which are

taken not only with the net but also with a basket in which a stone is put so that the basket may plunge into the water . . . "

Today, after four and a half centuries, notable changes have come over the fisheries off our east coast, in the species sought, the ships that pursue them and in the catching methods. But one factor remains unchanged — from the earliest days of

Canadian otter trawler, fishing on the Grand Banks, with its net alongside after a tow. While this ... ep produced mostly haddock, such trawlers take a variety of other groundfish species, such as cod ... different types of flatfish.

241

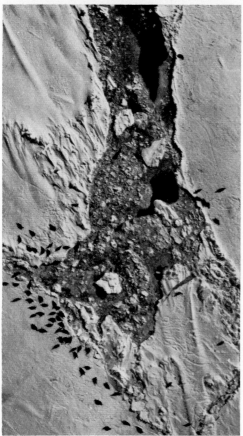

"Sworders" leaving Glace Bay, Cape Breton, Nova Scotia, for fishing grounds.

discovery to the present, the wealth of these waters continues to be a prize coveted by fishermen of many European as well as the two North American nations, and food from these teeming waters continues to follow multilaned routes to many parts of the globe.

Richly endowed as she is on the east coast, Canada is no less fortunate in the resource of her Pacific waters. Here, too, are found the requisites of a great natural heritage replete with variety, quality and abundance. Based on the all-important salmon, the west coast fisheries also have access to important stocks of halibut, herring and various groundfish and shellfish species which support a rich and multi-faced industry.

Rounding out the picture of Canada's fisheries are those of the immense stretches of inland lakes and rivers which comprise over one-half the freshwater area of the earth. The inland fisheries are widely dispersed over the central and prairie provinces and today are reaching ever farther into the northland.

From these vast resources of ocean, river and lake, offering some 150 species of fish and shellfish of commercial importance, Canada's 80,000 fishermen annually harvest two billion pounds for which they receive upwards of $100 million. From the catch, the processing industry, employing some fifteen thousand men and women, produces a wide variety of food items in fresh, frozen, salted, pickled, canned, smoked and other forms, together with an imposing list of by-products comprising chiefly animal feeds and industrial oils, all having a marketed value of some $200

Left: Aerial photograph of a seal herd on the ice-floes off Newfoundland.

Right: The old and new method of harvesting clams.

million. The United States is Canada's principal customer, but many other countries, principally in the Caribbean, South American and European theatres together with the Far East and Commonwealth areas, also represent important markets.

Atlantic Fisheries

The fisheries along Canada's Atlantic seaboard are shared by five provinces: Newfoundland, Nova Scotia, New Brunswick, Prince Edward Island and Quebec. From Grand Manan, New Brunswick, in the south to Cape Chidley at the northern tip of Labrador, including the deep indentations of hundreds of bays, coves and inlets, the protruding headlands and offshore islands, the entire shoreline stretches some 12,000 miles.

Dominant among the species taken by the inshore Newfoundland fishermen is the cod which swarm into

These P.E.I. fishermen use rake-ended, scissors-like tongs to bring up oysters from a Malpeque oyster bed.

A fisherman removes his lobster catch from a trap set off the coast of Nova Scotia.

coastal waters during the summer months to feed on vast schools of silvery little capelin which come in to the beaches to spawn.

Other species taken in Newfoundland's coastal waters include: Atlantic salmon, herring, mackerel, turbot and squid. Only two shellfish species are harvested, lobsters along most of the coastline and scallops in a relatively limited area on the province's west coast.

As in Newfoundland, the majority of fishermen in the Maritime provinces — Nova Scotia, New Brunswick, Prince Edward Island — and Quebec are employed in the inshore fishery. Throughout most of this huge area, which takes in the Gulf of St. Lawrence, the Bay of Fundy and numerous large bays, there is seasonally a great variety and abundance of fish and shellfish. The groundfish species, those living on or near the bottom, are well represented with cod, haddock, pollock, hake and different kinds of flatfish, these being

supplemented by so-called "estuarial" species such as salmon, alewives, smelt and shad.

A delight of the gourmet as well as the everyday meal planner are the shellfish caught throughout most of the Maritimes region. By far the most important of these is the lobster, taken in all four provinces, which has the distinction of being the most important income producer of all species in Maritimes waters. Because of fishing intensity and their high vulnerability to overfishing, lobsters are rigidly protected as to fishing seasons which vary throughout the lobstering district.

Oysters, a valuable crop, are fished both from public beds where they grow "wild", and from leased beds which are under cultivation. Prince Edward Island is one of the main producers of cultivated oysters, and the name Malpeque stands for an epicurean treat.

Clams are another important shellfish in many parts of the Maritimes

and are usually dug or raked. Stocks in deeper waters inaccessible to hand-diggers can now be exploited too as the result of the development of a mechanical clam digger by the Fisheries Research Board of Canada.

Among the most abundant of pelagic species in the Maritimes are herring, which are caught in weirs, gill-nets and purse seines. Herring also have a special significance for the sandy, windswept Magdalen Islands. For the fisherfolk there, this species constitutes the bulk of their landings.

Several other species of varying importance are caught by commercial fishermen of the Maritimes area. These include mackerel, which are taken almost everywhere, and others of regional rather than general importance.

"It's like Main Street on Christmas Eve", is the way one veteran bluewater Canadian fisherman is wont to describe the Grand Banks during the height of the fishing season. By night the scene is especially impressive as

The sardine industry of Southern New Brunswick relies heavily on weirs to catch the miniature herring. The weir is seined to bring the fish together into a mass for taking into the boats.

A fishway on the big falls on Newfoundland's Terra Nova River.

the amber islands of light move slowly across the vast ocean void, ever fishing. Here assembles the last great ocean-going schooner fleet, the dory fishers of Portugal, who come out under taut sails as they have for upwards of four centuries. Today their fleet also includes many otter trawlers dragging huge, cone-shaped nets across the bottom, and mingling with similar ships from France, Italy and Spain.

Fished for cod since their earliest days of discovery, these rewarding underwater plateaux have in recent years been contributing other food species in massive volume to the world's tables, including haddock, pollock, halibut, hake, redfish and a mixture of flatfish. Despite the intensive scouring over the centuries, the banks continue to offer new fishing lodes such as the untapped red-

Salmon being brailed aboard a purse seiner off the B.C. coast. This type of vessel is the largest in Canada's Pacific operations for the valuable salmon.

fish stocks discovered a few years ago and now exploited by at least five nations.

Another important offshore fishery is for scallops, mainly on Georges Bank off the Gulf of Maine. Within recent years new scallop grounds have been found by Canadian fisheries scientists on the southern part of St. Pierre Bank, which are said to be sufficiently extensive to support commercial operations.

Swordfishing, in which well over 100 boats engage, may also be classed as a deepsea operation although the fish are taken on the surface. The "broadbills", which average 200 pounds but individually often weigh up to 600 pounds, are captured by hand harpoons. Such a harpoon, equipped with an electrically charged head, has been proven successful in killing swordfish quickly and efficiently.

Daring and danger are epitomized in the sealfishery out of Newfoundland and Nova Scotia ports in the waning days of winter and early spring. Two species of northern seals, the harps and hoods, are hunted in sturdy, iron-prowed motor vessels along the Arctic icefloes on which the mammals whelp.

The two main sealing grounds are the "Northern Front", off Newfoundland's northeast coast, and the Gulf of St. Lawrence. In addition to the shipboard operation, landsmen also take varying numbers when drifting ice brings the seals within striking distance from shore.

Pacific Fisheries

When the first white pioneers arrived on the Pacific Coast, they found that fish, in this case salmon, had from some unknown time been a prime factor in the livelihood of the native Indian tribes, with many villages located close to choice river fishing sites. To this day the salmon species — sockeye, coho, pink, chum and spring — dominate the British Columbia fisheries in value, but the present highly-mechanized industry exploits many other fish and shellfish as well.

Notable after salmon are the hali-

A small salmon troller cruises slowly over sparkling Pacific waters.

but stocks, the largest on this continent, and the herring which habitually outrank in volume the combined catch of all other species on our Pacific Coast. Most of the West Coast fishing activity is carried on in waters close to shore, or sheltered by the chain of large islands which act as a natural breakwater against the ocean's turbulence along much of the British Columbia coast. The principal offshore fishery is for halibut, on the prolific grounds in the Gulf of Alaska and the Bering Sea.

The salmon are taken in coastal and estuarial waters when they make their annual pilgrimage from the ocean to spawn in British Columbia's rivers and streams. This fishery is a highly concentrated one, with something new being added almost every season, in vessels and catching equip-

ment, to make operations more efficient.

Pacific salmon are justly regarded as a quality product for which the demand, both on the domestic market and abroad, consistently remains high. For this reason they are intensively exploited, and, to avoid their being over-fished, the various populations are protected by regulations covering catching gear, and seasons designed to provide escapement of sufficient spawning stock to ensure adequate seeding.

In their freshwater habitat the salmon may face hazards in the form of natural and man-made obstacles, predatory enemies, pollution of streams by industrial wastes, or floods and droughts caused by indiscriminate removal of forest cover from the stream banks. Here further protection is provided by the federal Department of Fisheries which, by stream clearance programs, the building of fishways and by other remedial meas-

The Hells Gate fish ladders on the Fraser River aid the return of spawning salmon runs to this river system.

ures, seeks to preserve and enhance the salmon's spawning and early-life environment. So thorough has been this work that runs of salmon threatened with extinction have been successfully restored, and man-made spawning beds are bringing new stocks into existence.

Similar rigid protection is provided for the halibut and herring stocks, both of which are avidly pursued by the west coast industry. A case in point was the serious decline in halibut stocks which led to an agreement, in 1923, between Canada and the United States aimed at reviving them. Under a system of quotas the halibut grounds have become even more highly productive than at any previous time. Halibut are caught by the long-line method and are marketed as fresh or frozen.

Pacific herring, caught in purse seines, are also hedged by a protective quota system established and enforced by the federal Fisheries Department. These stocks, too, continue to flourish and support the province's important oil and fish meal industry.

Adding variety to the Pacific catch are such groundfish as gray cod, lingcod, sablefish, soles and mixed flounders. Among the shellfish species, crabs and oysters compete for supremacy while clams, shrimps and prawns also contribute a share to overall landings.

Inland Fisheries

For most Canadians the multitude of lakes, rivers and streams from coast to coast are mainly a holiday retreat. But there are thousands of others for whom the nation's 260,000 square miles of freshwater area are as much a commercial fishing territory as are the oceans for the salt-water fisherman.

Over 600 lakes are commercially fished but the major share of landings, understandably, comes from the larger and more accessible areas. Among these the principal producers are the Great Lakes, notably Lakes Erie and Huron, Great Slave Lake in the Northwest Territories, Lakes Winnipeg, Winnipegosis, Manitoba and The Pas in Manitoba, Athabaska Lake in Saskatchewan and Lesser Slave Lake in Alberta. New roads knifing into wilderness areas are gradually bringing previously inaccessible sources into range.

Ontario ranks as the largest fresh fish producer, followed in order by Manitoba, Saskatchewan, Alberta and the Northwest Territories. Principal species according to volume are whitefish, perch, pickerel, lake trout, herring, pike, suckers, sauger, and smelts.

As with the marine species, the freshwater catch is marketed in a variety of forms: dressed and whole, fresh, frozen and filleted. The highly regarded "Winnipeg Goldeye", which now come mostly from Ontario and Alberta, are smoked, and others are frozen in blocks, to be used eventually for certain specialty fish products appearing in glass jars.

Many of the inland areas are vulnerable to over-fishing and suitable safeguards have been devised to ensure productivity. However, some freshwater territories have peculiar problems for which new remedies must be prescribed. Such a complication was presented in the invasion of the Great Lakes by predacious sea lampreys, following the building of locks and canals. In particular, they are regarded as being largely responsible for the diminution of whitefish and lake trout stocks in the lakes.

To meet this challenge, Canada and the United States have joined, in

A British Columbia gill-netter hauling his net for salmon. Gill-netters, the smallest units of the fishing fleet on the Pacific Coast, are also the most numerous.

Fishermen lifting pound net on Lake Erie, Ontario. A large variety of fish is taken from this and other lakes in Canada's vast freshwater areas.

the Great Lakes Fishery Commission, in an all-out program to find ways of eradicating the sea lampreys. So far considerable success has been obtained by using electrically charged barriers to block the predators from their spawning streams, and more recently a chemical has been developed which, when introduced into breeding streams, destroys the young lamprey but is harmless to desirable sport and commercial fish. The lamprey control program is to be followed by a program of re-stocking with trout to boost recovery of these stocks.

Another marine species which has thrived in the Great Lakes is the smelt which were transplanted from their ocean habitat to some lakes adjoining Lake Michigan as forage for the local species. In some way — whether through a broken dam or overflow — the smelt found their way into Lake Michigan, continued on through Lake Huron, and eventually arrived in Lake Erie, where they flourished. In ten years the smelt populations have attained such proportions that they are now an important factor in the region's fishing industry. The bulk of the catch is taken in shallow waters when the fish congregate to spawn. This limits their availability to a relatively short period. To extend the fishing season for smelt, the federal Department of Fisheries is experimenting with gear which will take smelt in the lake's open waters and successful work has already been conducted with the midwater trawl.

The Northern Resources

Any discussion of Canada's fisheries resource would be incomplete without a reference to the potential of the vast northern areas of ocean and inland waters. Historically, these resources have been exploited chiefly by the native populations for food purposes. A limited commercial fishery has for many years been based on the white whale herds, particularly in the Churchill area of Hudson Bay. These mammals are hunted with harpoons and guns, chiefly from small boats, and are protected by a catch quota. A relatively minor fishery for Arctic char has also been launched as one facet of the general development of the northland.

Without doubt the most important factor in the north's fisheries future is the scientific research program that is now being carried out. These investigations, which have been going on for years, have been intensified as a result of the increased attention focussed on the overall resources of the northern areas. There is a general feeling that this region has a fisheries potential as yet unexploited; success or otherwise in this regard will be

A swirl of smoke clouds the harpoon fired at a humpback whale off the British Columbia coast. Air is pumped into the captured whale to keep it afloat until the "catcher" boat arrives to tow the whale to the factory.

revealed by the probing light of scientific research.

A high order of diplomatic and administrative ability is called for in dealing with problems associated with the international fisheries adjacent to our coasts. In the solution of such matters, Canada takes a leading role as signatory to seven international conventions covering fish stocks in which this country has an interest.

It is significant that the first international treaty of any kind which Canada signed in her own right was the halibut treaty with the United States in 1923. Two additional treaties of a bi-lateral nature, with the United States, over the sockeye and pink salmon resource of the Fraser River-Juan de Fuca Strait on the

A halibut fisherman takes in a big fish on his longline. Halibut fishing on the West Coast is closely controlled by international agreement.

Pacific and the jointly-shared fisheries of the Great Lakes.

Treaties of a broader nature include the International Commission for the Northwest Atlantic Fisheries in which twelve nations now participate; the International North Pacific Fisheries Commission in which Canada has as partners the United States and Japan; the International North Pacific Fur Seal Commission composed of Canada, Japan, U.S.S.R. and the U.S.; and the International Whaling Commission which is worldwide in membership.

Through these groups, through various committees on the home front, and by the efforts of its staff across the country, the federal Department of Fisheries seeks to preserve and expand Canada's rich heritage of ocean and inland waters for the benefit of today's population and for generations of Canadians to come.

EAS

by JAMES S. DUNCAN

This account, from the May, 1959, issue of the Canadian Geographical Journal, *formed part of an address by Mr. Duncan, then chairman of the Hydro Electric Power Commission of Ontario, to the annual meeting of the Royal Canadian Geographical Society in that year.*

IT IS EASY to understand why this colourful project, the St. Lawrency Seaway, with all its international connotations, should have captured the imagination of the peoples of the world. The Seaway will provide a deep-water channel of 27-foot draft, almost halfway across the continent, opening the heart of North America to a major portion of the world's salt-water shipping.

The old canal system in the International Rapids section ceased to operate when we raised the water levels at the power project on July 1st of last year. The remainder of the 14-foot system continued in use until the close of navigation last year. When this system was in operation it was necessary for steamship operators in the Great Lakes to operate two fleets: one which remained in the lakes and sailed between Fort William or Port Arthur and Lake Ontario, and another, composed of ships drawing only fourteen feet of water, much smaller and narrower in beam, which could travel between Lake Ontario and the St. Lawrence ports.

In addition to this, upwards of eighty per cent of the world's ocean freight traffic, which previously could not navigate beyond the port of Montreal, will now have access to the Great Lakes.

It is obvious that the elimination of trans-shipment and the direct access of larger ships with greater cargoes will result in lower shipping costs and therefore will accelerate international trade. These costs will be reduced in at least four ways. First, the operating cost per ton of capacity, because of the larger size of the vessels, will be lower. Secondly, the expenses involved in trans-shipment of cargo to smaller vessels or rail transportation will be largely eliminated. Thirdly, the risk of damage, weight loss and deterioration, always present in the transfer of cargo, will be removed. Fourthly, there will be a substantial saving of time.

It is perhaps a little early to estimate what the saving in cost will actually be, but I am informed on reasonable authority that the decrease in cost of shipping grain from the Lakehead to Montreal and other ocean ports will range from three to seven cents per bushel. The cheaper water transport which will ensue will accelerate the already rapid expansion of the industrial empire surrounding the St. Lawrence-Great Lakes Basin, and at the same time will assist in the gradual development of this area into a major centre of international trade.

The Seaway is but a small part of what is called the St. Lawrence and Great Lakes Basin, a vast drainage system covering an area of 680,000 square miles (nearly eight times the total area of Great Britain) and including the five Great Lakes, which contain nearly half the fresh water of the world.

The area bordering this system contains what has been described as the greatest concentration of industry in the world. More than sixty per cent of all Canadians live in the provinces of Ontario and Quebec adjoining the water-way. These provinces account for nearly eighty per cent of Canada's manufacturing and processing industries. They also share a large portion of Canada's abundant natural resources.

On the other side of the dividing line, the eight States adjacent to the

The Honore Mercier highway bridge and the Caughnawaga C.P.R. railway bridge at Montreal, which had to be modified to provide 120-foot clearance over the Seaway canal.

Seaway possess thirty-five per cent of the population of the United States. Almost one-half of the total American exports of non-agricultural products to overseas destinations originate in the Great Lakes Basin.

Physically, this inland water-way consists of five navigational steps as the river drops from the head of the lakes to the ocean. A fall of twenty-one feet between Lake Superior and Lake Huron is traversed by the locks at Sault Ste. Marie. The second step is found in the St. Clair River-Detroit area, with a drop of eight feet into Lake Erie.

In the Niagara River, between Lake Erie and Lake Ontario, Nature formed Niagara Falls, majestic as a cataract but also a formidable obstacle to navigation. Along with the rapids, this provides a drop of 326 feet, which is by-passed by means of the Welland Ship Canal, built by Canada across the Niagara Peninsula.

The fourth step is a fall of 225 feet in the upper St. Lawrence River between Lake Ontario and Montreal. This section includes the International Rapids, the site of some of the major works of the Seaway and of the power development. Finally, between Montreal and the sea there is another drop of twenty feet.

So much has been said and written of the present St. Lawrence Seaway that many of us forget the fact that Canada built a nine-foot seaway connecting the Great Lakes to the ocean, which was completed in 1850. The deepening of the locks, canals and channels of this system, after Confederation, was finished in 1904 and permitted vessels of 12½-foot draft and under to use its facilities.

The purpose of the latest Seaway project is to deepen the section between Montreal and Lake Ontario, a distance of approximately 183 miles, and the Welland Canal across the Niagara Peninsula, to a maximum of twenty-seven feet.

When Canada completed the Welland Canada in 1932 it was built to accommodate ships of 23½-foot draft. This was for a dual purpose. Primarily, of course, it allowed communication between the Great Lakes and Lake Ontario by large ships measuring 700 feet in length, which carry huge cargoes of coal and iron ore, petroleum, cement, grain, and so on, to ports between the Lakehead and Lake Ontario. At the same time Canada foresaw that some day the channels on the St. Lawrence would be deepened, enabling larger freighters to travel from the oceans of the world to the Great Lakes into the heart of the North American continent.

The deepening of the Welland Canal to twenty-seven feet, which was undertaken as a part of the new St. Lawrence Seaway, was greatly facilitated as a result of the work which was undertaken in 1932.

The new locks have a usable length of 768 feet and are 80 feet wide. They will enable lake freighters of up to 25,000 tons to travel between the Great Lakes and the ports along the lower St. Lawrence. Thus the new Seaway will accommodate vessels having a capacity nine to ten times larger than those which used the old St. Lawrence canals.

The twenty-one locks of the old Canadian seaway system have been replaced by seven, five of which are on the Canadian side and two on the American — the Eisenhower and the Snell.

It is interesting to note in this connection that provision has been made by Canada so that, if necessary in the future, two additional locks could be built on the Canadian side at relatively small expense. These additional locks would permit traffic to pass through the entire St. Lawrence Seaway, using Canadian structural facilities only.

Ports, such as Toronto for example, are spending millions of dollars to improve their facilities to meet the requirements of greater traffic and larger vessels. It is estimated that approximately $100,000,000 is being spent by the United States and Canada in the improvement of their port facilities along the Seaway system.

In accordance with legislation enacted in both the United States and Canada when construction was approved, the capital cost of this navigational project will be liquidated over a fifty-year period by means of a system of tolls on ships making use of the water-way.

It is imperative that these rates should not be set too high lest the objectives of this imaginative project — namely, to provide a cheaper form of transportation to and from the Great Lakes area — be defeated.

By far the largest tonnage of traffic on the St. Lawrence Seaway will move, of course, between American and Canadian ports, but I have seen one estimate which suggests that within a decade the volume of direct overseas shipments will be five times larger than it is at present.

We must not expect miracles. The build-up of traffic will be gradual. Problems of pilotage, of traffic congestion and transfer of overseas cargoes to other ports during the winter season, when the Seaway is closed to shipping, will be encountered.

The advantages of this enlarged water-way connecting the oceans of the world with one of the richest industrial, agricultural and mineral areas of the continent are, however, self-evident. An indication of the growing interest of shipping firms in the St. Lawrence Seaway can best be illustrated by the statement that some

years ago only seven or eight lines competed for overseas business out of the port of Toronto. Last year the port of Toronto had twenty-seven lines competing for business, with 150 ships serving European ports and South America. They are obviously preparing themselves to be ready competitively against the day, so rapidly approaching, when the 27-foot depth will give access to upwards of eighty per cent of the freighters which travel the high seas.

Transportation has always been vital to Canadian progress. A small scattered population, taming a vaster space than ever in human history was brought to man's use by so few people, natural resources remote from the centres of habitation, a dependence upon far away export markets — all these things have made an efficient system of transportation essential for the continued growth of our economy.

The Eisenhower Lock, the most westerly of the two United States locks on the Seaway, built near Massena, New York. The lift of this lock is 38 feet.

The Mountainous North: Looking south up the valley of the Bonnet Plume River, in the northern Yukon with part of the Mackenzie Mountains in the foreground.

THE FACE OF THE NORTH

by N. L. NICHOLSON

This is our challenge and our promise — the inhospitable north, whose riches are not to be won easily but which are well worth the winning. This account appeared in the September, 1958, issue of the Canadian Geographical Journal.

THE TERM "the Canadian North" has a different meaning for different people and in no interpretation of the term are there more divergent views than with regard to the area to which it refers. To a non-Canadian it may be all of Canada. To most Ontarians it may be the gold mining district of Timmins or the James Bay port of Moosonee. Yet both Timmins and Moosonee are in more southerly latitudes than Edmonton which to Albertans, at least, is merely the southern gateway to "the North".

A simple definition is elusive. Perhaps the best that we can say is that the north is far enough away from "civilization" to be considered "remote". One thing is certain, however. Its southern boundary is not a single line of latitude. It more nearly approximates to the northern limit of Canadian commercial agriculture. This is essentially a climatic boundary — the southern limit of the sub-arctic climate. Within this sub-arctic region there are less than four months with an average temperature of more

The Frozen North: A DC 3 transport aircraft on Lake Hazen in Ellesmere Island, at the base camp established by scientists of the Defence Research Board in 1957.

than 50° Fahrenheit, while the average January temperature is below 26° Fahrenheit, and may be as low as 36° Fahrenheit below zero. Thus the sub-arctic is a region of short, cool summers and long, usually severe winters. This straddles fifty-three per cent of Canada in a broad arc from the Alaskan border to the Atlantic coast of Newfoundland. But north of the sub-arctic and in patches in the mountains of British Columbia lies the arctic — an area covering almost one-quarter of Canada in which the mean temperature of the warmest month, although above freezing, is never above 50° Fahrenheit. But these simple definitions based on average temperatures give no idea of the climatic paradoxes which can occur in the North. Cool and short though the summers are, temperatures of over 100° Fahrenheit have been recorded

in the area about Fort Smith. This is in contrast to the lowest recorded temperature of 83° Fahrenheit below zero at Snag in the Yukon. Similarly, the precipitation of over eighty inches a year in northwest British Columbia contrasts with the average annual precipitation of only 2.59 inches at Eureka on Ellesmere Island — the lowest average annual precipitation figure for any place in Canada. Generally the snowfall of the north is light — less than half the amount which falls in Montreal, and yet parts of the Labrador coast receive twice as much as that city. Also, three per cent of Canada is covered with permanent ice and snow and all but a small amount of it in the southern mountains of British Columbia is in the North. In these areas of "ice-cap" climate the average monthly temperatures are always below 32° Fahrenheit.

Climatically then, there are three "Norths" — the permanent ice and snow fields, the arctic and the sub-arctic. But within the seventy-eight per cent of Canada's area which they embrace, the further variations are added as a result of the topography, for the western and eastern approaches to the North are guarded by mountains. In the west they include the highest peak in Canada — Mount Logan, 19,850 feet high; while in the east, though the mountain rim is less than 300 feet above sea-level on the island of Newfoundland, it exceeds 5,000 feet in the Torngat Mountains and 10,000 feet in northern Ellesmere Island. From these highland rims the land for the most part slopes to the myriad channels which break the "Far North" into a multitude of islands. A score of these are larger than Prince Edward Island, while

255

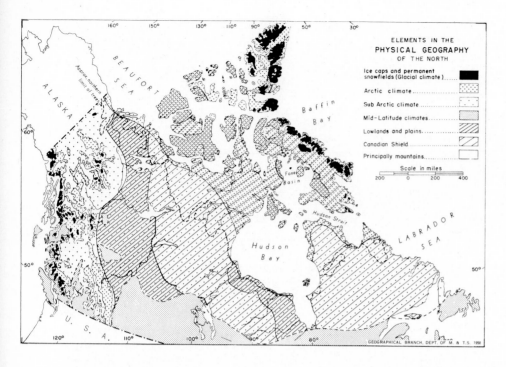

ELEMENTS IN THE
PHYSICAL GEOGRAPHY
OF THE NORTH

Ice caps and permanent snowfields (Glacial climate) ....
Arctic climate ....
Sub Arctic climate ....
Mid-Latitude climates ....
Lowlands and plains ....
Canadian Shield ....
Principally mountains ....

Scale in miles
200 0 200 400

GEOGRAPHICAL BRANCH, DEPT. OF M. & T.S. 1958

Baffin Island is almost as large as France, and Ellesmere and Victoria Islands are each larger than England and Scotland combined. Farther south the land drains to Hudson Bay and Foxe Basin. Locally the shores terminate abruptly, as along the west coast of Baffin Island or the west coast of Quebec. In other places they slope imperceptibly beneath the salt water, as is the case with the broad, poorly drained lowlands which flank the Manitoba and Ontario shores of Hudson Bay. Indeed, in Foxe Basin, Prince Charles Island is so indistinguishable from the waters around it that it remained undiscovered until aerial photographs disclosed its existence as recently as 1946.

But the descent from the mountains to the northern seas and straits is no gradual one. Surrounding Hudson Bay and Strait is the Canadian Shield — an immense stable block of ancient rocks, mostly granitic. Lacking hills of any size except along its mountainlike eastern rim, the Shield, when seen from the air, presents a monotonous landscape. Yet it is not without its variety, most of which has been produced by the geologically

recent glaciations. In places, the glaciers roughened the surface into a "rock-knob" type of landscape and the hollows between the "knobs" are now occupied by enormous numbers of lakes of all shapes and sizes. Elsewhere, as in the Labrador Trough, the landscape consists of a series of long, parallel ridges and valleys — all that remains after the work of the forces of erosion in areas of ancient folding. In places these valleys have become filled with water, producing striking finger-like islands such as the Belcher Islands of Hudson Bay or lakes like Lake Mistassini. In other places, the glaciers deposited morainal material on the surface — boulders, sand, silts and clay, in the form of sheets, or in isolated heaps and locally in the form of eskers, which look like railway embankments running across the country for 100 miles or so, and which mark the course of streams which once flowed beneath the ice. The western edge of the Shield is characterized by several large lakes. Lake Winnipeg, Great Slave Lake and Great Bear Lake are each about half the size of Nova Scotia.

Between the Shield and the western

mountains lies part of the interior plains of North America, which in their entirety extend from the Gulf of Mexico to the Arctic Ocean. Dominating the northern part of these plains are the Mackenzie River and the lower portions of its tributaries. In contrast to the rivers of the Shield, which are characteristically interrupted by rapids and falls, the Mackenzie system is one of the most magnificent navigable waterways in the world. The only break in navigation in the 1,700-mile stretch from the end of the railway at Waterways Alberta, to the Beaufort Sea is the sixteen miles of rapids in the Slave River south of Fort Smith. Impressive to the end, the Mackenzie River reaches the sea through the maze of channels in the delta which it has spread over several hundreds of square miles.

The contrast between this landscape and that of the western mountains could hardly be more striking, for west of the interior plains the Rocky Mountains and its northern extensions—the Mackenzie, Richardson and British Mountains — rise abruptly to heights up to over 10,000 feet. These, in turn, give way to the series of lower mountains, high dissected uplands and narrow valleys of the interior of the Yukon and British Columbia, only to be succeeded by the even greater heights of the Coast Mountains and the St. Elias Mountains before the Pacific Ocean is reached.

Nature has clothed these varying topographic forms in a variety of ways. Essentially, the arctic is non-forested and to its variety of low-growing plants the name tundra has been applied. The sub-arctic, on the other hand, is a forested zone generally referred to as taiga or the northern coniferous forest, or simply as the boreal (northern) forest. While it consists essentially of coniferous trees characterized by white and black spruces and tamarack with a sprinkling of such deciduous trees as white birch and poplar, it varies considerably in composition and density from place to place. Balsam fir and jack pine are predominant in the eastern and central portions, and Alpine fir and lodge-pole pine in the western and northwestern parts, particularly on the slopes of the mountains. In the southeastern parts there is a considerable intrusion of such species as the red and the white pines, yellow birch and sugar maple. Then in the northern parts the proportion of rock, muskeg and tundra gradually increases, for there is commonly no sharp break between the taiga and the tundra.

Similarly, within the tundra itself the nature and amount of vegetation varies with soil, water conditions and exposure to wind. Mosses and sedges are common, intermixed with streams, lakes, peat bogs and swamps, the latter often resulting from poor drainage because of the underlying permafrost (permanently frozen ground). But small willows, a foot or two in height, and bushes are common around the wet edges of the marshes or in the more favourably sheltered places. Sandy areas or rocky lower slopes are often covered with heaths of lichens and grasses. Many areas that are simply bare bedrock or disintegrated frost-shattered rock and glacial boulders have no vegetative cover. This is typical of the mountainous areas and the tops of rocky ridges.

The flora of the North has an economic significance in that it is important to the wildlife within the region whose numbers and distribution can be traced directly to the distribution of the plant life. Consequently, the wildlife can be primarily divided into that which dwells in the taiga and that of the tundra. One of the most remarkable animals is the musk-ox which, with Peary's caribou, finds its food in the arctic pastures of the Queen Elizabeth Islands of the Far North. Farther south the principal grazing animal is the Barren Ground caribou, which also spreads southward into the northern parts of the forested zone where, in the west, the mountain caribou is also found. The carnivorous animals of the tundra include the polar bear, the arctic wolf and the arctic fox and among the smaller animals are the arctic hare, lemmings, squirrels and mice. In an area in such intimate contact with the sea, sealife, too, is important. Various species of whales and seals and the Atlantic walrus are all found. And of the sea fish, the arctic char is the one most used for food. In addition, the fresh-water lakes support white-fish, lake trout and pike. Insect life is also abundant

The Traditional North: A fish camp established by Indians at Arctic Red River in the Mackenzie River valley, north of the Arctic Circle.

A prospective gold mine in the Barren Lands northeast of Yellowknife, N.W.T., supplied entirely by aircraft.

Converters in the nickel smelter at Thompson, Manitoba.

and birds like the ptarmigan make the tundra their permanent home. Others, like the whistling swan and several species of geese, choose to summer in the region. The boreal forest similarly supports a varied wildlife typified by the moose, which browse among the shrubs and low-growing trees, the woodland caribou and the fur-bearing rodents — the beaver and muskrat. The larger carnivorous animals include the black bear and, in the west, the grizzly bear, the coyote, timber wolf and red fox. The smaller ones include the otter, marten, wolverine and mink.

And what of man ? To what extent has he added further variety to the fabric of which the North is woven ? By definition, his civilization has not penetrated to any great extent and signs of his activities are like fly-specks on the map of Canada. In 1956, the Northwest Territories had a population of just over 19,000 and the Yukon Territory just over 12,000. Thus, excluding the northern parts of the provinces, the North has a total population of some 31,000 or almost the same as the population of cities like Sydney, Nova Scotia, or Kingston, Ontario. Commercial agriculture is so limited as to be virtually non-existent. However, in the Yukon there are some small farms as far north as Dawson but at the most such cultivated land does not exceed two square miles — out of a total of 207,000 square miles. Corn has been ripened on the banks of the Mackenzie at Norman Wells; potatoes have been grown at Fort Simpson for shipment farther North; cabbages the size of footballs can be grown at places like Aklavik and tomatoes at Coppermine, in soil carefully gathered in buckets. But can these activities be developed and expanded ? At the moment the main commercial activities still depend on furs, minerals and the forest. It was the search for furs that led to the first settlements in the North and the fur-trading posts of the Hudson's Bay Company still form the nucleus of scores of northern hamlets. But today, the number of fur-bearing animals is decreasing and the fluctuating prices for pelts make the industry a precarious one. Minerals, too, were an early lure to the North, from the days when Martin Frobisher sought gold on Baffin Island in the sixteenth century. Three decades later, the gold rush to the Stikine country established the northern boundaries of British Columbia and the gold rush to the Klondike established the Yukon Territory. Gold mining is still a major activity. Indeed, Yellowknife, with a population of 3,100 and the largest settlement in the Northwest Territories, is founded on it. Gold also led to the construction of Canada's northernmost railway — the White Pass and Yukon Route from the Pacific Ocean to Whitehorse. Eventually other minerals were discovered — oil at Norman Wells and later, with gas, in the Peace River country; uranium at Port Radium and, later, on the shores of Lake Athabasca in Northern Saskatchewan; nickel and copper at Lynn Lake in Northern Manitoba; iron at Schefferville; asbestos at Cassiar, just south of the Yukon border; and nickel at Rankin Inlet, 300 miles north of Churchill. A complete recital would take pages. It is to be expected that even more mineral wealth will be discovered as surveys and exploration proceed. But the development of many of the deposits will be dependent on adequate transportation facilities for moving ores to the south and perhaps overseas. More railways will be needed to extend the northward-creeping tentacles of steel which have already reached Schefferville and Lynn Lake and more roads to supplement the ribbons of gravel which now lead to Great Slave Lake and Alaska. But mining development, sawmills and

modern communities also require power. Here the North has undeveloped potential, particularly where the rivers spill over, or can be made to spill over, the rugged topography in the east and the west and where the chaotic drainage of the Canadian Shield has produced rapids and waterfalls. To create Kitimat, the Nechako River was dammed and made to run backwards through a mountain to drop sixteen times the height of Niagara and so generate power to refine alumina and create a community of 10,000 people.

One of the other "resources" of the North is its location with respect to Western Europe. The fact that the Hudson Bay route is almost as short a sea-route to Liverpool as that from Montreal was of prime importance in the construction of Canada's first northern port at Churchill and its railway to the south. But it was not until the air age arrived that man took a further look at the globe and realized that the shortest distances between the main land masses of the Northern Hemisphere were not those which followed lines of latitude across the Atlantic or Pacific but those

which followed great circle routes across Northern Canada. Today, several scheduled airlines cross the North, so that tiny settlements like Frobisher with 2,500 take-offs a month have become busy airports and may be destined to become large cities in the future. With the air age, too, came the need for observational data on the weather in the North. Because of this, the most northerly settlements in Canada were established in the Queen Elizabeth Islands. But if the locational advantages of the Canadian North have led to the developments in civil aviation, they have also created an awareness that attacks by high-powered aircraft could come from this direction in time of war. The reaction has been to construct radar warning systems across the North — the Mid Canada Line and the Distant Early Warning (DEW) Line. It is to be hoped that these will never be needed, but in the meantime their construction has aided northern development and their continual maintenance may stimulate other activities which will change the face of the North still more.

The icebreakers John A. Macdonald (*foreground*) *and* d'Iberville *at Slidre Fiord, near Eureka, Ellesmere Island, at 11:30 p.m., 17 August 1962.*

A research scientist at McMaster University works on an experiment set up at one of the beam ports of the university's reactor.

PATTERNS OF THE FUTURE

by N. A. M. MacKENZIE

I have been asked by the Directors of the Royal Canadian Geographical Society to forecast the changing patterns that will appear in Canada within the next few decades. I willingly accept the challenge, though in so doing I am reminded of the prophet Amos, who once protested, "I was no prophet, nor was I a prophet's son".

In discussing the future of Canada, I am well aware that careful consideration must be given to the nature and state of the world in which we live. Today no nation is an island unto itself: world events will play important and, in some cases, decisive roles in shaping the destinies of this — or for that matter any other — country.

Canada, I feel, is particularly vulnerable to the impact of outside forces. We are, in terms of the space we hold and occupy, one of the largest countries in the world, with great natural resources of minerals, fresh water, forests, and agricultural lands. But, relative to our size, we have a small and a scattered population. The severe problems resulting from exploding populations and limited resources, particularly in China, India, and Japan, and to a somewhat lesser degree in Africa and South America, are obvious to all observers of world development. Equally obvious is the fact that future policies of governments within these countries may well determine the shape of things to come in this Canada that is ours.

This assumption — and it is a serious one — is based in part on recent trends in the newly-developing countries and within the framework of the United Nations itself. Membership in the United Nations has grown beyond the expectation of its creators, but within it the idea or theory of "democracy" still prevails — or is used when it is useful to a particular nation or group of nations. It is not inconceivable, therefore, that a demand by some nation, or group of nations, for freer movements of peoples and readier access to surplus resources may some day win majority support within this great international organization. I need not go into details here, but is it clear that any such policy would change our own destiny, and violently alter — even eradicate — the patterns I am attempting to forecast.

In moulding the world of the future, the United States has more than a limited stake. Its own peaceful development and even its national survival will depend, in part, on its willingness and ability to protect Canadian and other North American territories and resources from non-American ambitions or actions; in part again, on its future use of Canadian resources for the maintenance of its own welfare and its — as well as our — high standard of living.

Already, willingly and even eagerly, we sell our minerals, oil, gas, and other "wasting assets" to the United States. Further, it is almost certain that with their rapidly expanding population and their ever-increasing need for fresh water, the Americans will again turn to Canada, to press for the common development of our fresh water reserves. This means that in the future, even more than in the past, the Government of the United States will deeply concern itself with our policies and actions.

Basaltic cliffs near Southwest Head on Grand Manan's rugged west coast, where such cliffs range up to 400 feet high and show the typical columnar structure seen here.

When we add to this real interest the Americans have in our natural resources the never-ending and ever-increasing financial, economic, and cultural interests, both conscious and unconscious, that they have already brought to bear on our own society, it is obvious that we shall, despite our best efforts, become in many respects an integral part of the North American "English-Language Community".

We shall retain, I hope, our political independence and autonomy, but in other fields more and more integration and interchange are, in my view, inevitable, and, in many ways, desirable. For integration and interchange should help the peoples of both countries maintain and improve their standards of living and contribute to their general welfare. But all this assumes, of course, that the world beyond our borders will leave us sufficient freedom of action to develop as we see fit.

The detailed discussion of our future, the future of Canada, must be thought of and described at two levels: first and immediately important, the national level; second, the provincial and regional levels. For Canada is very much a nation of "provinces" and "regions" as well as a nation made up of a variety of peoples.

Canada, nationally and provincially, is subject to the "winds of change." Whether we like it or not, we are influenced by the acts of violence and the revolutions that have been erupting in many part of the world, especially in Africa, Asia, and South America. Because we are relatively wealthy and have lots of elbow room within our country, the changes taking place within our borders have not yet reached the explosive level. Wisdom, intelligence and patience can ensure that it never will, but it will take all of these in large measure if we are to survive and prosper as a united and free nation.

Our basic problem is the "English language-French language" one. This has its roots in history and in our different culture, emotions and desires. These differences are natural and inevitable, but they can be lived with and they can contribute greatly to the enrichment of life in the whole of Canada, as well as provide an example to the rest of the world. Our acceptance of the philosophy and the policy of "the mosaic", rather than the "melting pot", for our nation is praiseworthy, but it is difficult to work out. We have not only the desires of those of "British" and "French" origins to deal with, but also the same feelings and desires on the part of many other groups that have come to Canada and who make Canada their home.

A good deal is being written and spoken about the special position of the "founding races", the English and the French. This, on other than sentimental grounds, does not, I believe, make sense. While we, the members of the "founding races", have made a great contribution to the creation and development of Canada, we were not the first to occupy the land nor were we the first Europeans to discover it.

Moreover, we are not different races, but peoples of the same mixed racial origins. Our differences are cultural and linguistic, not racial. In addition, none of us, however many years we have attained, were original settlers. These, the original settlers, are long since dead and gone and their descendants, individuals like myself, rather on ability and suitability for the work in hand and the posts to be filled. At the moment, I realize that this is not possible, but I am convinced that thoughtful and intelligent Canadians should accept this objective of a united Canadian nation in which everyone thinks and acts as a Canadian and is given equal op- and of those who have come to us from Asia and Africa. I especially like the contribution French Canada has made, and is making, and I hope that all of Canada in the years ahead will have opportunities for sharing in this.

But again, being realistic, we must accept the fact that the Atlantic Region is different from the Prairies;

The modern copper mine and town at Tilt Cove, set in rugged terrain in northern Newfoundland is a far cry from the original mine and settlement which started there in 1857.

have no better right to consideration than the sons and daughters of recent immigrants or, for that matter, those who of their own free will have left their own homelands and have made Canada their home.

It is my hope that some day we will achieve a degree of maturity and a civilized development which will make all of us "Canadians", and will ensure that opportunity and responsibility will be provided and assumed, not on the basis of racial origins or cultural backgrounds, but portunities everywhere in Canada. At the same time, I am sentimental enough to feel that we should permit and encourage the various groups that have come to Canada, and that make up Canada, to retain a pride in their origins and to retain something of their very attractive and valuable "folk ways" and backgrounds. Personally, I love our Highland Regiments, Pipe Bands and Scottish dances, music and poetry. In a similar way, I love the costumes, the music and the dances of European peoples, that Quebec and British Columbia have very little in common; that Ontario, with its wealth and concentration of population and industry, tends to overshadow the other regions within the Canadian framework. One inevitable result is that these other regions feel and believe that the sacrifices they seem to make in terms of the concentration of industry, finances, tariffs and the like in Ontario and Quebec do work to their disadvantage.

For these kinds of reasons, I feel

that the "future of Canada" must be considered region by region, and even province by province, for there are differences between and among the provinces within the regions.

Newfoundland has the longest association with Europeans of any of the Canadian provinces. There seems no doubt that it was here the Vikings landed; it was here that the fishermen from the western shores of Europe — the Breton, the Basques, the Portuguese, and the west-coast English — sought out the riches of the fisheries on "the Banks". The first European settlement in what is now Canada was made by Sir Humphrey Gilbert, on behalf of Queen Elizabeth and the English, in 1583. The history of Newfoundland since that time has been a stormy and interesting one. The country itself, apart from its fisheries, its forests, its minerals, and its water power potential, is a poor country and these natural resources are only now coming into their own in the sense of being profitably developed. The result has been that over the centuries since 1583 the people who settled, and live, in Newfoundland

have had a very hard life. It is a tribute to their character and their tenacity, toughness and courage that they have survived at all. They are now beginning, as a province of Canada and as a more closely associated part of the mainland, including the United States, to enjoy a marked improvement in their standard of living and their material welfare.

By one of those accidents of history, a substantial area on the mainland, Labrador, is part of Newfoundland. With the discovery of the rich iron ore deposits, and the probability of the early development of the great hydro-electric resources on the Churchill (or Hamilton) River, it seems that Newfoundland and its peoples have a much more prosperous future than they have known in the past. However, it is my opinion that most of these natural resources will find their way to the mainland, to Europe and to other lands across the seas. Secondary industries, apart from those of a local kind, are not likely to be developed, with the result that many of the young men and women of Newfoundland will continue

to seek and find their fortunes elsewhere than in Newfoundland. I hope that most of these young people, if they do leave Newfoundland, will come to the other provinces of Canada, for they are among our best citizens.

Prince Edward Island is rightly described as the "garden of the gulf" for it has been, and continues to be, a very attractive and, almost exclusively, agricultural community. One result has been that its population has remained constant and many of its young men and women over the years have, of necessity, migrated to other places. Natural resources seem to be limited to agriculture and fisheries, but Prince Edward Island has unusual "tourist attractions" for those wishing to enjoy holidays by the ocean during the summer months. The causeway connecting Prince Edward Island with the mainland, which the Federal Government has agreed to build, will make this tourist traffic to the Island easier and simpler and will inevitably increase the number of visitors, who will spend money and contribute to the economy of the

Island. Apart from this, and the developments in education, particularly in higher education, which are taking place as in the rest of Canada, I see no likelihood of significant or marked changes for "The Island" in the future that we are concerned with.

The economic conditions in Nova Scotia have improved considerably since World War II, particularly in the past decade, and this despite difficulties in one of its major industries, coal mining. Action by governments, provincial and federal, and the backwash of general prosperity that has marked the whole of the American economy, has contributed to this improvement in Nova Scotia conditions. But here again, unless there are discoveries of substantial quantities of oil and natural gas in the offshore waters of the Atlantic region, or unless tidal development of power in the Bay of Fundy materializes and changes the picture, Nova Scotia's growth and development is likely to be gradual and steady rather than spectacular.

New Brunswick, ever since Confederation, has been relatively less

Fishermen mending nets at West Pubnico, on Nova Scotia's historic south shore. This is a task which must still be done by hand, despite modern advances in fishing technique. The scene could be duplicated in many coves along Nova Scotia's 4,625 miles of coastline.

Until just a few years ago Roddickton was one of the many Newfoundland settlements accessible only by boat or aircraft.

prosperous than the rest of Canada. But here, too, the situation is changing, and has changed, because of the general improvement in the economic conditions pretty well everywhere across the continent, and more particularly because of the discovery of substantial deposits of minerals and the better and further development of water power, of the forests and of agriculture.

New Brunswick is particularly interesting in respect of the future of the whole of Eastern Canada, because its population is nearly equally divided between the English language and the French language peoples. The French are divided again between the Acadians and the "French Canadians", with their origins in Quebec, but this difference is tending to disappear, partly because of "nationalist" developments in Quebec and partly because of an appreciation by the

Acadians of the opportunities that could, and should, be theirs. However, at the moment, nationalism, both French and English, seems to be less militant in New Brunswick than in Quebec and some other areas in Canada, and one would hope in the interests of New Brunswick and of Canada, that this condition and feeling will continue. The development of substantial hydro-electric power on the St. John River and the possibilities of the development of tidal water power in the Bay of Fundy will bring changes to New Brunswick, and contribute greatly, along with the mines in the north east, to its industrial development.

Two proposals have been made within the last two years that are of considerable interest and could be very important, not only to the Atlantic region but to Canada and the United States. The first of these is the suggestion of Premier Louis Robichaud of New Brunswick that there be a political and economic union of the four Atlantic provinces. This proposal is being given serious consideration and has been turned over for further study by representatives of the various provinces concerned. Superficially, it would seem to have some advantages, in that it would make for larger units of development and possible economies in the expense of government and general overhead. However, there will be a good deal of resistance to it and it would not, fundamentally, change the situation or circumstances of the Atlantic provinces, though it might give them a stronger voice at Ottawa. In any event, developments along these lines are likely to be gradual and slow, if they do occur.

The second proposal seems to have come out of a meeting of Premiers of the Atlantic region. It suggests some kind of a "common market" consisting of the Atlantic provinces and the northeastern states of the United States of America. This is part of the history of the region, for had the American colonies which revolted against England in 1776 been successful in their attempts to include what is now Nova Scotia, New Brunswick, and Prince Edward Island, this area would be part of "the United States Free Trade Area", with very substantial financial and economic benefits to all concerned. Three of the Atlantic provinces are a natural part of the adjoining areas of the United States and have a great deal in common with the people of those areas. Their natural resources, which are their main source of wealth, could and would find better and more lucrative markets in the United States than they now have, and the manufactured goods which the people of the area must have could be purchased more cheaply if there were no tariffs and no boundaries.

This proposal, as I have noted above, is a part of the history of this area of Canada, and is significant, not because it is likely to develop as things are now, but because it indicates what would almost inevitably happen if Canada does not remain a united nation. This is another illustration of a small area of the world in which the future depends less on its own actions and decisions than on what happens elsewhere.

Quebec is, at the moment, the most exciting and important part and province of Canada. This because of the several major changes and developments described as "the peaceful revolution" which are taking place, but more important because Quebec can probably determine whether Canada will continue as a nation or whether it will break up. Personally, because I am "a Canadian" and because I believe that Canada has a contribution to make both in the Western Hemisphere and in the world, I hope very much that Quebec will remain a part of Canada. But one would not be realistic if one did not appreciate that this matter is very much in the balance. I don't believe that the rest of Canada would fight, in a military sense, to keep Quebec part of Canada. This not only because it would be contrary to our mentality and attitudes but, more important, because the end results would not be happy ones. However, I hope and expect that we will do our best to prevent a "break up" in every way possible. This means concessions, but concessions by both groups. It means, too, a greater and better recognition and understanding of each other's points of view, desires and ambitions — an understanding, too, not only of our own local and provincial interests, but of the whole of Canada and of all of the modern world.

Assorted pleasure craft at a dock in a quiet bay near Gananoque, Ontario.

Tadoussac, where the deep dark waters of the Saguenay merge with the St. Lawrence, was an important trading post before Quebec City was founded. Here, huddled together near the river, are some of its oldest houses.

If Quebec does decide to go its separate way, it will be interesting to observe the effects of this upon the French-language population of New Brunswick. Ontario and the other provinces will take care of the French-language groups within their own borders in their own ways, as Premier Robarts has already stated. But New Brunswick, as I have pointed out, is in a rather special position in this and other regards, and action of this kind by Quebec would confront New Brunswick with a particularly difficult problem and choice.

Surprisingly enough, the most concern and greatest resistance to the creation of a separate French language nation at the mouth of the St. Lawrence might well come from the United States rather than from the rest of Canada, for it would confront that country, the United States, with some novel and difficult possibilities.

But all of this speculation about the separation of Quebec and the break-up of Canada, and the union of the Atlantic provinces with the United States, is pessimistic in tone and outlook. I am, by nature, an optimist and I believe that the chances of preserving a united Canada are good, if we are convinced that this can be done and must be done.

Quebec, and particularly Montreal because of the position it occupies on the St. Lawrence River and as the eastern gateway to Canada, has been, and will be increasingly in the future, important. This importance is enhanced by the rapid social and educational changes taking place, by the development of natural resources, by the extent of these resources, and by the location of many new and major industries in this area. But here again, it should be noted that these industries exist to serve not only the people of Quebec but the rest of Canada and the world. These markets might be more difficult to enter if Quebec went it alone.

In any event, I envisage for Quebec, and particularly that part of it in the lower St. Lawrence Valley, an increasingly important future in every way, economically, financially and culturally. That Quebec will continue to be predominantly and increasingly French seems inevitable and proper. That the development of its great resources, water power, minerals and forest, will contribute greatly to its

Churchill, on Hudson Bay provides the shortest shipping route to Europe for grain from the prairies. The port is busy day and night during the short shipping season.

wealth is certain. But it will have to make its own adjustments with the rest of Canada and the United States of America, for its successful development and maximum welfare will depend on the nature and extent of these adjustments.

Ontario, because of its wealth, its population, its possession of industries and financial institutions, head offices of banks, corporations and the like, is the most important province in Canada and will play in the future, as in the past, a determining role in that future. Apart from personalities (in particular, Sir John A.

Macdonald and George Brown) Ontario was the most significant and influential party in the Confederation conferences a century ago. Whether Canada carries on as a nation, or whether it breaks up and continues its development along different lines, will depend very largely on Ontario, and on the kind of understanding and agreement that the people and government of Ontario work out with the people and government of Quebec. This understanding and agreement may be decided upon at interprovincial meetings or through the agency of the federal authorities, but

in the long run the decision and determination of Ontario is likely to be decisive, and this is one of the reasons I am optimistic about the future of Canada.

Quebec and Montreal, with their markets, their resources, their importance in respect of communications with the Atlantic and the Maritime Provinces, are so important and so valuable to Ontario that Ontario will do everything humanly possible to ensure that none of these are lost. It is my view that arrangements which will retain the benefit of the special relationships of Ontario and Quebec will be worked out, and that the rest of us across Canada will go along with these arrangements. We may resent some of them and be outspoken in our resentment, but all of us, I believe, want Canada to continue and will accept pretty well anything that is decided upon.

Canada west of the Great Lakes could probably get along without Ontario and Quebec. The French language groups in Western Canada are relatively rather small minorities and other ethnic groups outnumber them substantially, so the "St. Lawrence struggle" is not as important to the West as to the East. However, assuming, as I have done throughout, the continuance of "the Canadian Nation" the economic prospects for Ontario are most encouraging. This, because of the concentration of industry and finance already noted; because of the rapid growth in popu-

lation, exceeding all the other provinces; because of its wealth and natural resources; and because of its geographical position in the centre of Canada and adjacent to the great concentration of population and industry in the United States.

By tradition, Ontario has been conservative, but conservative in a practical and creative way. While this may make for a less colourful development than that taking place in Quebec or British Columbia, it is steady, substantial and basically sound. It seems almost inevitable that industry and emigrants will continue to locate in the southern regions of Ontario, adjacent to the St. Lawrence and the Great Lakes, and that Ontario will continue to dominate the economic and financial scene as far as Canada is concerned.

The three prairie provinces form a natural region, but here again there

are differences and each of them should be given separate consideration. Despite the fact that Manitoba is older than the other provinces and began its recent history as the "Gateway to the West", it has lagged behind some others in recent years. But with the general expansion in Canada, and the United States, Manitoba will grow and develop in the years ahead; this again because of its natural resources of minerals, agriculture, water power and forests, and the markets and income which these provide. Manitoba, too, because of the part that those of the French language have played in its history and development, like New Brunswick, though to a lesser extent, can have an important role in the whole area of French-language and English-language relationships as they may develop in a basically English-language North American environment.

Muriate of potash, mined and refined in Saskatchewan, in a storage bin of 35,000 tons capacity.

But Manitoba, like the other western provinces, will find it difficult to obtain, or even retain, any important part of the secondary and service industries of Canada — as illustrated by the controversy over the location of the "repair and workshops" of Air Canada.

Saskatchewan is the most agricultural of all of the Canadian provinces and produces more wheat and other grains than any other. But this one resource industry has made the Saskatchewan economy very vulnerable to weather, to pests, and to markets. The industrialization of agriculture, too, has made manpower less important and has helped to depopulate the farm homes of that province. However, the discovery of oil and gas and very substantial deposits of potash and other minerals, as well as some modest development of commerce and industry within the province, indicate that Saskatchewan will grow and develop in the years ahead, but almost certainly in a gradual and unspectacular manner.

Before leaving Saskatchewan, the contribution that its university has made and continues to make to the people of that province should be noted. While it, like other universities, has provided a good education for young men and women and has contributed through scholarship and research to the sum total of knowledge, it has been closer to its people than other institutions and has earned the interest and support of the people to an unusual degree.

Its "socialist" Government, under the leadership of Mr. Douglas, Mr. Lloyd and the influence of Mr. Coldwell and others, has provided the rest of Canada with a very interesting and important "testing ground" in areas of politics, economics and social services. But about the only really spectacular and bitterly controversial

In Yoho National Park the Kicking Horse River flows under a natural bridge in the rocks with a man-made bridge over it. High above looms glaciated Mount Burgess.

development, which took place during the years of CCF* Government, was the Saskatchewan Medicare plan. Now that the whole of Canada seems certain to organize and carry out some form of medical care for all citizens, the Saskatchewan experiment is unique only in being ahead of its time.

Alberta, for me, has been and continues to be, potentially, one of the wealthiest and most important areas in Canada. I feel this because Alberta has an abundance of pretty well everything, save access to the oceans. Its agriculture in a variety of forms, including mixed farming, is very valuable and, compared with any of the populous countries of Europe, could support as many or more people than those countries, e.g. Germany or France. It has great resources of coal and oil and of gas, including the "tar sands" in the north; it has

*Commonwealth Co-operative Federation.

forests; it has mineral wealth and water power. Its political experiment in social credit, brought about by the problems of the depression years, has resulted in a stable, rather conservative and seemingly efficient Government with no apparent likelihood of early change. Its population, like that of Saskatchewan, includes large numbers of the "ethnic groups", Germans, Ukrainians and others, and the American influences, particularly in the oil industry and in the southern areas of the province, are marked. All of this suggests that Alberta is less involved in the "Canadian struggle" than some other parts of the country are, and would be less affected by what may happen there than these other provinces.

It is often said, with justification, that British Columbia really belongs to another world as far as the rest of Canada is concerned. The great mountain ranges which separate it

from the prairies are both a physical and psychological barrier and contribute to this sense of isolation. Its history, too, is different from and has little in common with Eastern Canada. The Russians, Spaniards, and British from across the ocean, were the early explorers of British Columbia coasts. The American gold miners almost made it a part of the United States in the 1850's and 1860's. While Mackenzie and Fraser, Thompson and Simpson and the fur trading companies they represented — the Hudson's Bay Company and the North West Company — did penetrate the mountains and reach the Pacific, the early development of British Columbia was essentially a sea-borne development, contributed to substantially by the movement northward of restless Americans. So British Columbia is a country in its own right, very British in feelings and traditions, American in many ways,

The cannery at Butedale, on Princess Royal Channel, far up the British Columbia coast.

with a strong southward pull playing a continuing role in its development, and with less real interest and concern about "Canada" than any other part of Canada, not excluding Quebec. But, at the same time, it is interested in and anxious to see Canada continue to grow and develop as a nation, and to share in that growth and development.

Today British Columbia is enjoying a spectacular boom in nearly every aspect of its life. Its population is increasing very rapidly and its natural resources are being developed with great imagination and foresight. Its hydro-electric power, which is already great, will be magnified by the huge damming projects on the Columbia and Peace Rivers, and its forest and mineral resources, through the application of highly mechanized techniques, are being transformed into saleable products with ever-increasing efficiency and rapidity. Even agriculture and fisheries, though in a more modest way, are sharing in the general expansion. It, like Alberta, has experimented with a social

credit Government; its Premier, the Hon. W. A. C. Bennett, has given colourful and dynamic leadership; and its standard of living is probably the highest in the country.

Despite this, like its American counterpart, California, it has rather special problems of a social and human kind. These include a high divorce rate, drug addition, and many of the other characteristics that tend to mark a rapidly growing pioneer community. There is less of the sense of stability and security in British Columbia than in Ontario, due to these conditions and, probably, to the vulnerable nature of its economy and finances. If the bottom were to "drop out" in the United States or in other important areas of the world economy, British Columbia could, and probably would, be in serious trouble. However, because of its climate, its geography and its resources, its long-term prospects are among the most attractive in North America and it is certain to share in large measure in the development of the whole North American continent.

The other areas of Canada, the Yukon and the Northwest Territories, are fascinating and exciting. This because of the resources, mainly mineral wealth, that are being discovered there and because of the uncertainty of the nature and possibilities of those vast territories. Russia has shown, and is showing, what can be done in similar terrain, for it seems that there are more than six million of her peoples north of the Arctic Circle. But conditions in Russia are special ones and the power of government over individuals very great. Whether anything similar can be brought about, or will happen in northern Canada, is anybody's guess. But this area, or at least its resources, will be developed one way or another as the need arises, and will contribute in important ways to the wealth and welfare of the rest of Canada, of North America, and the world.

One of the interesting questions, and one that has been raised in rather acute form recently by Quebec, is the nature of the provinces' interest in and control over these northern areas

The magnificent scenery provided by the Cariboo Mountains at Bowron Lake makes a fitting climax to a canoe trip through the chain of lakes which parallels the boundaries of Bowron Lake Provincial Park, east of Quesnel in British Columbia.

and of the native peoples who live in them. One of the facts that is overlooked by Canadians is that the original partners in the Canadian Federation controlled rather small areas of territory. All of the Atlantic provinces, save Newfoundland, have remained in that position and condition, but other provinces, including Quebec and Ontario, have been expanded beyond recognition by the acquisition of territory which was essentially Canadian rather than provincial. British Columbia has toyed with the idea of taking over the Yukon but for reasons beyond the limits of this article, nothing has come of it.

However, in the long run, apart from the question of the importance of the Federal Government authority versus the provinces, the question of control in the north is probably not important, for, as already stated, the resources will be developed and will benefit, in one way or another, the whole of Canada and all of those who are Canadians.

These, then, are some of "the patterns of the future" of our country. These cannot be defined or determined in absolute ways or with certainty. This because of the unknown factors in the world around us and in the countries that are our neighbours to the south and across the Pacific, and because of the uncertainty about the answers that we will find to our own problems within Canada, as between Quebec and the rest of Canada. But my own expectation, as well as my hope, is that we will and must find intelligent solutions to our own problems which will ensure the continuation of Canada and its growth and development as a great nation, and that we can prevent major catastrophes which threaten and might destroy all civilization, including Canada.

Symbol of the future, Canada's first satellite Alouette I and a Thor Agena-B rocket leave the launch pad at Vandenburg Air Force Base, California.

ACKNOWLEDGEMENTS

The illustrations in this book come from a large number of sources, some of which we are unable to trace. Most of them were sent in to us by the authors of articles in the *Canadian Geographical Journal*, but many bear no record of their origin. Below, under the appropriate titles, are listed the contributing photographers or artists, or the organizations which produced the illustrations, in so far as we can determine them. Where a government department or institution is named, it is a federal one unless a particular province is specified.

Facing title page:

Quebec Department of Agriculture; International Nickel Company of Canada; Ontario Department of Travel and Publicity; Nova Scotia Information Service; National Film Board.

Colour plates:

Ottawa Tulips, Malak, plates courtesy of The Blue Bell; *Rock Garden*, Royal Botanical Gardens; *Harvesting Apples*, unknown, plates courtesy of The Blue Bell; *Grain Elevators*, Richard Harrington; *Rocher Déboulé Range* and *Engineers' Camp*, J. L. Charles; *Mount Rundle*, *October Scene* and *Big Eddy Rapids*, unknown, plates courtesy of the Southam Printing Co.

The Pattern of the Land:

Richard Harrington

Canada's Debt to the Indians:

Geological Survey.

Birth of Agriculture in Canada:

Public Archives; National Museum; J. E. Laughlin, from *Canadian Social History Pictures* published by Clarke, Irwin and Co.

Spreading Out the Pattern:

Lawrence J. Burpee.

Etienne Brulé and the Great Lakes:

Public Archives; C. W. Jeffreys.

La Vérendrye:

Public Archives; Burpee collection.

Voyageurs' Highway:

Public Archives; Hudson's Bay Company; Eric W. Morse.

Christmas with Samuel Hearne:

C. W. Jeffreys; Geological Survey.

Fraser Rides the Fraser:

Public Archives.

Pattern of a Nation:

Public Archives.

The Geographical Circumstances of Confederation:

Public Archives; Toronto Public Library; National Film Board; Canadian National Railways.

The People of Canada:

Public Archives; Donovan Clemson; Imperial Oil; Quebec Film Bureau.

Confederation Chamber:

Prince Edward Island Tourist Bureau.

La Ville de Montréal:

Montreal Municipal Tourist Bureau; Montreal Gazette.

Halifax:

Public Archives of Nova Scotia; Nova Scotia Film Bureau; Department of National Defence.

Ottawa of Yesterday:

Public Archives.

The Port of Vancouver:

Greater Vancouver Visitors and Convention Bureau; National Harbours Board; Richard Harrington.

My Home Town:

S. C. Ells.

Rafting on the St. Lawrence:

D. D. Calvin.

Patterns of Growth:

Burpee collection; Department of National Defence; Richard Harrington.

Memories of '85:

Public Archives.

The Poor Man's Trail:

National Museum; Canadian Pacific Railway.

Canada at the Turn of the Century:

Public Archives.

Conquest of the Northwest Passage by R.C.M.P. Schooner St. Roch:

Royal Canadian Mounted Police.

The First Trans-Canada Flight, 1920:

Department of National Defence; Mrs. A. B. Shearer; Wing Commander R. G. Ford; Winnipeg Free Press; Frank Ellis.

The Welland Canal:

Richard Harrington; Public Archives; Confederation Life.

Canadian Women on Active Service:

Department of National Defence.

Patterns of Change:

City of Toronto; Air Canada; British Columbia Government; Quebec Government; Steel Company of Canada; Hydro-Quebec; National Film Board.

Kitimat:

Aluminum Company of Canada.

The Trans-Canada Highway:

National Film Board; Canadian Government Travel Bureau; Provincial Governments concerned.

Knob Lake on Canada's New Frontier:

W. Gillies Ross; Iron Ore Company of Canada.

They are Changing the Face of Saskatchewan:

Prairie Farm Rehabilitation Administration; Saskatchewan Photo Services.

Land Utilization in Canada:

W. E. Shore; Manitoba Department of Industry and Commerce; Richard Harrington; G. D. Dwyer.

The Thompson Project:

International Nickel Company of Canada; George Hunter.

Teeming Waters:

Department of Fisheries; Nova Scotia Film Bureau; Spartan Air Services.

Highway to the Inland Seas:

National Film Board.

The Face of the North:

Department of National Defence; W. C. Wonders; International Nickel Company of Canada; Department of Transport.

Patterns of the Future:

Tom Bochler; Robert F. Leggett; David Baird; Nova Scotia Information Service; Ontario Department of Travel and Publicity; Fred Breummer; Manitoba Department of Industry and Commerce; International Mineral and Chemical Corporation (Canada) Limited; Canadian Government Travel Bureau; Government of British Columbia; Defence Research Telecommunications Establishment.

And if you enjoyed the DI Callanach *Perfect* series, we think you'll love these fantastically twisty crime thrillers . . .

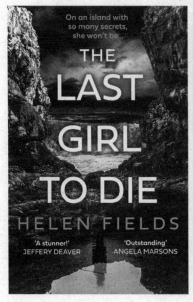
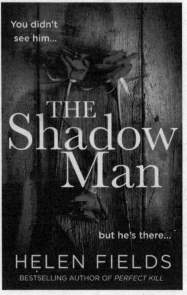

If you loved *The Institution*, then why not try
Helen Fields's iconic DI Callanach series?

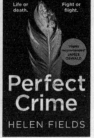

Available from all good bookstores now.

And as ever, to the word-dealers. The booksellers, the librarians, the English teachers, the bloggers and reviewers – where would we be without you?

To Margaret Baumber for talking books with me constantly and being my champion. To Ruth Arlow for coming to endless bookish events with me and keeping me laughing. To David, Gabe, Sollie & Evangeline for all the usual stuff. And if I've forgotten anyone – you know me, I'd forget my own head if it wasn't screwed on.

Acknowledgements

People contribute to books in a thousand different ways, some obvious, others less so. Occasionally it's just a passing comment from a friend or in a coffee shop queue or at the hairdresser that sparks an idea for a new twist or a line of dialogue. To all the people I simply cannot thank here individually – I'm still grateful.

To those I can name but whose efforts still go relatively unseen, I appreciate you each and every day. Publishing is a tough business. Keeping up the enthusiasm for every book, for every author, for every press release is unbelievably hard. So endless gratitude to Helen Huthwaite, Thorne Ryan, Elisha Lundin, Maddie Dunne-Kirby, Ella Young, Gabriella Drinkald, Samantha Luton, Hannah O'Brien, Tom Dunstan, Oliver Malcolm and Charlotte Brown.

And to my agents, Hardman & Swainson, who continue to stick with me in spite of all the stupid questions, my administrative errors and general author paranoia – I love you guys – Caroline Hardman (thank you is never enough), Joanna Swainson, Thérèse Coen and Nicole Etherington. Also, to Tory Lyne-Pirkis and all at Midas PR for helping spread the word.